IN SEARCH OF
J. D. SALINGER

IN SEARCH OF
J. D. SALINGER

IAN HAMILTON

HEINEMANN : LONDON

William Heinemann Ltd
Michelin House
81 Fulham Road
London SW3 6RB

LONDON   MELBOURNE   AUCKLAND

First published in Great Britain 1988

British Library Cataloguing in Publication Data
Hamilton, Ian, *1938–*
   In search of J. D. Salinger
   1. Fiction in English. American writers.
   Salinger, J. D. (Jerome David), 1919–
   I. Title
   813'.54

ISBN 0 – 434 – 31331 – 9

Printed and bound in Great Britain by
Billing & Sons Ltd, Worcester

ACKNOWLEDGMENTS

I am grateful to the following for their help and advice: Gillon Aitken, A. Alvarez, Martin Amis, Carlos Baker, Richard Boston, Michael Boudin, M. E. Broadbent II, Robert Callagy, Don Congdon, Susannah Clapp, Jonathan Coleman, Prudence Crowther, Norris Darrell, Linda H. Davis, Jason Epstein, Bert B. Davidson Jr., Donald Fiene, Mark A. Fowler, Robert Giroux, David Godwin, Simon Gray, John Gross, Henry Anatole Grunwald, Gerald Gunther, Leila Hadley, Hamish Hamilton, Stuart Hamilton, Ernest Havemann, Gerald Hollingsworth, Dan Jacobson, Elia Kazan, Herbert Mayes, Karl Miller, Edna O'Brien, Jonathan Raban, Ernest D. Raum, Charis Ryder, Winthrop Sargeant, Frederick Seidel, Christopher Sinclair-Stevenson, Jerome B. Schuman, Robert Shnayerson, John Skow, Ahdaf Soueif, Denys Sutton, Sarah Timberman, Patchy Wheatley, and Laurie Winfrey.

Chapter 1

1

Four years ago, I wrote to the novelist J. D. Salinger, telling him that I proposed to write a study of his "life and work." Would he be prepared to answer a few questions? I could either visit him at his home in Cornish, New Hampshire, or I could put my really very elementary queries in the mail—which did he prefer? I pointed out to him that the few sketchy "facts" about his life that had been published were sometimes contradictory and that perhaps the time had come for him to "set the record straight." I assured him that I was a serious "critic and biographer," not at all to be confused with the fans and magazine reporters who had been plaguing him for thirty years. I think I even gave him a couple of dates he could choose from for my visit.

All this was, of course, entirely disingenuous. I knew very well that Salinger had been approached in this manner maybe a hundred times before, with no success. The idea of his "record" being straightened would, I was aware, be thoroughly repugnant to him. He didn't want there to *be* a record, and—so far as I could tell—he was passionate in his contempt for the whole business of "literary biography." He was contemptuous too of all book publishers (so much so that for two decades he'd refused to let any of them see his work). When, in my letter, I vouchsafed that my "project" had been commissioned by Random House, I knew it would be instantly clear to him that I was working for the enemy.

I had not, then, expected a response to my approach. On the contrary, I had written just the sort of letter that Salinger—as I imagined him—would heartily despise. At this stage, *not* getting a reply was the essential prologue to my plot. I had it in mind to attempt not a conventional biography—that would have been impossible—but a kind of *Quest for Corvo*, with Salinger as quarry. According to my outline, the rebuffs I experienced would be as much part of the action as the triumphs—indeed, it would not matter much if there were no triumphs. The idea—or one of the ideas—was to see what would happen if orthodox biographical procedures were to be applied to a subject who actively set himself to resist, and even to forestall, them.

For instance, it was said—on "the record"—that Salinger had worked as a meat packer in Poland during the 1930s. Would it not make a readable adventure if some zealous biographer figure was to be seen trudging around the markets of Bydgoszcz "making inquiries" about a sulky-looking young American who had worked there for a week or so some fifty years before? Although this particular sortie was not actually on my agenda, the book I had in mind would, I conjectured, be full of such delights. It would be a biography, yes, but it would also be a semispoof in which the biographer would play a leading, sometimes comic, role.

And Salinger seemed to be the perfect subject. He was, in any real-life sense, invisible, as good as dead, and yet for many he still held an active mythic force. He was famous for not wanting to be famous. He claimed to loathe any sort of public scrutiny and yet he had made it his practice to scatter just a few misleading clues. It seemed to me that his books had one essential element in common: Their author was anxious, some would say overanxious, to be loved. And very nearly from the start, he had been loved—perhaps more wholeheartedly than any other American writer since the war. *The Catcher in the Rye* exercises a unique seductive power—not just for new young readers who discover it, but also for the million or so original admirers like me who still view Holden Caulfield with a fondness that is weirdly personal, almost possessive.

To state my own credentials: I remember that for many months after reading *The Catcher* at the age of seventeen, I went around being Holden Caulfield. I carried his book everywhere with me as a kind of talisman. It seemed to me funnier, more touching, and more *right* about the way things were than anything else I'd ever read. I would persuade prospective friends, especially girls, to read it as a test: If they didn't like it, didn't "get" it, they were out. But if they did, then somehow a foundation seemed to have been laid: Here was someone I could "really talk to." For ages I thought I had discovered *The Catcher in the Rye:* I had come across it in a secondhand bookshop in Darlington, County Durham, and had bought it on the strength of its first sentence:

If you really want to hear about it, the first thing you'll probably want to know is where I was born, and what my lousy childhood was like, and how my parents were occupied and all before they had me, and all that David Copperfield kind of crap, but I don't feel like going into it, if you want to know the truth.

What more audacious opening to a novel could be imagined—at any rate, by one whose own fiction at that time was darkly allegorical/ archaic and, in its speech, almost euphuistically remote from the dialect of his northern English tribe? And of course the *Catcher*'s colloquial balancing act is not just something boldly headlined on page one: It is wonderfully sustained from first to last. And so too, it seemed to me, was everything else in the book: its humor, its pathos, and, above all, its wisdom, the certainty of its world view. Holden Caulfield *knew* the difference between the phony and the true. As I did. *The Catcher* was the book that taught me what I ought already to have known: that literature can speak *for* you, not just to you. It seemed to me "my book."

It was something of a setback when I eventually found out that I was

perhaps the millionth adolescent to have felt this way, but I was by then
safely engrossed by *Beowulf* and the *Aeneid*, Book III, a student of
English literature at Oxford. Holden would say that this was where I
started to go wrong, started along the path that would eventually lead
me to the sort of literary folly I now had in mind, but I didn't know
this at the time. "My book" had turned into everybody's book: Everybody had seen in it a message aimed at *him*.

In gratitude for this sensation of having been specially confided in,
J. D. Salinger's readers have granted him much fame and money and,
if he has not altogether turned these down, he has been consistently
churlish in accepting them. Now he won't even let us *see* what he is
working on. Is he sulking? If so, where did we all go wrong? By
studying English lit.? Or is he teasing us—testing our fidelity and, in
the process, making sure that we won't ever totally abandon him?
These were the sorts of question my whimsical biographer would play
around with.

Of course, every biographer has a bit of the low tec in him, and
mine—having made his first move—now looked forward to "getting on
the case." I was already thinking of "him" as somehow separate from
"me": a convenience or a necessity? Anyway, I got "him" started by
firing off about two dozen form letters to all the Salingers listed in the
Manhattan telephone directory. Where did the Salingers come from,
I asked, and did any of these Salingers happen to know the novelist
J.D.? I was hoping to tap the well-known American hunger for
genealogy and, sure enough, the replies came storming back. But they
were neither entertaining nor informative. Nobody knew anything of
J.D. except that he had turned into a hermit, and several had never
heard of him at all.

On the other hand, many of them did claim a connection with Pierre
Salinger, John F. Kennedy's press secretary, and it emerged from what
they said that there were in fact two sorts of Salinger. One sort hailed
from Alsace-Lorraine; the other from Eastern Europe, perhaps Poland.
The French branch was far more numerous and self-knowing than the
Polish, and J.D.—it was soon evident—belonged to the more shadowy

East European line. Had he ever himself tried to find out about his origins and, failing to do so, become charmed by some sense of his own elusiveness?

It was at moments like this, I could now see, that my "biographer," my sleuthing other self, would need some rather severe guidance and restraint.

2

About three weeks after the first wave of answers had subsided, I got a letter from J. D. Salinger himself. One of *my* letters, it seems, had been received by his sister, and another by his son—both of whom are listed in the Manhattan phone book. Salinger berated me for harassing his family "in the not particularly fair name of scholarship." He didn't suppose he could stop me writing a book about him, but he thought he ought to let me know—"for whatever little it may be worth"—that he had suffered so many intrusions on his privacy that he could endure no more of it—not "in a single lifetime."

The letter was touching in a way, but also just a shade repellent. It was as frigidly impersonal as it could be, and somewhat too composed, too pleased with its own polish for me to accept it as a direct cry from the heart. And yet there could be no mistaking its intent. I tried it out on one or two of my more sardonic literary friends. One said that it was "really a kind of come-on": "I can't stop you" to be translated as "Please go ahead." Another said: "Who does he think he is?" and I suppose this was closer to my own response. But it was hard for me to be certain what I felt. I had already accepted a commission for this book. I'd been paid (and I'd already spent) a fair amount of money. According to my original plan (that Salinger might perhaps be lured into the open), it could be said that things were working out quite well. And yet this human contact, icy though it was, did give me pause. Up to now, I'd been dallying with the *idea* of Salinger; he was a fictional character, almost, and certainly a symbolic one, in the fable of Ameri-

can letters. He said he wanted neither fame nor money and by this
means he'd contrived to get extra supplies of both—much more of both,
in fact, than might have come his way if he'd stayed in the marketplace
along with everybody else. Surely, I'd been reasoning in my more
solemn moments, there was some lesson to be learned from his "career." To what extent was Salinger the victim of America's cultural star
system? To what extent its finest flower? American intellectuals look
with compassion on those Eastern bloc writers who have been silenced
by the state, but here, in their own culture, a greatly loved author had
elected to silence himself. He had freedom of speech but what he had
ended up wanting more than anything else, it seemed, was the freedom
to be silent. And the power to silence—to silence anyone who wanted
to find out why he had stopped speaking.

And yet here was this letter, obliging me to face up to the presence
of the man himself. He wanted to be left alone. He'd kept his side of
the bargain: by not publishing, by refusing all interviews, photographs,
and so on. He hadn't gone quite so far as to withdraw his books from
circulation, but perhaps it wasn't in his power to do so. He had, it
would appear, behaved with dignity and forbearance whenever some
eager college student had turned up at his door. Didn't he have the same
right to his privacy as you and I? Well, yes. But then again, not quite.
The Catcher in the Rye, Franny and Zooey, and so on are in the shops
and on the syllabuses, still likely to figure in any conventional account
of the best works of our time. Do we accord them special treatment,
saying of them, as we (or most of us) would not say of other books, that
we must suspend all interest in the author? On the face of it, we don't.
And yet is not Salinger, by claiming this treatment for himself, also
suggesting that other writers ought to do the same? After all, other
writers do draw the privacy line somewhere, saying "You can ask me
this, but not that." Salinger has decided not to play that game. But then
it could be said that by not playing it, by not giving *anything,* he has
exposed himself to a different sort of game: my sort, the sort that asks
him in reply, "What's *your* game?"

I wrote back to Salinger, saying that his letter had certainly made me think but that in spite of it I had decided to go ahead with my book. I would undertake, however, to observe some ground rules. Since up to 1965, he had been in the public domain, but thereafter had elected not to be, I would not pursue my researches beyond that date. I would also undertake not to bother his family and friends. He could still change his mind about seeing me, or about answering some questions, but I didn't suppose he would. My hope was, I said, that if he was eventually to read my book he might soften his view—not just of me, but of what was possible, decently possible, in a genre such as this.

To myself, I issued one or two instructions. I would not attempt to seek out his ex-wife, his children, or his sister. I would permit myself to write letters to people who had been friends of his during his writing (or publishing) years, but I would not surprise them on the telephone, nor persist in my letter writing if two of my letters were to go unanswered. I would make it clear, where I thought there might be any doubt, that Salinger was against what I was doing. And so on. I was trying to make myself sound decent—not just to Salinger, but to myself. On the one hand, I really didn't see why I should extinguish my curiosity about this Salinger phenomenon: I was by no means alone in wanting to know more about him. On the other hand, at what point does decent curiosity become indecent? In the end, I supposed that I would find this out as I proceeded, that I would recognize the border line when I ran into it. Even so, I didn't *have* to write this book.

This circular self-questioning persisted and was fairly constant for a week or two. And it was genuine; it felt genuine. But it didn't seem to be actually stopping me from moving on to the next stage of the operation. In November 1983, I set off for New York—or we did: me grappling feebly with the moral issues and my biographizing alter ego, now my constant companion, merely eager to get on with the job.

3

Somehow, in America, it was harder than ever to remember that this whole thing had started out as a rather stylish (as I saw it) literary game. First, it so happened, I had to cope with a few demons from my past, my New York past. I had spent many months in New York and Boston from 1979 to 1981, researching a biography of the poet Robert Lowell. This biography was authorized in that it had the token approval of Lowell's two surviving widows. Also, the poet's literary executors were sympathetic. There was, therefore, no problem about access; several thousand letters and manuscripts were stored in various libraries and dozens of Lowell's friends and acquaintances were, I soon found, prepared to talk. There seemed to be no requirement in this case for me to split myself in two.

But I also soon discovered that authorization, if you are writing a biography of someone who has died two years before, can be a narrow license. I had access, to be sure—to papers and to people. But papers that have not found their way into libraries (and some which have) can often be withheld, and people sometimes tell you lies. With Lowell, I found I almost had too *much* material—too many eyewitness accounts, too many items passed on to me in confidence, too many special interests. And the role of the biographer, even the authorized biographer, has its unpleasant aspects. For all that you enjoyed this magic-sounding right of access, you still had to be endlessly judging and rejudging limits of propriety. And to some extent you were always having to play one witness off against another. There were too many tightropes, too many injurable sensitivities, and later, when the book was done, too many denials and recriminations. Lowell had been loved by several people, but few of these people loved, or even liked each other. And yet all of them believed that their version of the man was the authentic one—it had to be because their love, which they knew to be authentic, made it so.

Compared to what I had been through with Lowell, this Salinger project might at moments seem bracingly unmessy. At any rate, there was little chance that I would become bewildered by a surfeit of material. But still, not to be authorized has some bad precedents in the United States: Unauthorized gives off a smell of sleaze. Describing my new project to a few New York acquaintances, I at once began to detect a pattern of response. People in New York wanted to know all that could be known about Salinger, this mysterious "celebrity," and yet at the same time they evinced a protectiveness toward him, as if his inaccessibility was a national treasure that I, the invader, somehow threatened to despoil. Freedom of information versus invasion of privacy: a quarrel within the American psyche that Watergate had simply tugged into the open. Several times during my first weeks in the States, I had the eerie experience of being advised by the same person 1) to "make sure you get onto that ex-wife. . . . She's probably sore at him. . . . You bet she'll talk" and 2) "Don't you think the poor man has the right to be left in peace, if that's what he wants? I hear he's deeply religious." One of Salinger's more vehement protectors, while arguing the "he's religious" line, also managed to slip me the name and address of a girl he claimed Salinger had lived with for several years—and this in spite of my protesting that I wasn't interested in the man's life post-1965.

The man's life. The writer's life. It became wearisome having to explain time and again what I wasn't even sure was true: that there had to be, somewhere, a line that could be drawn—that with other writers we knew more or less where to locate that line because the writers themselves at one stage or another had given us directions. We could tell from T. S. Eliot's *Paris Review* interview which bits of his "personal life" he felt we had a right to know about or ask about. It works like this in ordinary conversation: The limits of intimacy are signaled. We pick up the signals or we don't, but they are usually there. With Salinger, the signals were, well, shall we say, ill mannered, both hostile and provocative. "You'll get nothing out of me."

Of course, if Salinger was a Mallarmé we might not care so much. But he is, let it be confessed, a writer whose work is more than usually powered by autobiography. It actually admits to being so. Over three books, this author has offered us a central character whose curriculum vitae is in almost every detail like his own. . . . And so the argument went on. But it was all the time getting thinner and more effortful in the face of what often seemed to me dishonest or sentimental opposition.

As for my companion, he was already marking up his file cards. I decided to stick with *him* for just a little longer, and to listen more attentively when he explained to me that if this "job" was to be done, it might as well be done properly. There were several obvious next steps. First, there was the existing Salinger "record," such as it was. This record has been handed down from book to book, from magazine to magazine, over a period of some twenty-five years, without any significant alterations. Its fullest expression could be found in Warren T. French's *J. D. Salinger,* last revised in 1976.[1] The Warren French account, amounting to some fourteen pages, represented the best that biographical scholarship could come up with on this subject. It offered, we were meant to understand, as much as *could be known* without Salinger's cooperation. Our first task would be to put this proposition to the test; after all, maybe the record itself was a Salinger invention. Most of it seemed to have been compiled from statements he himself had made over the years. Evidently we would need to go through it, "fact" by "fact."

Just as it was taken for granted that the "record" was both true and unexpandable, so (necessarily) it was believed that everyone who had ever known Salinger was somehow sworn to silence. In New York, people kept telling me, "No one will talk," as if Salinger were a high-placed mobster who had ways of guaranteeing the loyalty of his lieutenants. Later on, I would learn of people like S. J. Perelman—willing to speak unsolemnly about everything under the sun and yet able to fall obstinately silent when asked about J.D. Was everyone like him? This side of things would be difficult to check without bending my own rules of conduct. It might well have been that there were blabber-mouths, or grudge bearers, or embittered ex-lovers who, with a bit of badgering, or after a few drinks, or just for fun would spill the beans.

The beans? Well, let us say, might tell me something that might later on connect with something else. What would happen if I ran into one of these? Would I stop my ears? Of course not. But perhaps the first question I would want to put to them would be: Why are you saying this? And what makes you different from the others?

I had the names of a few people who had known Salinger over the years. It seemed most unlikely that men like William Shawn or Peter de Vries or William Maxwell would wish to swell the literary historical record at the expense of their friendships with Salinger but, as my companion pointed out, it would be incompetent not to at least approach them. By letter. As agreed. Also, there was Salinger's agent, Dorothy Olding (of Harold Ober Ltd.). She, it was clear, had been my subject's chief protector for four decades. Obviously, I would get nothing out of her. But still, I ought to try.

4

While waiting, or not really waiting, for replies to the dozen or so "letters to his friends" that I'd sent out, I began my appraisal of the "record."

J. D. Salinger was born on January 1st, 1919. His father, Sol Salinger, was born in Cleveland, Ohio, and is said to have been the son of a rabbi, but he drifted sufficiently far from Orthodox Judaism to become an importer of hams and to marry a Gentile, Scotch-born Marie Jillich, who changed her name to Miriam to fit better with her husband's family.[2]

This paragraph alone could take a year or two to check. Where had these "facts" come from in the first place? For instance, the bit about his father's being the son of a rabbi and his mother's changing her name to Miriam. Warren French's footnote directed me to a 1961 article in *Life* magazine by Ernest Havemann.[3] I telephoned Havemann. "Who said that Salinger's father was the son of a rabbi?" "I don't know. I must have heard it somewhere." I looked up some Jewish *Who's Who's*. No Rabbi Salinger. Since I wasn't prepared to make a trip to Cleveland, I thought I'd leave this one for a bit.

But what about Sol Salinger himself? I looked him up in the *New York Times* index and found that he had once given a speech on behalf of the Cheese Importers Association and that he had worked for a Chicago firm called J. S. Hoffman and Co.—manufacturers of tasty-sounding items like Hofco Family Swiss Cuts and Hofco Baby Goudas, but mainly importers of meats and cheeses, from South America and Europe. I looked *them* up in the *Times*. The only mention of the firm records a sorry fall from grace: In 1941 the FBI seized thirty-two cases of Hoffman's Sliced Wisconsin on the charge that it contained "faked holes."[4] Although Sol was Hoffman's New York manager, there was no suggestion that he was tied up in this scandal.

From the Cheese Importers Association I got the names of several of Sol's colleagues and I rang around. Most of New York's cheesemen are Italians and they came over as almost mafialike in their suspiciousness. After all, what was a "biography" *for*, what made it different from something like a *police record*, for example? If I wanted to know about Sol why didn't I get onto his kid Jerry—he was still alive, wasn't he?; some kind of writer, they believed. But I did pick up a few bits and pieces. Solomon S. Salinger had died in the 1970s; he had been born in 1888 and had moved to New York—probably from Chicago—in 1912. He was admired in business circles for running a tight ship. In his later years he was notable for sporting a white mane and a magnificent white beard. "He looked like God," said one ex-colleague.

In spite of his appearance, though, Sol had always been something of a whipping boy for his boss, J. S. Hoffman. And he probably didn't get on with his son. Most of the Italians I spoke to were the sons and nephews of Sol's actual colleagues. In cheese, it seemed, there was a strong dynastic tendency, and Sol no doubt hoped his only boy would join the firm. "Let's just say I didn't ever see them together" was one comment. As for Jerry's mother, Miriam—or Marie—the cheesemen were chivalrously loath to say anything about her. Again: "Why don't you ask the boy? He and his mother were extremely close." I had read somewhere that Marie had been an actress, or had played in vaudeville (like Bessie in Salinger's Glass stories). There were reports too, on the "record," that when Salinger was a boy the Marx Brothers would often drop by the family apartment (and in an unpublished story of the 1940s, Holden Caulfield's mother is an actress called Mary Moriarity). I tried all this out on the Italians. "Yeah. She may have been. Why don't you ask the boy?"

Where had the family lived? I asked the cheesemen. From their few leads and from a search of the New York telephone directories, I was able to piece together what seems to have been a steadily improving list of Salinger addresses. When Jerome David Salinger was born at the New York Nursery and Child's Hospital on West Sixty-first Street, the family was living at 3681 Broadway. But in that same year they moved downtown, so to speak—to 113th Street, on the then- predominantly Jewish Upper West Side. (By 1931 the guidebooks described Salinger's earliest milieu as follows: "Dark-eyed beauties with high combs in their hair, and paradoxical high heels on their shoes, parade the avenues and survey the territory originally captured from the Jew, and now held against the northern onslaught of the Negro. This is Little Spain.")[5]

When Salinger was born, then, the neighborhood would already have been in transition. The Salingers, certainly, seem to have been restless. Between 1919 and 1928, the family moved three times, and always to the south. The New York that figures in Jerome's writing later on is largely the New York he would have remembered from the age of nine. In 1928, the Salingers took an apartment at 221 West Eighty-second Street, and it is from this address that their son would have made his first forays to the nearby American Museum of Natural History, or to the zoo in Central Park. As William Maxwell wrote in 1951: "A New York childhood is a special experience. For one thing the landmarks have a different connotation. As a boy, Jerry Salinger played on the steps of public buildings that a non-native would recognize immediately and that he never knew the names of. He rode his bicycle in Central Park. He fell into the Lagoon. Those almost apotheosized department stores, Macy's and Gimbels, still mean to him the toy department at Christmas. Park Avenue means taking a cab to Grand Central at the beginning of vacation."[6]

In fact, from the fall of 1932, Park Avenue meant home. The Salingers moved across the park to an apartment building on the corner of Park and East Ninety-first Street—a sure sign to all of Sol's colleagues that he was now an importer of real substance. He also had a motorcar of such splendor that it is still spoken of today with envy. Like Holden Caulfield, Jerome could from now on think of himself as an affluent big-city boy.

5

Replies to my letters had started to come in, and they were very nearly as discouraging as I'd supposed they would be. William Shawn, *The New Yorker* editor, was "not able" to speak with me, but he thanked me for my "courtesy and consideration." I had said to him, as to the others, that I didn't really *expect* him to "cooperate" but perhaps there was some "limited" way in which he might assist me. Shawn managed to sound almost rueful, as if in a kinder world there would have been nothing he'd have liked better than to talk candidly about his friend. I rather dismissed this as reflex *New Yorker*-ese. All the same, there was something faintly regretful also in the answers I received from Maxwell and de Vries. Again, neither of them felt able to tell me anything, but neither of them tried to warn me off. This did surprise me, rather.

And so did my fourth letter. It was from Dorothy Olding, Salinger's agent since the early forties and, in my mind, his spokesperson. Ms. Olding didn't suppose that she could help much, but she would be prepared to see me. I called her and we arranged a meeting in her office. The deal was that we would speak in confidence—and so we did. But what was happening here? Was this a put-up job? Had Salinger asked Olding to check me out? My companion was pleased enough to have the record put right on certain factual points, and believed he could already see ways in which the "Olding data," as he immediately began to call it, could be smuggled into our narrative without "revealing our source." Ever more sensitive than he, I came away from the meeting with a sharp sense that all was not as it had seemed.

Chapter 2

Salinger's childhood has never been publicly discussed. He attended schools on Manhattan's upper west side, where he apparently did satisfactory work, except in arithmetic. . . . At the time he should have begun high school in 1932, he was transferred to a private institution, Manhattan's famed MacBurney [*sic*] school, where he told the interviewer that he was interested in dramatics; but he reportedly flunked out after a year. In September, 1934, his father enrolled him at Valley Forge Military Academy.[1]

J D. Salinger has often said that he started writing at the age of fifteen—that is to say, during his first year at Valley Forge Military Academy. It has also been alleged by others that Valley Forge is the model for Pencey Prep, Holden Caulfield's alma mater in *The Catcher in the Rye:* a plausible theory, since Valley Forge, like Pencey, is only a shortish train ride from New York. We made this our very first "field trip" in December 1983.

The academy is based near Wayne, a small town in Pennsylvania, about half an hour's drive from Philadelphia. It was founded in 1928 and, according to its manifesto, the school's mission from the start was to turn out "young men fully prepared to meet their responsibilities, alert in mind, sound in body, considerate of others, and with a high sense of duty, honor, loyalty and courage. Valley Forge implements these goals and gives them structure through the values found in military discipline."² Pencey, it will be recalled, boasted of "molding boys into splendid, clear-thinking young men."

Holden, of course, thought all this "strictly for the birds," but there is evidence that such promo rhetoric might have had a pleasant lilt for Solomon S. Salinger in September 1934 as he mused on the troubled prospects of his son, Jerome. At Valley Forge, we were allowed to inspect Jerome's "201 File." In it we found Sol's original application form: It is hastily filled out, with irritated horizontal scratchings of the pen when asked about his son's religion—the answer appears to have been none—and there is a clear unwillingness to go into bureaucratic detail except on the matter of the school's fairly imposing fees. The decision to dispatch Jerome to Valley Forge was evidently taken in some haste. Sol's letter of enrollment is dated September 20 and the school's academic year was due to start on September 22.

A few days earlier Mrs. Salinger had taken Jerome and his sister to inspect the Valley Forge amenities—it fits with the sense one has of the father's exasperation that Sol himself chose not to make the trip. And when, shortly afterward, Valley Forge sent a lieutenant to New York to conclude the deal (Valley Forge, like most other such schools in 1934, was desperately short of funds), it was Mrs. Salinger with whom he dealt, not Sol. A cadet who entered the academy at the same time as Salinger wrote (in reply to a form letter we sent out to a list Valley Forge provided of Jerome's contemporaries) that there was indeed some tension between father and son:

I cannot imagine why Jerry's parents would send him to a military boarding school knowing his traits and sensitive personality. Perhaps his father, who was Jewish and a successful cheese importer in New York, felt he needed the discipline. He was very close to his mother, who was not Jewish. I met her briefly at the academy and remember her as an attractive and gracious woman, who obviously adored her only son.³

Jerry's last school had been The McBurney School, an expensive but none too chic establishment on New York's West Sixty-third Street. McBurney had links with the YMCA movement; rather like Valley Forge it was not an obvious choice for a worried Jewish father to have made—it was no cheaper and certainly no smarter than more local schools like Dalton or New Lincoln.

The year Salinger was enrolled at McBurney, 1932, was also the year in which Sol moved his family to Park Avenue—indeed, the two events were almost simultaneous. As an importer of luxury foodstuffs, Sol could have been among the few who prospered during this, the worst year of the Depression. And perhaps, therefore, Jerome's enrollment at McBurney was hasty, nouveau riche. Salinger himself in later years repeatedly declared that before McBurney, he attended a number of New York public schools. Only one of these has been identified—P.S. 109—but if the others were also public, this would support the impression that 1932 was something of a financial turning point for Sol.

The picture we have of Salinger at McBurney (gleaned from the school's files and yearbooks) is the one that will stay with us during the course of his school and college years. Academically, his performance was well below the average. His most dismal grades were in Latin and geometry, and he spent the summer of 1934 at Manhasset School in an effort to make up in these subjects. His English and journalism marks were also poor (in his first year at McBurney he was rated seventh in a class of twelve), and the overall rating of his headmaster, Thomas Hemenway, placed him in the fourth fifth of a class of forty—that is to say, somewhere between twenty-fourth and thirty-second.

His demeanor was silent, thoughtful, to one side of the main drift— the usual demeanor, indeed, of the artist-as-schoolboy. A contemporary told *Time* magazine: "He wanted to do unconventional things. For hours, nobody in the family knew where he was or what he was doing. He just showed up for meals. He was a nice boy, but he was the kind of kid who, if you wanted to have a card game, wouldn't join in."[4] He was nicknamed "Sonny" by his chums, perhaps with a hint of sarcasm.

The only school activities that attracted Sonny at McBurney were in the fields of journalism and dramatics. Like Holden Caulfield, he let himself become the manager of the school fencing team, but this no doubt came under the heading of Dramatic Art. (When Holden loses the "foils and equipment and stuff" in the subway, his Pencey team is on its way to play a match against McBurney). Jerome also served as a reporter on the *McBurneian*, and he acted in two school plays, taking a female part in each, and winning rave reviews. In *Mary's Ankle*, he played Mrs. Burns, and the *McBurneian* declared, "Some think Jerome Salinger . . . gave the best performance." In *Jonesy*, he "took the part of the well-meaning mother of Jonesy, giving a most excellent performance." His final report from McBurney described him as "very good in dramatics" and—more surprising—"good in public speaking."

There is no indication that he was much involved with sports. His McBurney records state that he liked Ping-Pong and soccer, but he seems to have been alarmingly accident prone. Before entering McBurney, he had on various occasions suffered a broken leg, a broken ankle, and a broken arm. In the middle of his freshman year, it is noted, he was struck on the head by a medicine ball—no great event, one might have thought, and yet his mother immediately demanded to know "how this could have happened in a supervised class." Jerome's only other recorded interest is in "tropical fish."[5]

The passion for acting seems to have been evident from very early on; it has been said (again, on what authority we know not) that at the tender age of seven, Jerome was the best actor at a summer camp in Maine. One might disregard this rumor if Salinger himself had not, later on, written a long story about a seven-year-old genius at summer camp. The Salingers, like the Caulfields in *The Catcher in the Rye*, probably had a summer home in Maine or New York State. Camp Wigwam, where Jerome is reputed to have won his acting prize, is possibly a model for Camp Hapworth in Salinger's last published work, "Hapworth 16, 1924," in which the genius Seymour Glass is also age seven. If young Jerome had anything at all like Seymour's sense of his own mysterious precocity, this would help to explain his sluggish academic showing.

Certainly it was not difficult—as my companion now repeatedly remarked—to perceive a connection between Jerome's juvenile attachment to the idea of performance with the heavily theatrical "man of mystery" stance adopted later on by JDS. Perhaps when Jerome Salinger was first escorted to Valley Forge, the theater of the place had an appeal for him. There is indeed something studied and artificial about the school's appearance: the dressed-up boy soldiers; the short-haired bushes, symmetrically spaced, as if they too were on parade; the cannons and flags that seem to be stationed around every corner of its spotless, neatly shaven grounds. The atmosphere is brisk, ready for anything, and, apart from the odd crumbling gable, shiny new, a boyhood dream of military competence and dash. For the secretive exponent of outsiderism, it might well have seemed like a perfect place to hide away, and for the performer who liked dressing up it offered a multitude of props, costumes, and disguises.

Liking it or not, Salinger was enrolled as a boy soldier. His character report from McBurney warned the colonels what they might expect. It said that he had been "hard hit by adolescence his last year with us," that he was "Fuzzy." On the boy's ability, the report declared that he had "Plenty." On his industry, however, the verdict was gloomy and abrupt: Jerome "did not know the word." Another school might have been cautious about taking him. The six-year-old Valley Forge could not afford to be fastidious.

Salinger has said that he hated life at military school, but the evidence is contradictory. He certainly didn't spend his time there in a state of sulk. As a half-Jewish New Yorker joining an odd school like this halfway through the curriculum he might easily have felt licensed to indulge an even deeper fuzziness than at McBurney. In fact, his career at Valley Forge is marked by a curiously companionable struggle between eager conformism and sardonic detachment. His co-students tend to remember the sardonic side:

What I remember most about Jerome was the way he used to speak. He always talked in a pretentious manner as if he were reciting something from Shakespeare. And he had a sort of sardonic wit.

I must say I enjoyed his company immensely. He was full of wit and humor and sizzling wisecracks. He was a precocious and gifted individual, and I think he realized at that age that he was more gifted with the pen than the rest of us.

We were both skinny adolescents and must have looked terribly young and boyish. I was immediately attracted to him because of his sophistication and humor. His conversation was frequently laced with sarcasm about others and the silly routines we had to obey and follow at school. Both of us hated the military regime and often wondered why we didn't leave the school. I believe Jerry did everything he could not to earn a cadet promotion, which he considered childish and absurd. He enjoyed breaking the rules, and several times we both slipped off the academy grounds at 4 A.M. to enjoy a breakfast in the local diner. It was a great surprise to me that he returned to school for a second year.

He loved conversation. He was given to mimicry. He liked people, but he couldn't stand stuffed shirts. Jerry was aware that he was miscast in the military role. He was all legs and angles, very slender, with a shock of black hair combed backward. His uniform was always rumpled in the wrong places. He never fit it. He always stuck out like a sore thumb in a long line of cadets.

The presiding genius at Valley Forge was the founder, Colonel Milton S. Baker—the model, everyone at the academy today assumes, for Pencey's headmaster in *The Catcher in the Rye*. Fund-raising was Baker's obsession, and he was immensely proud of having secured the school's survival through the Depression. One student writes: "Colonel Baker was no scholar, but he was a great promoter. . . . He was always seeking publicity in the papers. Some of it was downright 'tacky,' as the time his PR man had a cadet walk around on stilts. Indeed the corps would sometimes march—out of Baker's earshot—and chant: 'One-two-three-four, Butch's Advertising Corps.' Butch was the cadets' nickname for Baker."

Baker was very pro British. He wore a greatcoat like the ones worn by British officers. When he changed the cadet uniform in the fall of 1936, he used British army officers' "stars" for cadet officer insignia on the shoulder straps. In April of 1936, I still remember the time when Baker spoke in chapel and denounced Edward VIII for giving up his throne for Mrs. Simpson. Baker's concern was that Edward was shirking his duty, which of course he was! Some years later, Baker was awarded the OBE, which must have been the proudest moment of his life.

He was also a devout churchman—vice-president of the American Church Union. The Valley Forge chaplain was always an Episcopalian.

The colonel was a likely butt for Jerome's burgeoning sense of the absurd and it should be no surprise that when *The Catcher in the Rye* appeared, poor Baker was appalled. "I thought it was filthy," he told Salinger in 1963.[6] Other Valley Forge staff members would also have attracted Salinger's sardonic eye. There was Major John DesIlets, who wore a waxed moustache and was never to be seen without his swagger stick; Captain Horace Aitken, an aristocrat who hated cats and used to shoot them from the window of his quarters; Lieutenant Houston, who taught English and wore pince-nez (the cadets said they were made of plain glass and were worn to give him style); the officer (he won't be named) who was dismissed from the school for cursing in church and was later hailed as a hero by the boys. And among the cadets themselves there were more than a few eccentrics: the handsome cadet captain who served as crucifer in chapel and was busted to private after being caught in a nearby whorehouse; the cadet who rigged up the radio program *Gang Busters* to the loudspeaker system in the barracks; the upper-class bully who beat a new cadet for not answering a question quickly enough and thus forever cured him of his stammer. These were the real-life Ackleys, Stradlaters, and Marsalas, it would seem. And a cadet did fall to his death from a window in one of the dormitories—like James Castle in *The Catcher*. A former cadet testifies: "I did not know the details, but was aware of the accident. I did not know there was a reason beyond a 'slip' while trying to go from one room to another via the roof."

Salinger's own delinquencies seem to have been mild: sneaking out of school at night, getting drunk from time to time. There was one night, a cadet recalls, when Jerome became so impossibly drunk and "Holden Caulfield-ish," vowing to break out of school once and for all, that a close friend had to fell him with a knockout punch to prevent him from waking the militia. (The close friend was Salinger's roommate, one Ned Davis, thought by many to be a model for Stradlater: "Ned was a fine cadet, but was good-looking, tall, combed his hair constantly and believed himself to be the answer to a woman's prayer.") Most stories about cadet Salinger, though, are to do with his teasing, ironic manner: "His favorite expression for someone he did not care for was 'John, you really are a prince of a guy,' and of course the meaning never got through except to his friends." One day Salinger's mother came to visit the school. She commented on the red flashes that some of the boys wore on their caps (these were awarded for meritorious conduct of one sort or another). Salinger told her that she must at all costs avoid speaking with these boys. The flashes, he said, were worn as punishment for using profane language.

This, then, is the detached, mildly rebellious Holden Caulfield-ish Salinger one would expect to find. There was another side, though: the straight-faced joiner, the comrade-in-arms. In his second year at Valley Forge, Salinger was made literary editor of the class yearbook, *Crossed Sabres*. The literary editor was, in effect, the book's author, and the book itself can be taken as Salinger's "official" version of his years at Valley Forge. As an exercise in straight-faced irony (if such it was), the whole project is quite masterly. Here is the author's tribute, printed boldly in the center of an otherwise extremely empty page, to Colonel Baker:

When one speaks of Valley Forge Military Academy one thinks of Colonel Baker. The names are synonymous. All that Valley Forge has meant to us, Colonel Baker has meant to us. We, of the class of 1936, here regretfully take leave of this man, who has embodied all we ever hope to be. We shall carry his inspiration, the Valley Forge inspiration, to the four corners of the earth.[7]

Heartfelt or slyly subversive? Certainly, Colonel Baker could not take offense. And this tribute sets the tone. In another section of the year-book, there are two pages of class history in which the author muses lyrically on the four magical years he has spent at Valley Forge—no matter that Salinger had spent the first two of them being fuzzy at McBurney. The history begins with the eager cadet's arrival at the school:

The beginning of a new life! Prep school! Do you remember with what anxiety you waited for the Order telling you to report and, after it arrived, the feeling of trepidation on suddenly being faced with the realization that the die was really cast; that you were actually leaving your parents and friends—and accustomed habits—for a military school, about which you had read so much and looked forward to with longing? Do you remember the sharp emotion of bidding mother goodbye and the firm handclasp of father before you were hustled away by the important-looking cadets of the Plebe detail?[8]

The rhapsody goes on, from year to year: 1932 to 1936. In 1933 there is the pleasant sensation of drilling new recruits; in 1934 there is a new seriousness, an awareness that "in these last two years we will either make or break ourselves." And then, the final year:

We have grown, our horizon has extended, and our outlook has become more mature. Like those before us, we are only one of the innumerable classes which will graduate but we ardently hope that we shall not be forgotten by those with whom we have been associated. To our Alma Mater, nourishing mother, we say goodbye. To our memories of four happy years under your skillful guidance it shall never be goodbye. Our memories shall be ever vital and alive.

If we accept that whoever wrote this could not actually have *meant* it, then there is no need to challenge the probability that the author is indeed sardonic young Jerome: "Salinger the Sublime," as he is nick-named in the 1935 *Crossed Sabres*. On the final page of the 1936 yearbook Jerome excels himself in a rhetorical vein not dissimilar to the one that animates his elegiac prose. This time the contribution bears his signa-ture, and is offered as a class song for the boys of '36:

> Hide not thy tears on this last day
>   Your sorrow has no shame:
> To march no more midst lines of gray,
>   No longer play the game.
> Four years have passed in joyful ways
>   Wouldst stay these old times dear?
> Then cherish now these fleeting days
>   The few while you are here.
>
> The last parade, our hearts sink low:
>   Before us we survey—
> Cadets to be, where we are now
>   And soon will come their day.
> Though distant now, yet not so far,
>   Their years are but a few.
> Aye, soon they'll know why misty are
>   Our eyes at last review.
>
> The lights are dimmed, the bugle sounds
>   The notes we'll ne'er forget.
> And now a group of smiling lads:
>   We part with much regret.
> Goodbyes are said, we march ahead
>   Success we go to find.
> Our forms are gone from Valley Forge
>   Our hearts are left behind.[9]

However charitably we probe, no ironies can be made to surface here, no signals that between the lines the class song is other than what it seems. And yet it is almost certainly a spoof—an act of mimicry so consummately straight-faced that no one could possibly see through it. And it worked. To this day, Salinger's class song is enshrined in the Valley Forge school hymn book, along with works by Martin Luther and John Wesley, and is still sung at graduation ceremonies. The mode being what it is, fake sentiment is what the audience expects; so too is the mock-antique diction, the lachrymose team spirit. To achieve full, official piety, the hymn actually prefers a mimic author to a real one.

What is interesting, though, is that young Jerome seems to have been happy for the piece to be taken at face value, to be thought of as "by him." Cadets who were with him at Valley Forge particularly remember his conscientious labors on the yearbook and his authorship of the class song. Not one of them suggests that either the song or the history had been composed with tongue in cheek.

Of course, the "terrific liar" is at his most effective when he starts believing his own lies. Salinger's hymn is perhaps best thought of as an adroit finale to his whole performance in the role of good cadet. Although his contemporaries remember him as mocking and subversive, his teachers believed him to be "quiet, thoughtful, always anxious to please." The staff sergeant in command of his B-Company has said that Salinger was "a long way from the rebellious, nonconforming adolescent he describes in *Catcher in the Rye.*"

The mistake here, of course, is in thinking of Holden Caulfield as a nonconformist. There is in him, as there is said to have been in Salinger, a rather touching willingness to please, to keep the peace, to tell people what they seem to want to hear. Holden has an actor's ability to win over most of the grown-ups he has dealings with; if he can bluff his way out of a tight corner, he will do it. His true disaffection is a secret between him and us—and this is, of course, flattering to us.

Salinger's own acting career—his public one, that is—took a few steps forward at Valley Forge with his membership in the Academy's Mask and Spur Dramatic Club. The club was run by Lieutenant Norman Ford, who taught English and befriended Salinger throughout his time at Valley Forge. In 1936 Ford penned a musical comedy for performance by the Mask and Spur and later published a novel about a cheating scandal at West Point. Salinger's most extended triumph on the boards was in the part of Ralegh in R. C. Sherriff's *Journey's End,* a stiff-upper-lip drama set in World War I. Ralegh is the juvenile male lead, a fresh-faced young subaltern sent to the trenches straight from school and full of such lines as "Oh, but good Lord! That must have been simply topping" and "The Germans are really quite decent, aren't they?" He dies nobly in the final scene.

As well as belonging to the Mask and Spur, Salinger is listed as having been a member of the glee club, the aviation club, and the French club. A private for most of his time at Valley Forge, he was promoted in time to appear as corporal in the yearbook. Academically, he did enough to graduate: 88 in English, 84 in German, 83 in French, and 79 in modern European history. All his colleagues viewed him as "the writer." As one of them has put it: "Jerry was never in much of a hurry as far as moving was concerned. He was a very advanced thinker. I mean, he always came up with a different angle on things. When we wanted to spell a word, we'd hit him."

He was also the big-city boy: Very few New Yorkers went to Valley Forge. He knew about the Broadway shows, and he read *The New Yorker* and *Esquire.* He and a friend "used to talk all the time about how they were going to go out to Hollywood and become writers and producers. You know, they talked about cutting a wide swathe to the West Coast and making some of that big money." His class prediction (written by himself) foresaw him "writing four-act melodramas for the Boston Philharmonic Orchestra."

The *Crossed Sabres* job gave Salinger the chance to limber up in more than one literary manner. In addition to the pious material aimed at parents and members of staff, there are several pages of jauntily facetious stuff intended for the boys, and here we get a glimpse of the sophisticated Salinger at play. There are the class predictions: Willie Price will publish his own handbook called *My Wit;* Pat Patsowsky will run a roller-coaster monopoly in Atlantic City; Remo Tedeschi will be found singing "Ciribiribin" to a packed house at the Met; and so on. And there is a character rundown on each member of the Class of '36, with Jerome somewhat straining here to score a bull's-eye every time:

"Berg" Birgenthal is our most frugal cadet but says "business is business and I would not consider it under six percent. "Guy" Woodward is our best "nickel squeezer" and it is rumoured that "Guy" can get real groans from the Buffalo. "Hoim" Muller is the biggest chiseller but we must say that it's an art—we've been trying to learn it for years. Once again, "Dan" Comerford crashes through and this time is our noisiest member. "Dan" has a theory that the world is deaf. Our most timid member is Guy Woodward but we believe that it's merely a pose. "Bob" Jaegers loses by a blush.[10]

And thus it labors on, through something like a hundred cadet personalities; the only name missing from parade is that of Corporal Salinger himself. But then he is mine host, distributing the charm. There is genuine affection too in some of these class profiles. Just as Holden ends up "missing" even the most repellent of his Pencey schoolmates, so Salinger gives us a sense that he will probably remember many of these characters for years—as, indeed, most of them seem to have remembered him.

Holden at Pencey, of course, had no real friendships, and no "inner resources" to fall back on—no kings in the back row, no secret goldfish. Throughout The Catcher in the Rye he mourns for his dead brother. His author seems to have been luckier, as authors almost always are. If we are to believe his own account—as told many years later to the Saturday Review—it was at Valley Forge that Salinger first began to think of himself as a committed writer, and not just a writer of calculated set pieces for the school yearbook. At night, he said, hooding a flashlight under the bedcovers, he wrote stories. These stories are almost certainly now lost; we know that none was published. But the hooded flashlight, the air of secrecy and obsession, the sense of a momentous opening of doors—these are to recur time and again in Salinger's sparse recollections of his life at Valley Forge. By day, *Crossed Sabres* and the Mask and Spur. By night, the secret fictions. A military academy was perhaps the perfect place at which to acquire a lasting attachment to the surreptitious.

One might record as a nice footnote to Salinger's double life at Valley Forge the impressions of one of a pair of twins who served there with him: Remo and Romolo Tedeschi:

Yes, I did know Jerry Salinger, since he roomed two doors from me on the second floor. He was an upper classman and a corporal and I recall him as a pasty-faced, not too well-liked individual. He was not my favorite person . . . sort of a "wise guy" and rather cynical about everything. I happen to be a twin, identical really, and my brother Remo lived in the same hall, but at the other end from my room. He tells me that he liked Jerry Salinger and thought he was a regular guy. So there! You now have two diverse opinions.

Chapter 3

1

We traveled back from Valley Forge to New York feeling triumphant. Look at what had been amassed, so far: Salinger's school records, some telling items of juvenilia, frank testimony from contemporaries, some eyewitness location stuff from us, and so on. Material any biographer would have reason to be proud of, you'd have thought. And, sure enough, my companion now had a smug, workmanlike look about him—as if, no matter what the theoretical problems attaching to this case might be, he had journeyed with efficiency across the uncomplaining fields of Fact. He'd done his job. He had his Chapter 1.

But what, I wanted to ask him, had we actually achieved? So Salinger was bad at arithmetic: *All* writers are bad at arithmetic. He was sardonic, moody, a bit of an outsider; again, what writer isn't all these things, when young? We had some fresh data, to be sure, but how close had we really come to conjuring anything distinctive? Did we think we now knew Salinger any better than before? And when we made connections between the "man of mystery" we're in pursuit of and the juvenile's love of playacting, were we not simply bending the material to suit our plot? We still didn't have any close-ups, any illuminating mini-narratives. Would we have liked that boy if we had known him then? We didn't know.

And what about the life/work line of scrutiny? We had been able to dig up a few "real-life models," and there *was* some interest in seeing young Salinger foreshadowing young Caulfield. Or was it that this was what we wanted to find? We wanted there to be, from the start, some near-intolerable strain between the "anxious to be loved" side of Salinger and the other, darker side, the need to be untouchably superior. This was our reading of him as he had become, but was it really there, in embryo, at Valley Forge?

And it was not as if anything very comic or remarkable had happened to us in the process of pursuing this "research." We had written to Valley Forge, been invited there, and been given the run of the school's files. We had written to about forty of Salinger's contemporaries and had had some twenty-five replies. We had even been *saluted* on arrival by a tiny soldier and been called "sir" by a general. It had been too easy. "I suppose you ache to *interpret* him," scoffed my companion. "Well, at least he's started writing now. We'll have some texts to chew on."

We spent the next few weeks in New York and other public libraries putting together a file of Salinger's early, uncollected stories: no easy task, since in several cases these had been ripped out of the magazines they'd first appeared in. This was eerie, as if someone had got there ahead of us. We recalled, though, that in 1974, Salinger had "broken his silence" with a telephone call to the *New York Times* complaining about a pirated edition of these early tales. "I know I am known as a strange, aloof kind of person," he'd confided. "I pay for this attitude" but "some stories, my property, have been stolen . . . suppose you had a coat you liked and somebody went into your closet and stole it? That's how I feel." He had wanted the stories to "die a perfectly natural death," he said.[1] Twenty-five thousand copies of the edition were distributed before its phantom publisher disappeared from view, sought by the FBI. Perhaps *he* had been the vandal.

It was difficult to accept Salinger's analogy between a story that had appeared in a mass-circulation magazine and a coat that was hanging in his closet but, having tracked down some of this material, we could appreciate his resistance to republication. This rigorous, high-minded author had once tailored his prose to please the market. It was here, perhaps, that biography might be of help, real help, might even explain why a writer wrote the way he did. "Rationalization has dawned," said my companion. "Let's get back to work."

2

We know from Salinger's contemporaries at Valley Forge that by the time he left school at age seventeen, he had already decided on the shape of things to come. He was prepared to go along with his parents' now-revived expectations for a time—indeed, in June 1936 he applied for admission to New York University. His Valley Forge grades were adequate for college entry, and he was accepted for the fall semester. But secretly—"by flashlight," as it were—he had made up his mind: He was going to be a writer—a verbal performer, a composer (probably) of plays and stories, a professional.

The term "professional" crops up with regularity throughout the next few years; for Salinger it seems to have been a thoroughly specific designation. Being a pro meant making a living by the sale of words; it meant constant productivity, a tough, all-out commitment, and even a willingness to write below one's best in order to support the overall "career." The amateur or the part-timer could afford to indulge himself by writing only when the spirit moved; it was the pro's job to move the spirit, and, failing that, to be able to function in its absence. Time and again in his early years, Salinger's image of himself is of a working scribe who travels light but is never more than a yard or two from his typewriter. The image derives, no doubt, from Hemingway, as do several of Salinger's early affectations, but without any man-of-action overtones. The action, for Salinger, was on the page.

To function as a professional it was necessary to know the market and in the mid-1930s the market for short stories was healthier than many other sectors of the American economy. In 1934 the anthologist E. J. O'Brien, famous for his annual *Best Short Stories*, was in no doubt that the American short story was now at its peak of vitality and international prestige. "Five years ago," he told his British audience, "the English short story was the most memorable. The American short story had not yet stirred in its sleep. Now it is the English short story which strikes us as sterile and inbred. . . . It is high time that the young English story writer braced himself to the salt and bitter reality of life."[2]

This new American vitality had not escaped the notice of commercial publishers, and in particular the publishers of the rising new mass-circulation magazines. A magazine like *Esquire*, for instance, had won itself both an audience and some prestige by running Hemingway's "The Snows of Kilimanjaro" and Fitzgerald's "The Crack Up" in its early issues. There was a general willingness to promote the story writer as a new species of American star. Even the shamelessly commercial "slicks" (so called because of the slick, advertisement-ready paper they were printed on) were alert to the promotional possibilities of major literary names. Papers like *Collier's, Liberty,* and the *Saturday Evening Post* would pay around two thousand dollars for a shortish yarn, and even the more classy outlets like *The New Yorker* and *Esquire* were able to offer relatively handsome rates. As Brendan Gill has written: "Hard for writers nowadays to realize how many magazines were vying for short stories in the thirties and forties; hard too to realize how much they paid!"

The New Yorker and *Esquire* were, for Salinger in 1936, the quintessence of high sophistication. In the political 1930s, *The New Yorker*'s stance was relaxed, quizzical, dauntingly metropolitan; the cutaway and the monocle were necessary weapons in the cause of good humor and sound common sense. The notion of proletarian literature could be bruited elsewhere. *Esquire*, founded in October 1933, was even more explicit in its detachment from the political arena (and it also offered a novel, in color, dash of the salacious):

The magazine is, as its name implies, not for children. Nor is it, on the other hand, a dirty magazine, as some may have falsely told you. It is dedicated to the literate, if not the literary, and to the intelligent, if not the intellectual. Politically, it is non-partisan, as concerns the two major political parties. Otherwise it is something of an anomaly, because it is both anti-fascist and anti-communist.[3]

The well-off young American's fundamental right, according to *Esquire*, was to "mis-spend his life if and as he see [*sic*] fit." With superb timing, its first monthly edition (the first issue had been a pilot) appeared on the day on which Prohibition was repealed: December 5, 1933. More roguishly male than *The New Yorker*, it had the same languid air of know-how, of boulevard self-assurance, of—try as we may—not being able to keep an entirely straight face for the duration of an averagely verbose and solemn call to arms. *The New Yorker* could hardly have put the problem more urbanely than in its issue of November 25, 1935:

It's no fun to be a political anemic. We believe in technocratic doctrine—feel that it is sound and that steps should be taken. We deplore a system which tends to elevate a few persons and degrade many. Yet so fickle is the human animal, we find ourselves deriving an unwonted pleasure from signs of better times; that's how we know we are useless to reform movements. A reformer of any stamina hates recovery—he is happiest during a depression, knowing that only when great numbers of people are miserable is there any possibility of Change. We know it too; but when we walk out in the cool of the afternoon and see shopkeepers sprucing up and stores looking busy and people sitting in cafes and having a good time, believe us it takes all our strength not to feel good about it, for we have very little capacity for sustained dismality. We're not defending our temperament, merely pointing out a paradox; that Utopia's best friends are its worst enemies.[4]

This grown-up manner, its calculated agreeableness, its lofty but well-tempered detachment from the fray, its—some would say—complacency was to enchant the youthful Salinger, so much so that traces of it have stayed with him all his life and can be heard from time to time in the cadences of Seymour Glass. At seventeen, it seems, Salinger was ready to take it up as an ideal. He would tell his friends at Valley Forge that his ambition was to succeed Robert Benchley as *The New Yorker*'s drama critic (a typically "stylish" Benchley piece would run as follows: "I left *All Editions* at the end of the first act because I was sick of it and didn't want to see any more"); failing that, Salinger would probably go to Hollywood and write sophisticated screenplays.

At this point, Salinger's conception of a writing career was focused on these two key citadels: New York and Hollywood. It was a conception that had more to do with the world of mass entertainment (movies, plays, big-circulation weeklies, even radio) than with the world of Letters as this would have been perceived by, say, the editors of *Partisan Review* or by most university English departments. Partly by accident, partly by inclination, Salinger's literary route was from the outset established as metropolitan, not academic. And this separation has mattered quite a lot. To grasp how much, we need only wonder what Salinger's writing life would have been like if he had gone to Harvard or Yale. So maybe the arithmetic report does matter after all. Certainly, his career might have been very different if his first stories had been aimed not at *Collier's* but at *Partisan Review*.

It was in the 1930s that the split between these two worlds became overt—at any rate, from the point of view of the "serious" creative writer. This was the era of the "literary intellectual." From now on, it would not be enough for a writer merely to write poetry or fiction; not enough, that is, in the eyes of literary intellectuals. Henceforward popular success would be likely to taint a work with the stigma of commercialism, and writers would be obliged to take account of the "functions" and "responsibilities" of what they wrote. They would be expected to give interviews, make contributions to symposia, attend political assemblies, and, in general, show signs of living in society as intelligently anxious grown-ups. A novelist sans ideas or sans texts from which acceptable ideas might be construed would stand every chance of being regarded as lightweight. And if he was to get popular as well, that would be that. The so-defined—Steinbeck, O'Hara, Saroyan are names that come to mind—often got very bitter on this score. And so too, much later on, did Salinger.

In 1936, though, this could not have been anticipated. Nothing in Salinger's background or temperament, so far as we can tell, would have equipped him to regard a magazine like *The New Yorker* as frivolous or irresponsible (which is how *Partisan Review* saw it). His short spell at New York University evidently did nothing to solemnize his outlook: conceivably, he might have found himself caught up in student left-wing circles or he might have become captivated by *After Strange Gods* or the first issue of *New Directions*—he might, that is to say, have begun shaping up as a New York intellectual. But no; he left after a single year, leaving virtually no trace of ever having been there.

3

So far as Sol Salinger was concerned, this abrupt default must have seemed to mark the end of Jerome's formal education. The obvious, if not the only, next step would be for him to join the family business. As we have seen, this is what usually happened to a cheeseman's son. But there was tension between Sol and Jerry. Herbert Kauffman, a Valley Forge classmate who lodged for a while in the Salinger apartment, remembers dinner-table arguments in which Jerome would lash out sarcastically at his father—and unfairly, as Herb saw it. "Sol Salinger wasn't at all 'sensitive' in the way Jerome D. Salinger believed himself to be. Sol just didn't want his son to be a writer." Nor did he want his son to be an actor, which for a brief stretch in 1937 seems to have been Jerry's next-best ambition. Kauffman recalls that he and Jerry used to do the rounds of New York theaters, each hoping for a break.

But nothing broke, and for a few weeks the pair of them consoled themselves by taking work as "entertainers" on a cruise liner, the MS

Kungsholm. On a tour of the Caribbean, these young blades organized deck tennis and made themselves available as dancing partners for any unattached ladies who might need their services. Another friend of Jerry's, called Holden, was on this same cruise and, according to Kauffman, the name Holden Caulfield comes from a joining of his name to that of a movie actress called Joan Caulfield, on whom young Salinger later had a huge crush. (Much later, since in 1937 Miss Caulfield was fifteen; she did not star in films until after the war.) After his *Kungsholm* adventure, Salinger seems to have become resigned to abandoning his career in show business. That being so, he was left with little choice but to go along with whatever next step his father might insist on. It seems to have been decided that he would, after all, be apprenticed to the trade.

One of the stories we had come across in the New York Public Library was called "A Girl I Knew." It had appeared in *Good Housekeeping* in the late 1940s.[5] We read this story with particular attention, not because it was especially good (it wasn't), but because of what we took to be its documentary, real-life feel. The circumstances of the story fit neatly with everything we knew or thought we knew about the boy Salinger's predicament in 1937. To my companion, the piece was sufficiently studded with specific dates and places for him to hail it as "splendidly revealing." This seemed to me excessive. "You can't treat fiction as a source. Not unless you have some clear authority to do so." "But we have plenty of *unclear* authority. We know he had left college and was at a loose end; we know his father wanted him to go into the family firm; we know he went to Austria, to learn the trade. We also know that later on in the army, Salinger's job was exactly the same as . . ." "Very well. Let's say it *is* admissible; but let's also admit that we might be, that we are on shaky ground."

The father in the story, out of patience with his son's repeated academic failures, decides to send his boy abroad "to learn a couple of languages the firm could use." And his boy, who tells the tale, does sound familiar:

The particular college I had been attending apparently does not simply mail grades home, but prefers to shoot them out of some kind of gun. When I got home to New York, even the butler looked tipped off and hostile. It was a bad night altogether. My father informed me quietly that my formal education was formally over. In a way I felt like asking for a crack at summer school or something. But I didn't. For one reason, my mother was in the room, and she kept saying that she just knew I should have gone to my faculty adviser more regularly, that that was what he was there for. This was the kind of talk that made me want to go straight to the Rainbow Room with a friend.[6]

Instead, the boy goes along with Daddy's scheme, setting off on the SS *Rex* for Naples in July 1936. His destination is Vienna.

It was probably in the late fall of 1937 that Salinger made *his* European trip, and it is really no great impertinence to suppose that Sol Salinger's plans for his son were similar to those of the father in "A Girl I Knew." In Vienna, Jerome's mission was twofold: He was to improve the two languages he had studied at Valley Forge (French and German), and he was to apprentice himself to "the ham business." The language study came first. In the story, the boy is under orders from his father to take three hours of Linguaphone lessons daily, in addition to any colloquial material he might pick up. Salinger may well have done the same, although we do know that he was also required to work in an office, writing English advertising copy for an Austrian business associate of Sol's. Since we are treating most other things in "A Girl I Knew" as autobiographical, it's possible that like the hero of his tale Salinger lodged with an Austrian family in the city's Jewish quarter: not the safest place to be in 1937.

Altogether, Salinger, we know, was in Europe for five months, mostly in Vienna, but with visits to Paris and London. It was in the winter of 1937 that he made the trip to Bydgoszcz, where there was probably a family connection. It was here that he was supposed to learn the mysteries of the ham trade. In Bydgoszcz he "slaughtered pigs and wagoned through the snow with the big slaughter-master, who was determined to entertain me by firing his shot-gun at sparrows, lightbulbs, fellow-employees . . ."[7] It could have been during this visit that his father finally agreed that Jerome was not cut out for a career in import-export. Certainly, nothing further is heard on the matter after his brief trip to Poland. Nothing is heard, that is to say, by us, who have, in any case, heard little.

Throughout his European jaunt, Salinger was writing stories, sending them off to magazines back home and learning "as well as this can ever be learned, how not to mind when the manuscripts came back."[8] He was also writing plays and at this stage, it would seem, the playwriting ambition was as strong as if not stronger than the ambition to write stories. In "A Girl I Knew," the hero is working on a script whose substance would seem to confirm Salinger's Valley Forge class prediction that he would end up as a melodramatist. The boy's play is called *He Was No Fool* and features a cool, handsome, casually athletic young man—"very much my own type"—who is summoned from Oxford University to help Scotland Yard out of a tight spot.

"A Girl I Knew" is the only one of Salinger's surviving stories that draws directly on his European visit. It's a love story of the star-crossed type: The American boy falls in love with a Jewish girl ("she was probably the first appreciable thing of beauty I had seen that struck me as being wholly legitimate"), but she is already engaged. There are sentimental exchanges but no real blossoming. The boy goes back to America (to take another crack at college), and he later hears that the girl has died in a Nazi concentration camp. During the war the boy works for army intelligence and questions prisoners of war about the girl; later, he visits her old home in Vienna to seek news of her, but no trace can be found.

Salinger, it seems certain, was in Vienna during the first two months of 1938 and very likely saw, firsthand, Nazi street mobs on the rampage; they were by then moving around in the thousands. Austria fell to Hitler on March 12, 1938, and on that same day Nazi gangs raided Vienna's Jewish quarter. The probability is that by the end of February, Salinger had already moved on to Paris, but he could hardly have failed to take with him some troubling impressions of a city under threat.

Apart from the rather facile concentration camp plot twist in "A Girl I Knew," there is nothing in the rest of Salinger's work that draws on the experience.

4

On Salinger's return from Europe in the early spring of 1938, the problem of his prospects was deemed to be unsolved. His business apprenticeship had clearly failed, and he had had no professional successes as a writer. In "A Girl I Knew," the hero's predicament is identical: The idea of a business career is shelved, and he is given one last chance to try for the semblance of a college education—"the familiar moment came for me to advance one of my fragile promises to really apply myself this time."

If Salinger gave an undertaking of this sort, he didn't mean it. But he did go back to college. In the fall of 1938, he enrolled as a nineteen-year-old freshman at Ursinus College in Collegeville, Pennsylvania. And now, almost fifty years later, here were his deeply unauthorized biographers stepping off the bus from Philadelphia (Collegeville is about two hours from the city) in search of any scraps he might have left there.

The first thing to strike the visitor to Ursinus is that the place is miles from anywhere. There is no local town to speak of, and the bus service to more distant points is intermittent. It's certainly a place you might send your son *away* to. The next thing you notice is that the college itself actually looks like a college—a turreted, gray-stoned copy of some, perhaps specific, European model. And it is tucked away, most snugly, in its own extensive, leafy grounds. There is a retreatlike atmosphere, an air—almost—of asylum. That is to say, if you didn't like it there, you might not find it all that easy to escape. Which leads to the third element that has to be remarked: All the students seemed antique, otherworldly, in their clean-cut, well-adjusted pleasantness of bearing.

The idea of not liking Ursinus, of not liking anything, seemed far from their thoughts as they bustled smilingly about their proper business— not saluting this time, but now and again tossing us a cheery "Hi!"

I was all for leaving right away, but no—the job, the job. We searched through the 1938–39 files of the *Ursinus Weekly*, we got a list of Salinger's contemporaries and wrote to them, we quizzed the older-looking members of the college staff. The picture that emerged was consistent with the one we had already formed: of a boy humoring his parents, playing for time, and, since Ursinus was evidently where he had to be, making the most of whatever it was that marked him off from his co-students. The mystery is: why Ursinus? There was nothing Jewish about it, nothing military. It's a small liberal arts college, founded in 1869 by members of the German Reformed Church, and its aim was education "under the benign influence of Christianity." It drew on a middle-class student body of Pennsylvania Dutch background; most Ursinus students came from nearby suburban areas. The college's academic strengths were in prelaw, medicine, and chemistry; according to one of its alumni, Ursinus "placed little stress on literary, artistic, or highly intellectual pursuits."⁹ Perhaps this was the ingredient that caught Sol's eye. Or maybe Ursinus was simply the only place that would take this aging freshman. It was near Valley Forge; some local strings might have been pulled.

In any event, it was unlikely that Jerome would fit in there—and he didn't. His fellow students tend to remember him "for what he did not do, rather than for what he did."

He stood out in one respect: He was not working for a degree (as was everyone else I knew), did not care whether he received credit for the courses he took; and was considered a loner.

It was a good basic liberal arts college; its smallness contributed to closeness of students and professors. However, not always. The "not always" included Jerry Salinger. I do remember him and I remember him because it is my impression that he was not close to anyone—students or professors. Indeed, my recollection is he was pretty much a loner.

The word "loner" cropped up several times:

Although we talked on several occasions, I cannot remember why Jerry Salinger came to such a school. It seemed evident to me that he was bored and unhappy. I assumed he felt Ursinus had little to offer him. I can only conclude that he was marking time until he could move on. He was very much a loner. I don't think he gave himself to others, nor did he consider that others had much of value to offer him.

Generally he had no friends or companions. Jerry came from New York and looked on the college and students with disdain. He seemed so dissatisfied. . . . He never smiled, gave a friendly greeting or responded to overtures of acceptance. His manner was nasty. His remarks, if any, were caustic.[10]

In the freshman photograph, Salinger is at the end of the second row, his black hair brilliantined into a dashing quiff, his white tie and dark shirt marking him as just a touch more slick and urban than his fellows. "As I recall his physical appearance, Jerry Salinger was tall, slender, with dark hair and eyes. He had an olive complexion. His hands were long-fingered and sensitive. The nails were bitten short and were to-bacco-stained. He smiled infrequently but seemed almost mischievous when he did."

The girls at Ursinus mostly remember him this way. He was a New Yorker, he was older than the other boys, and he had been to Europe. One of them recalls:

The 'girls' were impressed by Jerry's good looks—tall, dark, and handsome, and we were in awe of his New York City background and worldly ways. Of course, there were other handsome men on campus—I married one; but Jerry was different—a loner, a critic, and definitely not one of the crowd. The boys, incidentally, were not impressed by or in awe of Jerry Salinger. My husband was not too kind just now when I asked him how he felt about Ursinus's claim to literary fame.

When this handsome, suave, and sophisticated New Yorker in the black Chesterfield coat (complete with velvet collar) hit the campus in 1938, we had never seen anything quite like it. He gave the impression of having "been around" more than the rest of us. We were enchanted by his biting and acerbic manner. . . .
Most of the girls were mad about him at once—including me—and the boys held him slightly in awe with a trace of envy thrown in. Jerry Salinger was a decidedly different phenomenon at Ursinus. His avowed purpose in life was to become a famous writer, and he declared openly that he would one day produce the Great American Novel. Jerry and I became special friends, mostly, I am sure, because I was the only one who believed he would do it. He felt that his English professors at Ursinus were more interested in how he dotted his *i*'s and crossed his *t*'s than they were in developing his literary style.
When we knew Jerry, he *was* Holden Caulfield, although when *The Catcher in the Rye* burst upon the literary world, he expressed surprise when I recognized him as Holden. I guess he never knew his adolescence was showing.

The woman talking here is Frances Thierolf. Frances or Franny is one of Salinger's favorite girl's names in his fiction, both early and late. When Frances Thierolf married, her name changed to Glassmoyer, and Salinger wrote to her saying that Glassmoyer "was the funniest name he had ever heard, and gallantly offered to join us on our honeymoon. He promised to write a book about me, and while I claim not the slightest resemblance to Franny Glass, the name did seem something of a coincidence."[11]
Salinger's one surviving teacher at Ursinus, Dr. Calvin Yost, remembers "nothing about Salinger as a person or as a student." Dr. Yost had to check with the dean's office to determine that he did indeed have a Jerome Salinger in his newswriting and journalistic practice class and that he gave the boy a B. One other classroom glimpse comes from a fellow student:

Ursinus College had a popular English teacher named Charles Mattern. He has
since died, but I remember him telling me at a class reunion that he was often
asked if he remembered J. D. Salinger, who by that time had become very well
known. He had had him as a student but did not remember him personally but
he had saved all the compositions his students had written. Learning of Salinger's fame, Mattern had searched out Jerry's papers. He said he routinely gave
him C's and found no great worth in them "then or now."

Luckily, Salinger did leave his own mark on Ursinus, although not
everyone seems to have noticed it at the time. For nine weeks he wrote
a column in the college paper, the *Ursinus Weekly*, and he served as the
paper's drama critic, reviewing three productions during his short stay.
The title of his column made it quite clear that this boy (the column
was signed JDS) was only passing through. It was called "The Skipped
Diploma: Musings of a Social Soph." and it began as follows, with an
item headed simply "Story":

Once there was a young man who was tired of trying to grow a moustache.
This same young man did not want to go to work for his Daddykins—or any
other unreasonable man. So the young man went back to college.[12]

This cool, world-weary note is struck time and again. One week JDS
portrays himself as applying for a job as a driver and odd-job man—
does it matter, he asks in his mock letter, that he recently lost his driver's
license, needs sixteen hours' sleep a day, and has no practical experience
beyond having once unblocked Aunt Phoebe's sink? "It is my family's
unanimous opinion," he declares, "that I am precisely the young man
to fulfill the requirements desired."

On academic matters JDS is similarly scornful. In "A Campus Dic-
tionary," he defines "written exam" as "an unpleasant event which
causes callous to form on the first joint of the middle finger" and "eight
o'clock class" is "continued slumber without the formality of pajamas."
There are several other jibes at the curriculum and at those "kiddies"
on campus who are serious about this kind of thing.

In another column, JDS finds himself on the Philadelphia–New York train; a "ruddy-faced gentleman" sits down beside him and starts talking. The dialogue could be an early sketch for Holden Caulfield's chat with Mrs. Morrow on the same train, and around the same time of year (this column is dated December 12, 1938):

MR. X: College feller?
US (cautiously): Yes.
MR. X: Thought so. Heh! Heh! Larry, that's my oldest boy—he goes to college too. Plays football. You play?
US: N-no.
MR. X: Well, I guess you need a little weight. Heh! Heh!
US: Heh! Heh![13]

It turns out that Larry is not only a fine football player; he is also an assistant scout master, helps old ladies across the street, and is "the indifferent object of Miss, Mrs. and Grandmother America's violent affections." When Mr. X suggests to "us" that we and Larry might like to get together sometime, he is told: "The truth is, unfortunately, that for generations our family has been suffering from beri-beri." Mr. X (retreating slightly): "Oh."

It is indeed feeble stuff, but at Ursinus it no doubt came across as stylish and a little daring. "Ursinus, even today," a student writes, "has not lost the flavor of what it was and is—a stimulus to the student life, with high academic standards and an approach that holds fast both the idealist and the realistic interrelated life." Another says, "My days at Ursinus remain my fondest and happiest of memories. Proper manners and etiquette were part of everyone's behavior. It was the custom to dress for dinner every evening. We were in college to pursue excellence. We also felt it was a privilege to attend college; therefore we had to make the best possible use of it and had the obligation to pass on to others as much as possible." Yet another calls his Ursinus days "idyllic." In more than twenty letters from contemporaries of Salinger, there is not one whisper of complaint; indeed, some forty-five years on, the idealism, the gratitude are still vivid and emphatic. From Salinger's point of view, he was *surrounded* by types like Larry X.

In each of Salinger's "Skipped Diploma" columns, there are four or five crisp paragraphs: In addition to the digs at academic life, there are gossipy items on recent plays and films. The tone is always bright and knowing, with a hint of "I've seen it all" thrown in:

Having bounced on the velvet seat of its pants all the way from Europe, *Oscar Wilde* is now in New York, with Mr. Robert Morley purring very convincingly in the title role.

Weaned on Broadway, John Garfield (now appearing in *Four Daughters*) smokes cigarettes out of the side of his mouth, puts his feet on pianos, and grips Sweet Young Things by their shoulders, much more convincingly, we think, than does even Don Ameche.

The air of benign superiority, the very royal "we," is borrowed from *The New Yorker;* the magazine ran a show-biz column signed "Lipstick" that JDS seems to have studied with some care. "You will find us, this Thanksgiving, munching our drumstick by footlight"; "Frances Farmer surprised us with an excellent portrayal of the 'wayward gal.' Frances, by the way, has everything Hedy Lamarr forgot to get"; "This play we recommend oh-so-highly."

In his movie reviews (three or four sentences apiece), JDS is noticeably hard on young male romantic leads. He has a running gag about the Latin heartthrob Don Ameche, and is caustic about Tyrone Power—he "knits his eyebrows rather effectively, thereby proving his existence." Our columnist loves Mickey Rooney, the Marx Brothers, and the Lunts (although there is a seed of suspicion here that bears fruit in *The Catcher in the Rye:* "If you do something *too* good, then, after a while, if you don't watch it, you start showing off"); he deplores Charles Boyer, Shirley Temple ("I throw tomatoes at all small children resembling Shirley Temple"), and the film partnership of Bing MacMurray and Fred Crosby.

There are also several sneers at "Eleanor You-know-who" and her husband's "already well-excavated New Deal party" and one chirpily condescending epitaph for Hemingway—Ernest, it seems, has "underworked and overdrooled" since *The Sun Also Rises, The Killers,* and *A Farewell to Arms.* And, one week, we are given a clue on the matter of Salinger's own reading at this time:

The following books have been recommended to us very persuasively: "The Growth of European Civilization," "Short French Review Grammar and Composition," "The Literature of England," "The Art of Description" and "Man's Physical Universe." You tell us about them.[14]

Even by the standards of undergraduate arrogance, the whole performance in these columns is notably self-assured—another act of Salingeresque mimicry, although at Ursinus he was playing to an almost empty hall.

Again, as at Valley Forge, there are two voices. Writing in the newspaper as JDS, Salinger is laconic and airily delinquent. Writing as Jerome Salinger, the *Ursinus Weekly*'s drama critic, he is leaden and agreeable, stretching his paragraphs to make sure a good word is said about almost everyone concerned, especially the girls. "As Mrs. Conway, Dorothy Peoples, '39, played a very difficult part with the most intelligent understanding. As Kay, Joan Maxwell, '42, was extremely convincing, . . . Jean Patterson, '43, was most attractive and carried her part quite adequately, and . . . Marion Byron, '43, undoubtedly has theater in her blood. There was a breathless quality in her voice which, if regulated, may some day lead her to the professional footlights."[15] "As the Gracie Allen-like Adelaide, Roberta Byron was without reproach, upholding her leading role throughout the play, and looking most attractive."[16]

Of Salinger's ripe praise, Roberta Byron writes: ". . . it *must* have been with tongue in cheek. It was an absolutely dreadful play with no redeeming features. . . . I am sure my performance could only have been reviewed with personal sympathy on his part."[17] As Holden Caulfield might have said: "The terrific liar strikes again."

Chapter 4

1

S o far we had met Salinger in the third person, or as seen by others—
in most cases from a distance of more than four decades. His contemporaries had long since learned what sort of lives *their* education
had prepared them for. More than once as we read through our letters
from "girls" like Frances Thierolf or Roberta Byron, we had to remind
ourselves that these were now women in late middle age. The Jerry
they remembered had, even for them, a touch of hindsight, a touch of
"J. D. Salinger." This could hardly have been otherwise.

We did have some nice details that might have gone unrecorded, and
we had a fair grasp of Salinger's botched education. What had his
parents—or was it just his father—been thinking of? What had they
expected to happen when they packed him off, age fifteen, to a military
academy? Was it merely punitive, or had they really hoped that by this
means he would one day turn into a splendid, clear-thinking college
graduate?

We also had a (probably) sound general sense of what the boy
Salinger was like. We might even, now, begin to feel with some confidence that we *wouldn't* have liked him much if we had known him
then. The "Skipped Diploma" was pretty hard to take. But then, would

we have liked Holden Caulfield much if we'd met *him*? Ignorant, sex-obsessed, lumpishly inquisitive—that's how Holden comes across to "old Luce" in the book:

> "In her late *thirties?* Yeah? You like that? . . ."
> "I like a mature person, if that's what you mean. Certainly."
> "You do? Why? No kidding, they better for sex and all?"
> "Listen. Let's get one thing straight. I refuse to answer any typical Caulfield questions tonight. When in *hell* are you going to grow up?"[1]

What was happening here, though? Were we reading the life in order to illuminate the book, or vice versa?

Missing from our search for Salinger, it had to be acknowledged, was any vivid sense of presence. What we needed was the first person, off-the-record voice of Salinger himself. It is in this voice that Holden wins us over all the time. What we needed, really, was what turned up next.

We knew from the "record" that Salinger lasted but one semester at Ursinus, and that in the spring of 1939 he enrolled at Columbia University for a Friday evening class run by Whit Burnett, the editor of *Story* magazine. Burnett was something of an evangelist; for him, the short story was a Cause. With Martha Foley he had kept his small periodical afloat since 1931, and although much of what he published now seems thin and dated, he had some notable firsts to his credit: William Saroyan, Joseph Heller, Carson McCullers, and a dozen or so others. There was often a cozy, self-satisfied air about the project, and some-times Burnett's extramural anthologizing seemed born of overdesperate goodwill: 100 Authors Select Their Favorite Stories *(This Is My Best, The World's Best)* or Speak Their Minds *(This Is My Philosophy)*. He was always devising some new promotional wheeze: a Philosophy Book Club, a Literary Game called Detect the Author, a Factual Fiction series in which "the facts behind the story" would be printed alongside the author's "imaginative" text (he hoped to sell this gem to *Reader's Digest*). Few of these schemes ever worked out, but Burnett's ingenuity was irrepressible; when one grand project failed, he would usually have half a dozen new ones to propose. And through it all, he did keep the magazine alive.

In 1939 this mattered quite a lot. *Story* magazine was an important and much respected outlet for new writers. It offered a "serious" alternative to the big slicks and was more hospitable, more tuned in to the marketplace than, say, the newly founded *Kenyon Review* was likely to be. It conferred both prestige and professionalism. Norman Mailer (or Norman K. Mailer, as he was when he first published there) speaks for the epoch's highbrow pros when he recalls:

The magazine was its own legend, and young writers in the late thirties and the years of the Second World War used to dream of appearing in its pages about the way a young rock group might feel transcendent in these hours with the promise of a spread in *Rolling Stone*.[2]

The voluminous files of *Story* magazine are housed in the Firestone Library at Princeton University, and—sure enough—when we burrowed into them, we came across a bundle of letters, written over twenty years, from J. D. Salinger to Whit Burnett. It was an odd moment, finding these letters just at the point when our chronological pursuit was beginning to cry out for some first-person intervention, some "expressive heart" (to use a phrase we will be hearing more of later on). By now the young Salinger was much more "alive" to us than the New Hampshire recluse had ever been. Indeed, so close up was our focus on these early years that all connection with the present-day or even the "mature" Salinger had become a shade tenuous and theoretical. Our subject, at this stage, was a kind of patchwork apparition: elements of real-life young Salinger research overlapping with bits of Holden Caulfield. And we were, for the moment, in a world of promise, of beginnings: The quarry, in our mind's eye, was an on-the-make young college dropout plotting his first literary career moves. And here, perfectly on cue, we had his voice: We could listen in. It was as if a fictional character *we'd* invented had been suddenly supplied with lines invented *by himself.*

It had been evident from a first glance through that these were not just business letters. They were, if anything, too garrulously self-promoting, the letters of a son to an adopted father. Salinger's demeanor is tough, wise-cracking, mock-boastful, and, now and then, plain boastful. Most of the time he is putting on a performance for Burnett, addressing him as a junior near equal. Every so often the tone shifts into something exaggeratedly respectful, almost sycophantic, but the essential bumptiousness is never totally suppressed. Even with the most private-seeming revelations, there is a touch of "Look how well I'm telling this" to be discerned.

From a biographer's angle, though, these letters were a find. They told us where Salinger was and what he did for the next five years or so (after the war, the letters tail off and, by the end, they *are* business letters, with Salinger refusing rather grandly to do business). They also gave us the chronology of his early stories, the circumstances of their composition, and what he, the author, thought of them. Most telling of all, they introduced us to the man's obsessive strain, to the conviction which he seems to have held right from the start that he was elected or ordained for some high literary office.

2

When Salinger's friend William Maxwell interviewed him in 1951, he came away with the information that after Valley Forge, JDS "attended several colleges, but he didn't let the curriculum interfere with his self-imposed study of professional writers. Sometimes, the curriculum and his plans coincided. . . ."[3] And as at Ursinus, sometimes not. Again, though, one notes the stress on "professionalism," on Salinger's "self-imposed" apprenticeship to a marketable trade. The authors he most admired were Sherwood Anderson, Ring Lardner, Scott Fitzgerald: These three had almost classic status in his mind. And the writer who

most intrigued him at this point (he'd just turned twenty) was William
Saroyan.

Salinger first read Saroyan's story "Seventy Thousand Assyrians" in
Story magazine when he was seventeen, and he had loved it. By 1940,
Saroyan was at the peak of his celebrity, and Salinger was evidently
captivated by the older writer's ability to move successfully between the
stage play and the story. Salinger believed that this skill would soon
become his own. He was also more than a little susceptible to the
Saroyan charm, balanced somewhere between heartwarming lyricism
and treacly cuteness. Salinger would have done well to be wary of this
influence, but that is by the way. What matters for the moment is that
the idea of Saroyan seemed to him compelling. Here was a natural, a
pure, untutored *gift*, and—so far as the boy Salinger could tell—the
critics were always disposed to bully writers of this kind, to force them
away from their true instincts. Saroyan, he believed, was in danger of
acquiescence. He, Salinger, would need to be on his guard against these
"teachers." And this makes it all the odder that he should have chosen
to enroll in a creative writing class. Again, there is a whiff of compro-
mise, as if he had said to his parents: "I will continue my education if
you wish. But as a *writer.*" He could thus be presented to the world
as a student at Columbia University, and his integrity would be intact.

When Salinger, in 1964, recalled his classes with Burnett, he was
carefully ambiguous about their benefits. Of Burnett he wrote:

He usually showed up for class late and contrived to slip out early—I often
have my doubts whether any good and conscientious short story course con-
ductor can humanly do more. Except that Mr. Burnett did. I have several
notions how or why he did, but it seems essential only to say that he had a
passion for good short fiction.[4]

Salinger particularly admired Burnett, he said, because he didn't use
fiction to gain advancement in "the academic and quarterly magazine
hierarchies." He was different from those parasitic types the young
Salinger had come across in college: He was a free lance, and he had

done it all himself. This opposition between, on the one hand, the tough, slugging-it-out, "real" literary world and, on the other, the protected, self-serving, college-boy milieu of the literary-critical career-ist had it seems, for Salinger in 1939, already taken root. Burnett's lowbrow bustle and enthusiasm were precisely what Salinger, the surly, boastful, college dropout, was in need of at this time.

This was education, but not Education. Salinger has recalled one particular class of Burnett's in which Faulkner's "That Evening Sun Go Down" was under discussion. What Salinger liked about this session was that no discussion actually took place. Burnett simply read the story out loud. He did so with no theatrical flourishes; he "forbore to perform. He abstained from reading beautifully." And this is what separated Burnett from literature's "exploiters": the recorders, tapers, podiumizers, and televisers who were (by 1964) "all over the place." Not once throughout the reading, Salinger remembers, did Burnett "come between the author and his beloved silent reader."

It is, of course, faint praise to assert that Burnett's gift as a teacher was that he made no attempt to teach, and there is no certainty that this was how Salinger actually viewed him at the time. At first, he seems to have treated his new instructor with suspicion verging on contempt. Certainly, his demeanor in class was one of ironclad detachment. Whit Burnett recalls:

The first semester at Columbia, Salinger just looked out the window. The second semester he continued to look out the window. He turned in his first story at the end of the second semester, then two more . . . he was the kind who ingests and then comes out with very edited material.[5]

Hallie Burnett (Whit's wife and later his co-editor on *Story*) also remembers Salinger's air of studied noninvolvement. "But then suddenly he came to life. Several stories seemed to come from his typewriter at once." It would seem, she said, that for two semesters he had been engaged in "purposeful reverie."[6]

The reverie paid off in January 1940, when Burnett agreed to publish one of these class pieces in *Story* magazine; it was called (what else could Salinger's first published story have been called?) "The Young Folks." Salinger got the news of its acceptance just two weeks after his twenty-first birthday. He was ecstatic and almost immediately began to weave fantasies about how his enemies and disparagers would react when they heard that he was now a Published Writer. To be in print at last, and in a prestigious magazine like *Story*, was an important vindication, a way of showing Them that he had had it in him all along. To judge from his letters, for the next few weeks he was fairly buzzing with self-admiration and not at all disposed to keep quiet about it.

"The Young Folks" appeared in *Story*'s issue of March–April 1940. It's a short piece, mostly in dialogue, but written with considerable care. It would have been evident to Burnett right away that here was a young writer with some feeling for the sentence, its balances and flexibilities. Salinger's aim is for a light but firmly packed effect.

Lucille Henderson sighed as heavily as her dress would allow, and then, knitting what there was of her brows, gazed about the room at the noisy young people she had invited to drink up her father's Scotch.[7]

One can imagine the short story student Salinger counting the ingredients here. In thirty-seven words we are given Lucille's appearance, bodily and facial; her character, affected and irresponsible; and her location, a party she's in charge of but not paying for. This is what the instructors would call economical, and it is just a bit too pleased with its own thrift.

A similar effect is strained for throughout this small, sad tale. William Jameson—"large nose, flabby mouth, narrow shoulders"—is hanging around on the margins of a college-kid party. The prettiest girl in the room is being courted by three clean-limbed Rutgers types, and William is pretending to concentrate on his fingernails. Lucille takes pity on him and introduces him to Edna. Edna herself had been sitting in the corner for three hours hoping that somebody would catch her eye. She is, of course, the last thing Jameson needs—dumb, plain, and

pretentious. He tried to make his excuses—he has to get up early in the
morning to write a paper on a "rat" called John Ruskin—but she lures
him out onto the porch. And all the time she is telling him about her
boyfriend Barry from Princeton. Jameson listens to some of this and
then lurches back inside—to resume his position on the social fringe.
Lucille asks Edna what happened and is told that Jameson had turned
out to be a little too warm-blooded: "Well, I'm still in one piece. Only
keep that guy away from me, willya?"[8]

Edna is a thinly penciled prototype of Sally Hayes in *The Catcher in
the Rye*, and there are variants of the same model in several other stories
later on: the girl phony, empty, snobbish, treacherous—and, in Edna's
case, not even "terrifically good-looking." Jameson is more loutish than
Holden—indeed, there is something almost Ackleyish about the way
he treats his fingernails—but then all we hear from him are half sentences and grunts: "Don't getcha," "Wudga mean?" Salinger has not yet
discovered the interior monologue. Indeed, the whole story is determinedly external—a short story by a playwright, with Salinger mainly
concerned about exercising his already considerable gift for crossed-
wires dialogue.

"The Young Folks" is neatly done and Salinger was to remain fond
of it for many years. For a time, he even thought of turning it (back?)
into a play with himself starring in the part of Jameson.

Having enjoyed one professional success, Salinger now wanted
more—and quickly. A few things had happened as a result of his first
publication. A literary agent called Jacques Chambrun offered to represent him and Salinger did send Chambrun one story he could try to sell.
(Nothing further came of the association and shortly afterward Salinger signed up with Harold Ober.) Salinger also noted that the big
magazines were beginning to send him little cheer-up notes along with
their routine rejection slips. He didn't like this sort of pseudoencour-
agement. He'd have preferred a straight rejection.

But Salinger did have one more success in 1940; if, indeed, he regarded it as a success. A story called "Go See Eddie" was accepted by
the *University of Kansas City Review*. We learn from this that Salinger

wasn't simply limiting himself to Burnett and the slicks: He was also
sounding out the more academic little magazines. Was this a once-only
success? Had Salinger been bombarding the universities with stories?
Or was it an isolated act of condescension on his part? It would be
interesting to know. What seems certain is that no other story by
Salinger has appeared in any college magazine.

In 1940, he was probably glad to have notched up his second publication, even though he was in general beginning to get depressed that the
big magazines were proving unsusceptible. He began to wonder if he'd
shot his bolt. Perhaps he ought to revive his career on Broadway.
Perhaps he ought to give up altogether. In this fidgety, depressed state,
he decided to get out of New York and for the next few weeks his
letters are from Cape Cod and Canada. During this summer out of
town, he wrote a long story set in a hotel (probably the Manoir Riche-
lieu at Murray Bay in Quebec), and on Tuesday nights he played bingo,
or maybe even organized it. So far as we know, the only job Salinger
had held on to was his *Kungsholm* jaunt of 1937; it was just possible that
he was doing the same kind of work at Murray Bay.

Back in New York in September, he is full of confidence again. He
has started work on an autobiographical novel, and he is turning out
the stories at a decent rate. Money is very much on his mind; he'd even
had to remind Burnett to send him his twenty-five dollars for "The
Young Folks." The novel perhaps should wait until he had pulled off
a big score with the slicks.

Salinger's twenty-first year ends with a presidential election, and he
reluctantly decides that he will give his first vote to Roosevelt. At
Ursinus he had made a habit of sneering at FDR and the New Deal
(playing up to his conservative audience, perhaps), and he had seemed
to nourish a particular distaste for Roosevelt's wife, Eleanor. But in 1940
he was ready to prefer FDR to Wendell Willkie. He had taken against
Willkie on the basis of some radio interview he'd heard. There is no
evidence that Salinger's political awareness extended much beyond a
sort of wry impressionism: All politicians were phony but some were

phonier than others. As for the European war, he seems to have accepted that he would shortly be involved, but Europe was not weighing on his mind. His round-the-clock preoccupation, to judge from his letters, was with the burgeoning (or not burgeoning) career of J. D. Salinger, as he was now determined to be called.

Although J.D. was now pouring out the stories at a hectic rate, it was to be several more months before he was able to build on the triumph of his *Story* publication. The breakthrough came in the summer of 1941, when *Collier's* took a short piece called "The Hang of It." It was printed in the magazine as "A Short Story Complete on This Page" and it had all the right *Collier's* ingredients—a bungling young army recruit, a kindly but exasperated sergeant, and a rather cloyingly ingenious trick ending. The story's narrator has a son in the army and the son can't do anything right: He can't march properly, can't fire a rifle, and his backpack falls apart when it's inspected. The narrator is reminded of a boy he had known back in World War I, a boy called Bobby Pettit. Pettit too had been a bungler, but when chastised by Sergeant Grogan he would always vow, "I'll get the hang of it."

Switch back to 1941, the present day—a big parade is being held at Fort Iroquois, and the narrator and his wife are up there on the reviewing stand to see their son perform. Sure enough, the boy marches out of step and, on presenting arms, contrives to drop his on the floor. The narrator laments these foul-ups to his wife, and she retorts that if anyone is to blame it is surely the boy's colonel. We are now set for the final scene:

Then, when the parade was over and the men had been dismissed, First Sergeant Grogan came over to say hello. "How do you do, Mrs. Pettit."

Grogan, we register—and *Pettit.* Then . . .

"Think there's any hope for our boy, sergeant?" I asked. The sarge grinned and shook his head. "Not a chance," he said. "Not a chance, colonel."[9]

Salinger's feel for the market was remarkably assured for a twenty-two-year-old. "The Hang of It" was perfectly timed. It appeared in *Collier's* on July 12; at the beginning of July, it had been announced that U.S. Army troop strength had reached 1.4 million—eight times larger than it had been a year earlier.

In March 1941, Lend-Lease began, and in April the first U.S. "shot in anger" was fired at attacking German submarines. America could soon be in the war, and army stories would be in vogue. Salinger probably wrote "The Hang of It" in May 1941, aiming at a new audience: the apprehensive young recruit. And it offered consolatory uplift: soft-hearted drill sergeants, old colonels who made mistakes when they were young, inept rookies who would one day get it right and become colonels themselves, and so on. The message was: grit your teeth and persevere—a sound Valley Forge type of commandment, and, in Salinger's *Collier's* presentation, full of easy, calculated charm.

"The Hang of It" was J.D.'s first major magazine appearance but it also marked the loss of his literary innocence. He had written to length and to formula and he had also, it would seem, perceived that a genial, tough-but-tender cuteness of address came to him easily. It was a manner that he could switch on more or less at will. Beneath the charm, though, there was a shrewd weighing of the odds. Up to now, Salinger had been encouraged to think of himself as "uneducated." The enemy in nearly all his early stories is the Ivy League smoothy; the guy with the right university background is the one who gets the girls. Outside New York, the young Salinger could pose as a sophisticate. He had his Broadway know-how, he had been to Europe. In city circles, however, there must always have been a Scott Fitzgerald-style discomfiture about his college pedigree. Who else did he, or anybody, know who had been schooled at Valley Forge and polished at Ursinus, Collegeville?

With this in mind, it seems possible that the prospect of war, although alarming in all the obvious ways, was also not without a certain attractiveness for Salinger. He may not have known much about Harvard Square, but he did know about parade grounds. He knew the routines of army life, its codes and nuances. If it was to be the fate of his generation to be called to arms, then Salinger was already a couple of years ahead of most "regular" college graduates of his age. His eccentric schooling might now be reckoned an advantage. This would have meant a lot to him. "The Hang of It," for all its commercial acumen, was also, for Salinger, an exercise in self-esteem.

3

If Salinger still needed to impress his father, the *Collier's* triumph would presumably have helped. It was the kind of magazine that businessmen kept in their outer offices. And the story itself could even be said to carry within it a message meant for Sol: Give a boy some time to get "the hang of it" and he might turn out to be as successful in his way as his revered, perhaps once-faulty, dad. But Salinger was, again, the master of two voices, and to his literary friends he was already making a separation between his "commercial" and his "real" work. When, also in 1941, he finally broke into the pages of *Esquire*, it was with a good-humored but very *de haut en bas* parody of precisely the sort of story he had just contributed to *Collier's*. "The Heart of a Broken Story" starts out, its narrator tells us, as a story for the slicks: "What could be finer, I thought. The world needs boy-meets-girl stories. But to write one, unfortunately, the author must go about the business of having the boy meet the girl." Of course, in *this* story, as it unfolds, the boy doesn't meet the girl, except in his imagination. Thus, the potboiler for *Collier's* never gets written. Instead, we have a satire for *Esquire*. [10]

And this might seem a nifty enough way for Salinger to square his conscience, but it never really worked. He was trying to get the best of both worlds, and he knew it. What is remarkable, though, is the expertise with which he was able to concoct the kind of material that *Collier's*—and, come to that, *Esquire*—would go for. He had obviously studied the magazines themselves with considerable care, but an on-the-make apprentice pro would also have been on the lookout for any other market tips he could pick up. Whit Burnett read Faulkner decently and he ran a usefully prestigious magazine, but there were other, more mean-eyed instructors around town and it seems possible that Salinger was, so to speak, attending their classes on the sly.

The editor of *Esquire* in 1942 was Arnold Gingrich (who helped Scott Fitzgerald in his last years by commissioning the Pat Hobby stories) and for Salinger he would have been an object of curiosity for some years. It is more than likely that J.D. would have read, a year earlier, Gingrich's glowing foreword to the reissue of a book called *Trial and Error* by Jack Woodford.[11] Throughout the late thirties, Woodford's short story writer's manual had been the standard how-to text for up-and-coming literary pros. Gingrich in his foreword pleads that he himself had learned everything he knew from Woodford's book: "He showed me a formula as simple as warming up canned soup." In 1940, Gingrich was one of the people Salinger had to win over, and *Trial and Error* was his book of rules. Salinger might easily have checked it out.

On the matter of boy-meets-girl stories, for example, Woodford advises hopefuls to "open story with a beautiful female creature meeting a beautiful male creature; make it evident to reader that they *ought* to fall in love." This established, you wheel in the Complication: "Something dark and threatening must fall athwart their love." The Resolution will, of course, be happy: "Marriage or some comparable arrangement." "You will be tempted to have the heroine murdered by the hero in the end. Don't. It is almost impossible to sell such stories, even if they are really 'arty,' whatever art is." The "whatever art is" jibe crops up quite often in the Woodford curriculum; he advises readers that "anyone can write; you don't need to have any particular equipment. . . . Professors who write perfect English are the worst writers in the world . . . it's the *idea* that counts, not the syntax." It would have to be agreed that *this* was the kind of teacher talk that Salinger might have responded to. Even if he didn't read the Woodford book, this was a boom period for shorter fiction and the Woodford ideology was in the air.

Woodford goes on to offer some illuminating hints on the construction of a story. In a five-thousand-word yarn, he says, you must have an opening incident that contains both movement and dialogue. Ideally, you should begin a story with the bit you originally thought of as its middle—you should go from the middle to the beginning to the end. All "expository matter" is bad and wherever possible should be converted into narrative and drama. Dialogue is good: "A story that is 75 per cent dialogue is at least ten times as easy to sell as one that is 50 per cent dialogue. . . . NEVER have less than 25 per cent dialogue." As to characterization, this is defined as "expository matter not in quotes whose purpose is to establish the characters as real," and it is always to be regarded with suspicion—it "should be held down to as low as 10 per cent of entire story wordage."

These, then, were the rules—or some of them—and whatever we may think of Woodford's jaunty philistinism, no aspiring pro in the 1940s could afford to despise it altogether. Salinger's ambition was to manipulate the slicks, but there were times when they manipulated him. Several of his early stories conform quite readily to Woodford's doctrines. To have secured his first sale to *Esquire* with a satire on commercial potboilers must have given him some comfort, but this was not a trick he could get away with more than once. He was obliged to heed the Woodfords; it would be a year or two before he could afford to echo the contempt of George Jean Nathan:

A two million circulation, like a buzz-saw, is something not to be monkeyed with . . . a two million circulation must have its constant assurance that there is a heaven, that thousands of blind, one-legged newsboys have become bank presidents, that marriage is the beginning of all happiness, and that it is as great an honor to be superintendent of the Excelsior Suspender Company as to have composed *Tristan and Isölde*. [12]

In 1941 Salinger would have liked to think he was doing what Scott Fitzgerald had to do. Fitzgerald had died a year earlier, and his legendary aspects were fresh in everybody's mind. Salinger, in his letters, always spoke warmly of him and took heart from the knowledge that it was the *Saturday Evening Post* that had supported the writing of *The Great Gatsby*. In later years he would denounce Fitzgerald's association with the magazine. For the moment, though, he believed that he—Fitzgerald's successor—could perform a balancing act, which the master himself could never master: between the Nathan and the Woodford worlds, between integrity and commerce.

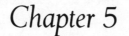

Chapter 5

1

Aged twenty-two, Salinger was still living in his parents' apartment on Park Avenue. The fees he had received from *Collier's* and *Esquire* made it possible for him to present himself to the world as a working writer, but they didn't add up to a living wage. The topic of money was often on his mind. In one sense, he didn't need it—his background was wealthy middle class. In another, it was what he needed most of all.

But he also craved respectability. And for this the ideal place to publish still had to be *The New Yorker*. It was a big metropolitan magazine but it offered a Nathan-like stylishness and poise—and it paid about the same rates as *Esquire:* modest but not to be despised. Salinger had already had several rejections from this quarter and by 1941 his admiration was beginning to turn sour. Almost worse than nothing, there had been one moment of near triumph when the revered journal did accept a piece he'd written about a boy who ran away from prep school. The boy's name was Holden Caulfield. But the editors changed their minds: In the current political climate, runaways were, in the end, not to be encouraged.

Salinger was furious, having made quite a noise about getting an acceptance. Also, it seems that at least part of his annoyance had to do with the special feelings he entertained on behalf of this particular short story. In a letter to a friend, he admits without equivocation that the boy-hero Holden Caulfield is a portrait of himself when young.[1]

Reading this letter, we biographers allowed ourselves a minor surge of self-esteem. We felt, I suppose, just for a moment, rather as policemen do, or torturers, when the confession finally gets signed. And all we'd had to do was nose around in libraries. But how absurd to feel even fleetingly triumphant. After all, the Salinger we were on the track of was surely getting less and less lovably Holden-ish each day. So far, our eavesdropping had yielded almost nothing in the way of human frailty or warmth. The first-person voice we'd been so pleased to come across had spent most of its time boasting or pushing its career. And this was not just because these letters were addressed to an editor he was anxious to impress.

Halfway through our Burnett researches at Princeton, we had learned of a further cache of letters: They were in Texas and were addressed to one Elizabeth Murray. We had come across this woman's name in a biography of Eugene O'Neill. In the fall of 1941, Salinger had been dating O'Neill's daughter Oona. He had been introduced to her by someone called Elizabeth Murray. According to the biography, the romance had always been fairly uneasy, and Salinger had all along had serious reservations about Oona's personality. Be that as it may, these letters evidently belonged to a more intimate realm of feeling than the Burnett material. We set off for Texas—or to be more precise, for the Harry Ransom Humanities Research Center at Austin.

We did so with a faint sense of unease. A year earlier, I had presented a book program on BBC-Television in which the Texas archive had been mildly ridiculed—the usual line about laundry lists, Somerset Maugham's shoelaces, and the like. The institution had been praised for its world-beating collection of modern literary manuscripts, and on the whole was treated with a quite proper respectfulness. But there had been this whimsical edge to my own introductory material, whimsical enough for me to wonder if I would be recognized when I arrived.

I was, but it didn't seem to matter. Maybe my jokes had been too deadpan. After all, if you actually *do* collect Somerset Maugham's shoelaces, your sense of the ridiculous must get mildly anesthetized after a bit. Anyway, the Salinger material was made available. I was not allowed to photocopy any of it, but I could transcribe as much of it as I liked—provided I used the library's own pencils and yellow legal pads. I couldn't quite see the reasoning behind this, but never mind. I also had to sign a form agreeing not to reproduce the material without the library's permission, and it was made clear on the same form that I would need Salinger's permission too. I signed, as I had signed a similar form at Princeton, because otherwise I would not have been allowed to see the letters. At the back of my mind, though, I was skeptical about the legal weight of these enforced undertakings. Was there not a doctrine of fair use to be invoked somewhere along the line? That is to say, I suspected that in spite of all this bureaucracy it would still be possible for me to use some small amount of the material I'd come to study. Or, failing that, I could paraphrase it. Texas presumably wouldn't object, and Salinger's objections might be deemed unreasonably restrictive. My companion was prepared to put the whole weight of his worldliness behind this, or some similar, position.

After all, as he argued, if I could neither quote nor paraphrase, then what was the point of my being allowed to see the stuff at all? What was the point, really, of its *being there*? So far as he could tell, anyone who made the trip to Austin, or who just happened to be passing by, could pop in, sign a form, and get to browse through the library's dossier on Salinger. In this sense, it was already published—albeit in a limited edition. Did Salinger know this material was sitting here? Well, even if he did, he couldn't get it back, or order it to be destroyed or locked away. The copyright was his, but the physical object, the letter itself, was the property of Texas. And Texas could show it to the world as often as it pleased. But it could not reproduce it. Most peculiar.

While I was waiting for the Salinger file to be hauled up from the vaults, I thumbed through the library's card index. Needless to say, the first name I looked up was HAMILTON, IAN (1938–). Even Texas couldn't be *that* comprehensive. But it was; to my horror, more than a dozen letters were listed under my defenseless name. Why, anyone could just walk in and . . . My companion indicated that the Salinger dossier was now sitting on desk three.

On the whole, apart from the Holden Caulfield "confession," the Murray letters were a disappointment. They provided several more facts, to be sure (as well as a wealth of unidentifiable Christian names of mutual friends), and they were a bit more open than the letters Salinger was in the habit of writing to *Story* magazine. But they were still, in the main, performances. On one occasion, a long letter to Murray is, apart from the odd word, identical with a letter he writes on the same day to Whit Burnett. Even when Salinger is depressed, there is no real letup in the self-consciousness of a letter's actual composition. And the cocksureness is still there, the wisecracks, the slick nightclubbing charm. Although it is clear that he is fond of Elizabeth Murray as a slightly older confidante, there is no romance between them (she was, it seems, the sister of a friend from Valley Forge) but one's sense, nonetheless, is that in these letters Salinger is as exposed as he can allow himself to be—which is to say, not too exposed.

Our chronology, however, did get an extra dimension. We felt closer to the man's moods, and to his anger. There is a steely unpleasantness, a hint of menace almost, in this writer's determination to succeed, to prove himself the best. Other writers, even favorites like Fitzgerald and Ring Lardner, get disparaged: Only Tolstoy is allowed the inside track. This championship impulse is evident in his letters to Burnett, but rendered jokingly most of the time. Writing to Murray, Salinger lets his own rather aggressive self-centeredness seep through. He is even, now and then, prepared to acknowledge that it's there—at any rate, in his writing—and to lament that he doesn't quite know what to do about it.

2

During the period when he first began dating Oona O'Neill (late 1941), Salinger was restless and irritable. He was unable to settle at Park Avenue. He takes off to the country for a while, or rents himself a room in the city for a couple of weeks, and then spends most of his time not using it. He would like to be in love. He would like to have his own place to live. He would like to have his stories appear in *The New Yorker*. In other words, like other young Americans in 1941, he was waiting for something, something big, to *happen*.

On December 7, 1941, the Japanese bombed Pearl Harbor, and Salinger for one was surprised by his own feelings of patriotic outrage. Earlier in the year—during his restless phase, no doubt—he had volunteered for the draft but had been rejected because of what he'd been told was a mild heart complaint. Now with war declared, he found himself wanting to make some sort of contribution. He even wrote to Milton S. Baker at Valley Forge asking if the colonel could recommend a defense job for which Salinger could volunteer.[2]

Four months later, though, the volunteer was reclassified and drafted for service in the army. On April 27, 1942, he reported to Fort Dix and from there he was transferred to Fort Monmouth in New Jersey for a ten-week instructor's course with the Signal Corps. He didn't in the least object to his army chores; his writing had been mediocre lately and in a way he quite welcomed a short break. At Fort Monmouth he mainly attended Signal Corps lectures and was also given the job of drilling new recruits. None of this held much novelty for Salinger, the ex-cadet. When, later on, he heard of William Saroyan's misery during his first weeks of army service, he was able to be almost avuncular in his solicitude. He himself knew the ropes, how to fit in; Saroyan didn't.

This break from writing was well timed. It gave Salinger a chance to sit back and take stock. From the strictly career point of view, he had reason enough to be pleased with what he had achieved. He was still only twenty-three; his work had appeared in three major magazines, and he had very nearly got into *The New Yorker*. So far, so good. But what comes next? Salinger, it seems, had begun to have doubts, solemn doubts, about the whole business of authorship, doubts which were to prove crucial later on. What did it mean to bring a character to life? From the start Salinger had shown himself to have a proprietorial, almost parental, attitude toward the people in his stories—he'd wanted to *be* Jameson onstage. This would intensify later on; indeed, it would swell into a damaging obsession. At the moment, though, it manifests itself as a mild, nagging doubt. Is there not a kind of sadism, an ugliness, in creating characters simply in order to arrange, readably, for their suffering and destruction? Ought not the author to behave more kindly, more protectively, toward these children of his imagination?

Later, Salinger will favor fictional techniques that give him the illusion of having, as it were, delivered his characters' destinies into their own keeping: the interior monologue, the letter, the long telephone call—these are all ways of making it seem that the "I" figure is in control of what is happening to him, that the parent of his tale, the author, has granted him full independence. Of course, if the characters are meant to believe in their own freedom from authorial designs, it need be no surprise if the author himself begins to partake of some similar delusion, begins to think of his characters as if they were his "real children"—creatures who have been imagined into "life," who must be looked after, sheltered from the hurtful scrutiny of critics, the casual deconstructions of the academics, the editorial intrusions of magazine editors and publishers. And of biographers who want to take them back to where they came from.

In 1942, none of these thoughts had taken shape. Salinger's unease then was much more to do with the authorial detachment he himself had been guilty of so far. He suspects that he might simply have been using fiction as a means of handing out punishments he would wish to see inflicted in real life. His changed situation—the patriotism aroused by Pearl Harbor, the camaraderie he feels with his new army buddies, the whole atmosphere of crisis and self-sacrifice—seems to have encouraged him to ponder his motives in this way. Not surprisingly, though, he feared what might happen to his work if he became more generous. Shades of the pulpit would need to be watched out for.

In June 1942—as if believing that a bit of seniority might help— Salinger decided he would make a try for Officer Candidate School, and he wrote off for references to Colonel Baker at Valley Forge and to Whit Burnett. Baker responded with a glowing testimonial; he had evidently not forgotten that full-page spread in the 1936 *Crossed Sabres*. Salinger, he said, has "all the traits of character" required in an officer. He has "an attractive personality, is mentally keen, has above-average athletic ability, is a diligent worker and thoroughly loyal and dependable."[3] Burnett was rather more cagey. He praises his former student's imagination and intelligence, and believes him "capable of swift and decisive action"; he would indeed, Burnett believed, be a "credit to an officer's rank if he sets his mind in that direction."[4] In other words, if he applies himself—the familiar refrain from Salinger's school days.

Nothing seems to have come of this first application. In July, most of Salinger's Signal Corps class transferred to Signal OCS (also based at Fort Monmouth). He himself, though, was given an instructor's job with the Army Aviation Cadets and posted south to the U.S. Army Air Force Basic Flying School at Bainbridge, Georgia. Salinger was clearly annoyed that he had not been granted a commission; as a military school graduate, he might have expected the elevation to be almost automatic. In 1943 he tried again. He had been posted by then to a cadet classification squadron at a base near Nashville, Tennessee, and it was from there that he wrote once more to Colonel Baker. He claimed this time that he had been accepted for OCS but had heard nothing since. This was not as unusual as he made it sound. As the army rule book said: "The status of applicants who are accepted but not selected may remain in abeyance indefinitely."

In an army briefing manual of the day, OCS interviewers were advised to ask applicants questions like "Can you give us instances in which, as a boy, you took the lead in normal 'gang' activities outside the home?" and "Were there obstacles to your educational development during college years? If so what did you do about such obstacles?"

Members of the selection board were instructed, in italics, to look throughout the interview "for indication of the applicant's skill in getting other people to work together and to exert group effort."[5] It is hard to think that Salinger would have emerged from such an interrogation without quite a few demerits.

3

"The Long Debut of Lois Taggett" (published in *Story*, September-October 1942) is set in a New York "society" world that Salinger himself seems to have been on the fringe of during his time between leaving college and entering the army, a Stork Club world with prosperous young girls getting nervous about their marriage prospects but filling in the in-between time by frivolously Doing Things—singing nights at Alberti's, fixing up to have a screen test, designing their own clothes. In winter such girls would maybe take a cruise to Rio or enroll for a course on Flemish painting at Columbia, but they were all in wait for Mr. Right and would chatter about little else.

Salinger's own sister, Doris, had been married in 1935, when he was sixteen, and her marriage hadn't worked. From early on, Jerome was a keen, unenchanted student of the institution. His stories are full of impetuous, mistaken unions. In "Lois Taggett" the portrait is mercilessly bleak. All the vengefulness that is never far away when Salinger turns his pen to the subject of treacherous girl phonies is here placed in the care of a character called Bill. Bill marries the debutante Lois Taggett for her money, but one morning some months after the wedding, he sees her asleep in bed: "her face was jammed against the pillow, puffy, sleep-distorted, lip-dry" and, in that second, Bill falls in love with her. The next two weeks are an idyll for the pair of them; and then an odd thing happens. Lois is sitting on Bill's knee, and they are listening to Chick Webb's Orchestra on the radio; it's playing "Smoke Gets in Your Eyes." Bill picks up a cigarette from the ashtray, but instead of dragging on it, he holds it between his fingers like a pencil and begins making small circles in the air with it, just over the back of Lois's hand:

"Better not," said Lois, with mock warning. "Burny. Burny." But Bill, as though he hadn't heard, deliberately, almost idly, did what he had to do. Lois screamed horribly, wrenched herself to her feet and ran crazily out of the room.[6]

"Deliberately," "idly," "horribly," "crazily," "did what he had to do": It is as if Salinger himself is performing in a kind of trance. Later in the same story, Bill breaks Lois's foot with a golf club—loving her hugely as he does it. Lois leaves.

It is a strange moment in Salinger's fiction and maybe just the kind of moment he was thinking of when he brooded on questions of authorial intent. In this story, the empty-headed debs he so often ridicules and mimics finally get the punishment they deserve. Lois, it should be said, later goes into a depression and then marries again—this time to a fat bore who has an allergy to colored socks. They have a baby, and it suffocates in its crib. By this means Lois is finally becalmed; her "long debut" is over, she is no longer "grand" or "phony."

Salinger's own girlfriends during his early twenties seem to have been plentiful. In his presentation there were two kinds of girl: those he despised immediately and those he fell in love with and afterward semidespised. In his letters, he is supremely offhand: A "girl" will be described as a "flash" or a "number" or a "little girl." Oona O'Neill, it seems, could not be written off so easily. She was beautiful, she was the daughter of a famous playwright, she was city-smart. With her friends Gloria Vanderbilt and Carole Marcus she formed a glamorous triumvirate much gawped at by the columnists. And when Carole Marcus got engaged to William Saroyan, Salinger might easily have read it as a Sign. From the perspective of Fort Bainbridge, Georgia, Oona seemed more urgently desirable than when he had actually been with her in New York. He began wooing her by mail. And all seemed to be going smoothly until Saroyan was posted to a base at Sacramento.

Carole went out to be near him and took Oona along with her as chaperone. Carole Marcus tells the tale:

Oona was receiving a letter almost every day from a boy named Jerry in New York. Some of the letters were fifteen pages long, and they were very witty with comments on all kinds of things. I told Oona I was afraid that if I wrote to Bill, he'd find out what an idiot I was, and decide not to marry me, so she marked the clever passages in her letters from Jerry and let me copy them, as my own, in my letters to Bill.

When Bill's two-week training period was up and I went to see him at camp, he was terribly surly. I asked him what was the matter and he told me he'd changed his mind about marrying me. He said he thought I was a sweet girl but that "those lousy glib letters" I'd been writing had made him wonder.[7]

In fact, Saroyan *did* marry her (twice), and a later twist came when Saroyan pressed her in 1951 to read a fine new book he'd just finished—it was *The Catcher in the Rye*.

Salinger was presumably none too pleased by Saroyan's early verdict on his prose, if he heard of it; certainly his rating of this author was never to be quite the same again. In this same year, he wrote to Whit Burnett about an anthology *(These Are My Best)* Burnett had just brought out and made a special point of denouncing Saroyan's contribution. And it was not long before he had further reason to feel bitter about Oona. There had been gossip items in the press linking Oona with the fifty-four-year-old Charles Chaplin. Salinger pretended indifference, but there was a sourness that refused to be suppressed. And some weeks later, when Oona married Chaplin, Salinger made no effort to disguise his sense of physical revulsion.

Salinger's letter on the subject of Charles Chaplin makes nasty reading (and it is this letter that he duplicates and sends to both Whit Burnett and Elizabeth Murray) and one fails to locate in it any powerful sense of loss. Even so, maybe because of his setbacks with Oona, marriage was on Salinger's mind throughout his time in the Deep South. There is breezy talk of various girlfriends he might honor with his hand. But everything depends on making a few more inroads on the slicks. His self-questioning gets suspended for the present, and the stories are beginning to flow smoothly once again. Often he is working on four stories at a time, and he has gone back to his old method of dividing his output into commercial and noncommercial brackets. And he is looking toward Hollywood. One big killing in the movies would buy him the freedom to set up as a full-time writer after the war. If this meant manufacturing rubbishy material, so be it.

In 1943, Salinger believed he had hit the jackpot when the *Saturday Evening Post* bought a story called "The Varioni Brothers" and there were indeed rumblings from Hollywood. But nothing came of these. Paradoxically, "The Varioni Brothers" is a parable on the evils of commercialism. "Pure" novelist Joe Varioni squanders his talent writing lyrics for his brother Sonny's tunes. The brothers make a fortune but at high cost to each of them: Joe is accidentally killed by a mobster, and Sonny spends the rest of his days trying to piece together Joe's masterpiece from the scraps of paper he has left behind—a foreshadowing of Buddy Glass's efforts on behalf of Seymour.

As to Salinger's own noncommercial stuff, he was still plugging away at *The New Yorker* but getting more and more disillusioned. He talks of wanting to write a novel but when, after "Lois Taggett" appeared in *Story*, Houghton Mifflin wrote to him suggesting that he apply for one of their fiction writing fellowships, he turned them down. And when Whit Burnett started up a publishing venture called the Story Press and began urging Salinger for a "longer work," he was only briefly tempted. The novel was *there*, evidently, and it would be—from Salinger's account of it in his letters—a first draft of *The Catcher in the Rye*. But the actual writing down of it could wait, should wait, until the moment was exactly right. And in 1943 it was not easy to predict when that would be.

4

In the autumn of 1943, the FBI paid a visit to McBurney School to check on Salinger's school background—he was being vetted for admission to the Counter Intelligence Corps. He was still fretting about his failure to get a commission and the best he had been able to manage at his latest posting, to Patterson Field in Fairfield, Ohio, was a fairly menial job in public relations. In a story written around this time (called "Once a Week Won't Kill You") the dumb wife character tells her sensitive husband that with his French and German, he ought to get *at least* a commission in intelligence: "I mean, you know how *miserable* you'll be just being a private or something. I mean you even hate to *talk* to people and everything."[8] This time, his application was successful. In October 1943 Salinger, demoted from acting staff sergeant back to corporal, was transferred to Fort Holabird in Maryland to be trained as a special agent.

The Counter Intelligence Corps was a fairly recent army invention; it had previously been known as the Corps of Intelligence Police, and its duties had been rather fussily domestic: conducting "loyalty investigations" into the background of servicemen who were under consideration for sensitive appointments and looking into so-called disaffection cases. "Disaffection," according to a CIC document of the time, was quite simply "a state of mind indicating a lack of affection for the United States."[9] In practice, this involved taking a suspicious view of anyone of German, Italian, or Japanese descent. As can easily be imagined, it was not a popular branch of the service; there were stories of intelligence policemen being planted in barracks in order to sniff out possible subversives.

It is unlikely that Salinger was required to do anything of this sort. By the time he joined the CIC it was urgently expanding its range of activities, and in December 1943 its functions were fundamentally reshaped. From that month, the domestic duties of the CIC would be handed over to the military police and all CIC operatives would be trained for overseas duties. It is probable that Salinger's very recruitment was part of this expansion. Between December 1943 and May 1944 about eight hundred American special agents were shipped to England to be trained there in "theater intelligence duties" before being assigned to specific fighting units. Salinger's posting came through in January 1943.

Up to this point it has not been at all clear how Salinger felt about the war. There was a burst of patriotism just after Pearl Harbor but since then he had shown no sign—in his letters or his stories—that the hostilities were weighing on his mind. He has coped with army life rather as he coped with life at Valley Forge—by keeping to one side of things, by putting up a serviceable front. Apart from his eagerness to get a commission (and this had nothing to do with any sense of service), he seems to have been content to muddle through from week to week, his chief concern being always to clear the time and space in which to be a writer.

Now it was different. There was every possibility that he would, after all, be called upon to fight or, at any rate, to engage with the enemy in combat situations. He might well be killed. Not long after his departure for Europe, Salinger sent three stories to the *Saturday Evening Post*. The magazine accepted all three, and—at *Post* rates, maybe two thousand dollars per story—this was close to being the big score he had been dreaming of. But these stories were not just out of stock, and one of them in particular deserves much more than a second glance. It's called "Last Day of the Last Furlough."[10]

Salinger knew that by the time the *Post* printed this story he would probably already be in action, lost from view. He had said his good-byes; his family and friends would already have begun to worry about him. Set in this context, the story can be read as a kind of letter home, a last letter, possibly. Who says? Well, Salinger's own instructions could not be more specific. The hero of the tale is called John F. Gladwaller, and his army number is 32325200, and this, we biographers can now reveal, was Salinger's own army number. The message is surely clear: Those close to him (close enough to recognize his number) should attend to this story with special care.

There are a dozen or so other clues. Gladwaller loves Tolstoy and Scott Fitzgerald; he has a snappy wardrobe and an adoring mother; he is confused about girls but he adores children. He also has a close friend called Vincent Caulfield, whose wild kid brother, Holden, seems to have been killed in action. Everyone close to Salinger would probably have known that Holden was the hero of the novel he had such high hopes for. If Holden is dead, where does that leave Salinger the writer? The story must have made harrowing reading at the time: It appeared in July 1944, a month after Salinger was known to have gone into combat.

In the story, Babe Gladwaller (as he is nicknamed) is on his last weekend at home before being shipped overseas. Several times in the course of the tale he makes it plain that he doesn't expect to survive. When his father reminisces proudly about World War I, Gladwaller turns on him and protests that it is just this kind of pride that causes wars in the first place. Gladwaller believes in this war, but he also believes that if he gets out of it alive, he will have a moral duty to keep quiet about it. Children should be taught to laugh at wars: "If German boys had learned to be contemptuous of violence, Hitler would have had to take up knitting to keep his ego warm."[11]

After this outburst, Gladwaller feels embarrassed even though he means what he said. Later in the story he speaks out again, this time to himself. He has an adorable young sister called Mattie, and when he is with her he can be "happier than [he has] ever been in [his] entire life." The lyrical moments he enjoys with Mattie mean more to him than his books, his girlfriend, than himself, even. For Mattie, and for what she represents, he is prepared to die: ". . . this is my home . . . this is where Mattie is sleeping. No enemy is banging on our door, waking her up, frightening her. But it could happen if I don't go out and meet him with my gun. And I will, and I'll kill him. I'd like to come back. It would be swell to come back. It would be—"[12]

In case he doesn't "come back" Gladwaller gives Mattie some advice. She will grow up one day, he says, and she will be plunged into the phony adult world. What he wants to tell her is that she must always try to live up to "the best that's in you. . . . If you give your word to people, let them know that they're getting the word of the best."

If you room with some dopey girl at college, try to make her less dopey. If you're standing outside a theater and some old gal comes up selling gum, give her a buck if you've got a buck—but only if you can do it without patronizing her. That's the trick, baby. . . . You're going to be smart when you grow up. But if you can't be smart and a swell girl, too, then I don't want to see you grow up. Be a swell girl, Matt.[13]

Robert Lowell was once asked by an interviewer if a poet he admired was not "on the verge of being slight and even sentimental." Lowell replied that "if he hadn't dared to be sentimental, he wouldn't have been a poet. I mean, his inspiration is that."[14] Salinger's inspiration is of the same order and will continue to be so, but he doesn't yet know how to keep it "on the verge." In 1944, not many writers did.

Chapter 6

1

The idea of J. D. Salinger as special agent, as a thief of secrets, an impersonator, was obviously of considerable appeal to us: cloaks and daggers, messages in tree trunks, radios in attics—this surely was our kind of world. Literary biographers are a thwarted tribe; they are gumshoes at heart and they yearn for their subjects to make contact with the realm of action. More often than not, though, unless they have a T. E. Lawrence or a Hemingway to celebrate, they are doomed to monitor merely interior upheavals. There is thus a tendency always to inflate *any* contact their subject might have had with the outer, public chaos of his time.

And with Salinger, it was so *appropriate* to be able to portray him as a spy, to reflect that even in uniform this man was in disguise. It was suggested to us by an ex-army acquaintance that perhaps Salinger is *still* a spy, or that somewhere in his spying past there is a secret so secret that he now has no choice but to dwell perpetually in shadows, in daily fear, no doubt, of some terrible exposure. It was easy enough to dismiss this as nonsense, but not so easy to suppress our own thirst for even just a sip of melodrama. It was with narrowed eyes that we moved on to the next stage of our "investigation."

But where to look? After all, the point about armies is that—like spies—they thrive on anonymity. Troop movements are easily researched, but try tracing the movements of a single trooper. On Salinger's army life in America, we had letters to assist us. After his posting to Europe, though, all his mail had to pass through the censor's office. The few letters we did have from 1944–45 were fairly cryptic. In the archives of *Time* magazine (which did a cover story on Salinger in 1961, an event we shall come to later on) there are transcripts of interviews done with some of Salinger's army buddies, and also a résumé of his army record—a bare outline, really, but enough to tell us his unit and division and to give us some idea of where he was, or should have been, or might have been during most weeks of 1944. We sent in a request to Washington for further information, citing the Freedom of Information Act, and we were told—quite properly, it seemed to us—that we would need permission from our subject. We made a trip to the National Archives in Suitland, Maryland, just outside Washington, and burrowed through the regimental files. In these there were some daily intelligence reports that could have been in Salinger's handwriting. The reports were to do with the interrogation of German prisoners of war, and the prose did have one or two nonbureaucratic flourishes. But we wanted them to be by him too badly for them to have really been by him.

Our story, then, would have to become even more thin and conjectural. And yet—or was it therefore?—we had this powerful intimation that we were near to the crux of the matter, the biographical turning point, the shaping crisis; we had this sense that 1944–45 was where the "secret" might be found. The best we could do was to set down what we had, and then stand back from it—the silhouette, the stencil might show through. But we had to keep in mind that perhaps we were already in search of a Salinger who had changed from the callow self-advancer we'd already met. There was, in his last story, a pathos verging on the sentimental, which had not been allowed to show itself in the tough stories of his early youth. There was also a groping for the

Larger Statement: a small but significant lapse of self-sufficiency, it could be said.

By March 1944, Salinger was stationed at the headquarters of the Fourth Infantry Division at Tiverton, in Devon, the setting for the first section of his famous postwar story "For Esmé—with Love and Squalor." We visited Tiverton and even advertised in the local paper, but we knew that we'd find little here except the hill he used to walk down from his camp into the town and the church in which the soldier in the story first encounters Esmé. This wasn't biography; this was tourism. We did have the evidence of one ex-army colleague who said that Salinger would often visit the town's Methodist church to listen to the choir, but absolutely nothing at all on a pert little girl aristocrat he might have met in the tearoom just across the street. We would have rather liked to link Salinger with the extraordinary events of EXERCISE TIGER—a U.S. Army exercise in which 749 servicemen perished in a mock invasion of the Devon coast—but we found no evidence that he had any close-up involvement with it. He would have *known* about it, though, and—like everybody else—he would have been ordered not to talk. Was he therefore sending out a signal when he had Sergeant X meet Esmé on April 30, 1944? EXERCISE TIGER took place on April 28 and 29.

From Salinger's letters, we could learn that during the pre-D-Day buildup he was writing hard and had actually completed six chapters of the Holden Caulfield novel. He was convinced, we discover, that a new element of warmth can be detected in his work, and that he might finally have outgrown his old destructive habits. And this, of course, is a development from the authorial worries that had afflicted him in 1942. Then, the urge toward warmheartedness was abstract, willed. He was stuck in the South, his army work bored him, and he was locked into an irritated or condescending aloofness from most of his buddies. In 1944, the difference was that Salinger begins to experience—for maybe the first time in his life—a sense of tribal solidarity.

In England, he was made to feel like an American, an American soldier at whom the Devon locals were inclined to stare. And with the

Normandy invasion looming, even the dumbest of his colleagues had to be regarded as comrades-in-arms. Outsiderism would not be easy to sustain in combat; fighting soldiers are necessarily committed to one another's care. A new note of feelingful camaraderie begins to show itself, both in his letters and in his stories. In "The Last Day of the Last Furlough," Vincent Caulfield tells Babe Gladwaller: "G.I.'s belong together these days. It's no good being with civilians any more. They don't know what we know and we're no longer used to what they know." Babe thinks about this for a moment, then replies, "I never really knew anything about friendship before I was in the Army."

There is also a new tendency for his stories to have "heroes." Until now the "great men" in Salinger's life and imagination have been dead literary heroes; he could nourish his own romantic pose of singularity by forming friendships, so to speak, with other superior spirits like Tolstoy and Scott Fitzgerald. From 1944 onward there is no slackening in Salinger's reverence for the magically great and gifted; his new position, though, permits him to concede that one or two of his living fellows might be worthy of his admiration. "Great men" begin appearing in his work. In "The Last Day of the Last Furlough," we have our first glimpse of Vincent Caulfield, the sage older brother who will eventually turn into Seymour Glass. And in "Soft-Boiled Sergeant," written around the same time, we meet a sugared army version of the ampler spirit: a heroic combat veteran, ugly, taciturn, spiritually battered, and yet quietly generous to those weaker and more frightened than himself. A nerve-racked young recruit is helped toward manhood by the sergeant's cool, paternal ministrations and is thus thoroughly won over to the military ethos. "I met more good guys in the Army than I ever knowed when I was a civilian."[1]

"Soft-Boiled Sergeant," "The Last Day of the Last Furlough," and "Both Parties Concerned" were the three stories that Salinger had sold to the *Saturday Evening Post* before setting off for Europe. He had been elated by the sale and had even donated some of the proceeds as prize money for a *Story* magazine short story contest. When the first two appeared, though, Salinger found his titles had been changed—"Both

Parties Concerned" and "Soft-Boiled Sergeant" had been dreamed up
by the *Post*'s editors (Salinger had called them "Wake Me When It
Thunders" and "Death of a Dogface"). There had been no consultation. Also the stories were tricked out with more than usually cute
illustrations. His triumph had turned sour. He would never again, he
vowed, expose himself to this kind of editorial manhandling.

Whit Burnett, thrilled by Salinger's generous donation to his magazine, wrote back suggesting that since Salinger didn't want to be rushed
on the Holden Caulfield book, it might be a good idea for him to collect
his short stories together in a volume. He suggested calling such a book
The Young Folks:

All of the people in the book would be young, tough, soft, debutante, social,
army, etc. Perhaps the first third of the book could be stories of young people
on the eve of war; the middle third in and around the army, and then one or
two stories at the close of war.

Burnett had some qualms about the commercial possibilities: "It is
dangerous if it fails," he warns, since booksellers might be nervous
about any follow-up book by the same author. But on the other hand,
"I have more faith in your writing than in that of 90% of the young
people I have run into."[2]

Salinger's reply was cautious, but even so he provided Burnett with
a list of the eight stories he thought his best: "The Young Folks,"
"Elaine" (a new story he has just submitted to *Story*), "The Long
Debut of Lois Taggett," "The Last Day of the Last Furlough," "Death
of a Dogface" ("Soft-Boiled Sergeant"), "Wake Me When It Thunders" ("Both Parties Concerned"), "Once a Week Won't Kill You,"
and "Bitsy" (now lost). He confirms that work on the Holden book has
been suspended for the moment.[3]

2

Salinger was with the 12th Infantry Regiment of the Fourth Division when it landed on Utah Beach on June 6, 1944. We have no record of what *that* felt like and the words of the regimental historian don't exactly bring the scene alive. The regiment, we are told, landed "under heavy shelling, moved rapidly inland across the inundated area, made a 45 degree right turn and attacked with lightning speed an alert and determined enemy. By night, we had advanced two miles inland." From here the regiment pushed on to Cherbourg. The only way we can locate Salinger in all this is to assume that he was doing what, as a CIC agent, he was supposed to be doing. At each newly captured town or village, agents would make for the "communication centers, cut off the telephones and impound the mails. They would then begin interrogating the hundreds of prisoners who were rounded up in the so-called Civilian Cage: on the look-out here for collaborators and for German army deserters in civilian clothing."[4]

Between June and August, the 12th moved from Cherbourg down to Paris—an often hazardous march, but perhaps not as bad as many of the ordinary soldiers would have feared. According to Salinger's letters, he himself had had one or two close shaves on the way, but his general tone at this point is relaxed, almost jaunty, as if he were quite happy, for the time being, to have come through the first weeks of the campaign "with all his faculties intact." And his own account of the 12th's entry into Paris on August 25 is no less ebullient than that of the regiment's normally unexcitable historian: "The regiment rode in triumphal procession through the Porte d'Italie and down streets jammed from wall to wall with thousands of joyous Parisians. Paris was free— the biggest news the world had heard since D Day."[5]

Salinger was only in Paris for a few days but typically he did not allow all the excitement to distract him from his literary objectives. He had heard that Ernest Hemingway was in town, holding Liberation Day court at the Ritz Hotel and he decided to pay him a visit. They had never met; according to one of Salinger's army friends, Salinger

suddenly said, "Let's go see Hemingway."⁶ Salinger's account of the
visit in his letters is close to reverential: The two authors seem to have
spent most of their time praising each other. Hemingway certainly
turned on the charm, telling Salinger he had seen his picture in *Esquire*
and asking to see some of his new work. Salinger showed him "The
Last Day of the Last Furlough" and Hemingway read it and said he
liked it.

Nothing, it seems, could have been cozier, although there is in print
a story that on some later occasion Hemingway visited Salinger's unit
(as a war correspondent he was, as it happened, attached to the Fourth
Division) and "got to arguing about the merits of a German Luger he
was carrying as opposed to the U.S. .45, and blasted the head off a
chicken to prove his point."⁷ Salinger is said to have been greatly
shocked by this and to have later incorporated the incident into "For
Esmé—with Love and Squalor." There is no firsthand evidence to
authenticate this tale, but we do learn from Salinger's letters that he had
little patience for Hemingway's macho posturing. Salinger's war
heroes rarely have a taste for war.

But that literary encounter in the Ritz Hotel would, for Salinger,
have been like touching base, the base that mattered. In the view of at
least two of his fellow CIC agents, Salinger the soldier was never for
long separable from Salinger the professional word spinner.⁸ He was,
they say, a conscientious soldier and especially good at the interrogation side of his job. Nobody, however, believed him to be deeply
committed to the war. "He liked the work but he was not a military
man—he talked about wanting out. He wasn't popular—he was the
kind of person that if he didn't like you it showed on him." His only
real commitment was to writing: "He lugged that little portable typewriter all over Europe. I can remember him down under a table pecking away while we were under attack near a front. He wanted to be
a good writer, and he wrote all the time."

The same colleague recalls that he would read Salinger bits from his
letters home, "and Jerry would incorporate these into his stories."
Another remembers him in much the same way, though more acidly:

"We worked together as a pair on several occasions. I didn't think of him as a friend. I was from poor people and he was from rich people. We generally got along on a live-and-let-live basis. In my opinion, he would look down on me and I sometimes thought he was a little belligerent. When I felt I didn't agree with him, I would just walk away. There was no animosity, but he was a kind of lone wolf."

This soldier also remembers Jerry pecking away at his typewriter: "He didn't join in the drinking and card playing. Even during the hottest campaigns, he was writing, sending off to magazines." As to the war: "I had the feeling he was just tolerating it as long as he had to and figured when it was over he would just get back to the good life he enjoyed before." (It should be kept in mind that this testimony comes from one who was much shocked when, long after the war, his young daughter was given *The Catcher in the Rye* as a set text at school; he considered the book "horse crap.")

By September 4, 1944, the 12th Infantry had begun pushing toward Germany and we can trace its painfully slow progress on the map from the "cold, dreary Schnee-Eiffel forest," not far from the Siegfried Line to the cold, but not so dreary Hürtgen Forest, south of the Aachen-Duren highway. The battle for the Hürtgen Forest has been widely chronicled, and all the histories agree that it was one of the toughest and bloodiest episodes of America's European war. The Germans were determined to hold the forest, believing it to be vital to the defense of the Roer Dams, Düren, and the Cologne Plain, and their forces outnumbered the Americans by four to one. The conditions were appalling: It was a bitterly cold winter, and most of the terrain was "deep, adhesive mud" clogged with mines, booby traps, and fallen trees. Nothing—men, supplies, equipment, reinforcements—could be moved quickly or without risk of explosion. A gain of five hundred yards was thought to be a heroic day's work, and it was. The Hürtgen Forest casualties were on a scale that "appalled even D-Day soldiers."[9]

The battle dragged on for a month: By December 7, the 12th had cleared its sector of the forest. The division history records that "the horrors of Hürtgen can never be forgotten by the men who were there" and this was echoed by Mack Morriss, writing in *Yank* magazine in December 1944. Of the survivors Morriss says: "Behind them they left their dead, and the forest will stink with deadness long after the last body is removed. The forest will bear the scars of our advance . . . the infantry has scars that will never heal, perhaps."[10]

Will never heal. Salinger himself wrote an elegy for the Hürtgen Forest dead in a story called "The Stranger." Babe Gladwaller, who has survived the war, visits Vincent Caulfield's ex-girlfriend in New York. Vincent was killed in the Hürtgen when a mortar exploded in his face; he was standing around with Babe at the command post when it happened. Babe wants to give his friend's girl a poem Vincent wrote for her. It's an uneasy visit: Gladwaller feels, not for the first time, a huge separation between those who *know* about what happened in the forest and those who have only *read* about it. Earlier in the story he has listened to a jazz record of Bakewell Howard playing "Fat Boy" and had heard in it "the music of the irrecoverable years, the little, unhistorical, pretty good years when all the dead boys in the 12th Regiment had been living and cutting in on other dead boys on lost dance floors: the years when no one who could dance worth a damn had ever heard of Cherbourg or St.-Lô or Hürtgen Forest or Luxembourg."[11]

The battle for Luxembourg began on December 16, 1944. At dawn on that day the Germans struck along the greater portion of the American First Army front in what was to become known as Von Rundstedt's Ardennes offensive, or the Battle of the Bulge. For ten days the 12th was heavily engaged in the defense of Echternach and in other, more successful line-holding operations in and around Luxembourg city. Salinger, we have reason to believe, was in the thick of it, and it was probably during this period that he was most vigorously "digging foxholes to cowardly depths," as he is said to have put it jocularly to an old girlfriend from Ursinus. For some days friends of his back home believed that he was among the captured or killed at Echternach; after five days of bloody fighting, the town fell to the Germans on December 21. To suffer these reverses so soon after the heroic effort of the Hürtgen must have been sickening; and there was more to come:

As the advancing 212th Volksgrenadier Division, reinforced, pushed its spearheads down the roads and valleys, it was met in the various places by all of the resources the Fourth could muster. It was an assorted crew. Two battalions of infantry, a company of cooks, military police and mechanics, two battalions of engineers and reconnaissance troops, and any other miscellaneous troops in the area were shoved into the line to halt the enemy. The Germans were stopped, Luxembourg was saved.

This was on December 26. The line held by the Fourth Division was the barrier behind which Allied forces in the south were able to reorganize. The ten days had been costly but in army terms they had provided "crucial breathing space"; General Patton sent a telegram praising the Fourth's "outstanding accomplishment." On the same day, back in New York, Whit Burnett noted in a memo: "Salinger well. Letter and phone to his mother. December 27."

For the first three months of 1945, the 12th pushed forward into Germany, crossing the Rhine at Worms on March 30: "towns and cities fell rapidly" as they advanced, and with each victory the CIC agents would round up the local Nazi bigwigs, seal party buildings, and check out suspicious Germans "whose presence might constitute a threat to authority." On May 5, the day of the German surrender, the 12th set up its command post in Göering's castle at Nauhaus. Shortly afterward the CIC agents who had served with the regiment since D-Day were given a new posting—to an intelligence detachment set up to assist the denazification of Germany.

The evidence we have suggests that Salinger might not have been included in this posting. Indeed—and we must speak with some caution here—it seems likely that by the time the 12th sailed back to the United States in July 1945 our subject was going through some sort of nervous breakdown. "Breakdown" might, for all we know, be too severe a term for whatever it was that afflicted Salinger around this time. According to a letter he wrote to Ernest Hemingway in July of that year, he was hospitalized in Nuremberg and under treatment for a condition that threatened to earn him a psychiatric discharge from the army.

There are other letters too from this period in which he speaks with
a lacerated bitterness about the war, the waste of life, and about the
back-home Armistice Day patriotics, which he despises. In these letters
there is both anguish and anger. On the other hand, the letter to
Hemingway is almost manically cheerful: Indeed, its voice is precisely
that of the eager, wisecracking, full-of-himself young Salinger of 1939.
This letter burbles on, boastful, flattering, facetious, as if to an old
chum—although the probability is that he had met Hemingway but
twice.

This Hemingway letter was written in July, and Salinger finally got
his (nonpsychiatric, we assume) discharge from the army in November.
In between, another odd thing happens. He gets married: his bride a
French girl he can hardly have known for more than a few weeks. This
contributes to the general picture of, at best, impulsiveness; at worst,
a kind of desperation. In a story published in the *Saturday Evening Post*
three days after Salinger's discharge from the army, Babe Gladwaller
is also desperate. Babe is back in New York. He is on the edge of a
nervous collapse; everything reminds him of the war, and almost everything makes him break into tears. He wants to apologize to everyone,
he says, and also to tell everyone what happened: "the thing that was
really terrible was the way your mind wanted to tell civilians these
things." We are reminded of Babe's vow to "keep quiet" about the war
if he got back alive.

The story itself is almost on the brink of tears. Salinger was still in
the army when he wrote it, and there is a possibility that between his
hospitalization and his wedding he had some August leave back home.
Babe anyway knows what it feels like to walk the "three long blocks
between Lexington and Fifth" and see an apartment-house doorman
walking his wire-haired between Park and Madison:

Babe figured that during the whole time of the Bulge the guy had walked that
dog on this street every day. He couldn't believe it. He could believe it but it
was still impossible.[12]

3

There is this same fragile, precarious tone of voice in the few other snatches of autobiography that center on Salinger's last year in uniform. As early as November 1944—during the Hürtgen Forest fighting—he was writing almost elegiacally about the old life in New York. He used to go "pretty steady" with the big city, he says, but he finds that his memory is slipping. He has forgotten bars and streets and faces. The New York he now recalls most vividly is the New York of his childhood—"the American Indian room in the Museum of Natural History" where, like Holden Caulfield, he once spilled his marbles on the floor.[13]

In prewar days, Salinger had been able to mask his nervous alienation by working hard at his big-city poise; even in late 1945 there is a lingering determination to keep the slick one-liners smiling through. The strain is evident, though, in a short self-description he sent to *Esquire:* "After the war I plan to enlist in a good, established chorus-line. This is the life . . ."[14] The effort to sustain a debonair persona in New York would have been too much for Babe Gladwaller, and there is no reason to suppose that Salinger felt differently. Certainly, all the war service stories that he wrote around this time are focused on a single subject: the war-damaged survivor pitiably suspended between two worlds—the world of combat and the world of civilian readjustment.

There are four stories that are, shall we say, afflicted in this way. Two of them feature Babe Gladwaller: "The Stranger," in which Babe visits Vincent Caulfield's girl, and "A Boy in France," one of the very few Salinger stories to attempt a description of front-line conditions. Babe is sheltering in a foxhole, he is exhausted and afraid, a nail has been ripped from one of his fingers, and the finger throbs. Babe, it is evident, has had enough. He dreams of home: of having just bathed, put on clean clothes (a blue polka-dot tie, a gray suit with a stripe), made coffee, and put a record on the phonograph: "I'll listen to the music, and I'll bolt the door. I'll open the window. I'll let in a nice, quiet girl—not Frances, not anyone I've ever known—and I'll bolt the door." As the dream fades, he takes some papers from his tunic pocket: some gossip column press cuttings about Broadway, which he crumples up and throws away, and a letter from his sister, Mattie—sweet, gossipy, and artless, but ending with a PPS: "I miss you. Please come home soon." On reading this (for more than thirty times, he says) the soldier "sank back into the hole and said aloud to nobody 'Please come home soon.' Then he fell crumbly, bent-leggedly asleep."

In the other two stories, the autobiographical Babe is missing and, perhaps in consequence, their treatment of the crisis is less cloying, although each does come close to surrendering control. One of them is unpublished, and the other is perhaps the most celebrated of all Salinger's shorter works: "For Esmé—with Love and Squalor." The unpublished piece, "The Magic Foxhole," is set mainly in France. The hero's name is Gardner this time, but he is Gladwalleresque in all essentials. Gardner is wrecked by the war. In combat, he keeps on meeting a ghost soldier dressed in a strange, futuristic uniform. Gardner interrogates him and discovers that the "soldier" is his own yet-to-be-born son, a boy called Earl. Earl is now aged twenty-one and is a combatant, it seems, in World War III. Gardner decides that he must kill this phantom offspring: If Earl dies, maybe the next war will never happen. The story ends with Gardner, still hallucinating, confined in a military hospital, a victim of what the authorities call battle fatigue.

In "For Esmé," Sergeant X suffers from a similar fatigue. Some months after VE Day, he too had been hospitalized. He is now back with his unit in Bavaria. The book in his hand used to belong to a "low official in the Nazi Party, but high enough, by Army Regulations standards, to fall into an automatic-arrest category." On the book's flyleaf are the words "Dear God, life is hell." Sergeant X "put his arms on the table and rested his head on them. He ached from head to foot, all zones of pain seemingly interdependent. He was rather like a Christmas tree whose lights, wired in series, must all go out even if one bulb is defective." In the exchanges that follow between Sergeant X and the vacuous but well-intentioned Clay—"his jeep partner and constant companion through five campaigns of the war"—we learn that X has served in something very like the CIC, that he was in Normandy and in the Hürtgen Forest, and that he has had a nervous breakdown.

Salinger's three war survivors—Gladwaller, Gardner, Sergeant X—are wounded in the nerves. Gardner doesn't recover, but both Gladwaller and Sergeant X are permitted healing intimations. In both cases, the therapy arrives in the shape of a radiantly innocent young girl. In "The Stranger," Gladwaller's Mattie does a charming "little jump from the curb to the street surface, then back again" and this is enough to stir Babe's faint hopes of recovery. "Why was it such a beautiful thing to see?" In "For Esmé," Sergeant X opens a package from the precocious little girl he'd met in England a year earlier, a few weeks before D-Day. Esmé has sent him a shockproof watch as a "lucky talisman": It had belonged to her father, who'd been killed in action.

It was a long time before X could set the note aside, let alone lift Esmé's father's wristwatch out of the box. When he did finally lift it out, he saw that its crystal had been broken in transit. He wondered if the watch was otherwise undamaged, but he·hadn't the courage to wind it and find out. He just sat with it in his hand for another long period. Then, suddenly, almost ecstatically, he felt sleepy.

You take a really sleepy man, Esmé, and he *al*ways stands a chance of again becoming a man with all his fac—with all his f-a-c-u-l-t-i-e-s intact.[15]

4

Unsurprisingly, Salinger's career plans seem also to have gone into retreat during these last months of 1945. In September, Simon and Schuster wrote to him, suggesting that they might publish a collection of his stories, but he told them that he would rather wait. (The sender of the letter, Don Congdon, recalls that for some months after Salinger returned to New York, he, Congdon, pursued him on behalf of S&S. Salinger seems to have liked Congdon well enough and came close to signing up on more than one occasion, but after meeting some of the company's top brass, he decided to say no.[16]) Also in 1945 Whit Burnett brought out (with Lippincott) an anthology called *Time to Be Young: Great Stories of the Growing Years.* Nothing from Salinger is included in the book's fifty or so essays and short stories. Very likely, he was asked to contribute and refused: Burnett does include a few of his Columbia discoveries among the mainly famous names. It would seem that Salinger broke with Burnett earlier in this same year. He had been given a contract by Lippincott/Story Press for his own *The Young Folks* volume of short stories, but the deal was suddenly called off. Shortly afterward, Burnett brought out *Time to Be Young.* Salinger felt badly used. Many years later (in 1963) Burnett wrote several times to Salinger asking permission to reprint work in anthologies, and his letters were always passed on to Ober for reply. In the end Salinger's ex-mentor wrote despondently to Dorothy Olding that it hadn't been his fault that the Lippincott arrangement had collapsed: "We almost broke with Lippincott at the time because they wouldn't take this book, although I do not think I made my point as emphatic as that to him when we had our final lunch together in the Vanderbilt Hotel and had to tell him that the book was turned down."[17]

It might be thought that with his volume of short stories spurned, Salinger would soon have got back to work on his Holden Caulfield novel. He had never been wholly certain about *The Young Folks* scheme and repeatedly during the war he had talked of wanting the time and solitude in which to tackle his longer work. In 1945, though, he seems to have decided that this too should be shelved: "I am a dash man not a miler, and it is probable that I will never write a novel."

Babe Gladwaller had said that soldiers had a moral duty not to speak about the war and then had found that he for one could speak of nothing else. Salinger's predicament in 1945 seems to have been similar. All his responses as a writer were tuned to the horrors he had witnessed and endured. It would have been hard to resurrect the schoolboy innocence of Holden Caulfield at a time like this. And yet he recoiled from the idea of writing a war novel:

So far the novels of this war have had too much of the strength, maturity and craftsmanship critics are looking for, and too little of the glorious imperfections which teeter and fall off the best minds. The men who have been in this war deserve some sort of trembling melody rendered without embarrassment or regret. I'll watch out for that book.[18]

Chapter 7

"Well, now you have your crisis." My companion was looking shrewdly diagnostic. Indeed, for days now there had been something distasteful in the smug, scientific way he'd set about rearranging his file cards. It was as if, having located the malignant source, he could simply sit back and watch the poison spread. All would be "symptomatic" from now on. It didn't seem to matter to him that we hadn't, even in his terms, proved anything that ought to have surprised us. After all, we had to some extent *created* a brash young Salinger who, if he went to war, would almost certainly crack up. But just as we liked the idea of casting our man as an undercover agent, so we warmed to the notion that he might, if only for a moment, have been mad. We liked the idea of him as a mysterious controller of his fate, but we also wanted to see him as maimed by some glamorously dreadful trauma.

"But take a look at the map, the real map," I insisted. Right from the beginning, my companion had carried around with him a couple of beige folders; on the inside covers of each he had drawn vertical and horizontal lines, creating a neat little box for every month of Salinger's life, 1936–65. His writing life. Thus, in the box for September 1936 you'd find Salinger's entry to Valley Forge; in January 1940, his first publica-

tion in *Story* magazine; in June 1944, his arrival, plus friends, on the
beaches of Normandy; and so on. If the "date" was confirmed by the
evidence we had, it would be marked in red ink. If it was conjectural,
a faint gray pencil would be used. And if we hadn't a clue where
Salinger was in, say, October 1945, then that slot would stay blank.
Whenever my companion began to crow, I would usually urge him to
reconsult his folders: "the map," as he was wont to call them.

Certainly, there were some healthy clumps of crimson here and
there, and the pencilings were almost quixotically extensive, but what
about those empty bits? These covered most of 1944–45 (I had had to
restrain my companion from penciling in *troop movements*, which he
often seemed to think he'd copied from J.D.'s personal Dataday). Aside
from three key confirmed dates—Salinger's hospitalization, his wedding, his discharge from the army—we had what I would call a blank
all the way from September 1944 until the end of 1945. True enough,
we had the fiction, and we could deduce states of mind from this—
especially from the Gladwaller material, which we were explicitly invited to treat as autobiographical. But surely we should be careful to
stop short of any final diagnoses?

My companion had the good grace to seem troubled for a moment,
or was it just that he had learned by now to fall silent whenever he
suspected any faltering of my resolve? When he *did* speak (forgetting,
no doubt, those early voices in New York, which, as I remembered it,
we'd both instinctively recoiled from) the best he could come up with
was "The wife, maybe, is the key." "We agreed not to pursue the wife."
"But that was the *second* wife. We didn't even know about this one
when we started. And in any case, it was all of forty years ago."

I let him summarize "the wife so far." She was French—we knew
this from Salinger's letters—and her name was Sylvia. According to
army friends of JDS, she was a doctor, but there was some indecision
as to whether she was a psychologist or an osteopath. "You know, one
of those doctors who is almost a doctor." They were married in September 1945. We had a glimpse of them as a couple at Christmas 1945,
idyllically happy and living in Gunzenhausen, Germany. Although

Salinger had been discharged from the army in November 1945, he had
signed a "six months civilian contract with the Defense Dept."[1] His
duties, we had good reason to believe, were to do with denazification.

Why had he signed on? Was it so that he could stay in Europe with
his new wife? Maybe she couldn't leave. Or was it that, like Babe, he
couldn't yet face civilian America? And what were his feelings as a half
Jew as he went about his business of picking up and interrogating
Nazis? Was this something he wanted to do more of or less of? "I was
surprised," a friend has said, "when he got married. He was so anxious
to come home and then he decided to stay out there and get married."[2]

The marriage lasted eight months. Salinger did take Sylvia back to
the States, probably in May 1946 when his contract would have expired.
But "she could not separate herself from her European ties," a friend
has explained. "She went back to France and got a divorce." Salinger
himself announces the end of the marriage from a hotel, the Sheraton-
Plaza, at Daytona Beach, Florida: a setting similar to that in his story
"A Perfect Day for Bananafish." In the story, Seymour Glass is recovering from a nervous breakdown, or is meant to be, and he is having
trouble adjusting to his wife's altogether foreign dispositions. Seymour
kills himself. Salinger, in his Sheraton letter, declares that for the first
time since his wedding he has been able to finish a short story. It is
called "The Male Goodbye."[3]

"We ought to trace her. There must be records of the marriage. If
she was a doctor, she must be on some lists. Except we don't have her
maiden name. But maybe she kept his . . ." His voice tailed off: Even
he, and even as he spoke, was able to see that here was an area that might
be ankle deep in dynamite. The information we had painlessly managed
to assemble was simply not enough to assure that the seeking of more
would not, in itself, and maybe in the very moment we began it, tear
open some old wounds. "But if we are scared off here by a damage that
we can't anticipate, why isn't that same fear preventing us from trying
to find out what Salinger did next?" "It's *her,*" I said, "not him. She
didn't write a book." And just for once, he let me have my way.

2

In 1946, J. D. Salinger seems to have found himself facing a dead end. His stories were no longer going to appear in book form; his novel was not the work he wanted to be writing at this hour. The "trembling melody" he believes would be appropriate to what he and others have just been through was elusive, maybe altogether out of reach. There is evidence that during this period he turned to writing verse; certainly, the kind of requiem he seems to have been yearning for was more likely to be captured in a song than in the consecutive, magazine-aimed narratives he'd trained himself to knock out under fire.[4]

For the next two years, 1945 to 1947, Salinger was silent so far as new, published writing is concerned. Two stories did appear in magazines but they were both, in a sense, old stuff. Ironically, it was in these troubled, creatively uncertain years that he at last made his debut in *The New Yorker* with "A Slight Rebellion Off Madison," the Holden Caulfield story that the magazine had accepted and then sat on in 1941. It appeared on December 21, 1946, but was tucked away in the back pages. The other story, "A Young Girl in 1941 with No Waist at All," was based on his youthful spell as entertainments organizer on the MS *Kungsholm,* and is really about the prewar lull, the breaking of the peace. It was tucked away among the fashion pictures in the May 1947 issue of *Mademoiselle.*

In *Mademoiselle*'s notes on contributors—or "Mlle. Passports"—Salinger solemnly announced that he "does not believe in contributors' columns." All he is prepared to say about himself is that "he started to write at eight and never stopped, that he was with the Fourth Division and that he almost always writes of young people."[5] Salinger as man of mystery might be said to have made his first appearance on this day. He was twenty-eight now, a combat veteran; for the first time, there is something faintly poignant in his determination to write "almost always . . . of young people."

For the moment, though, he seems to have been content to drift, to play for time. He began to be seen in Greenwich Village clubs and bars;

he even joined in small-stake poker games with other literary war veterans. The Hemingway biographer A. E. Hotchner remembers Salinger around this time as "lankly, darkly handsome" and insufferably arrogant: "He had an ego of cast iron." Hotchner met him once or twice for Wednesday night poker games at the Charlton Street apartment of Don Congdon, the Simon and Schuster editor who was still (at this stage) hoping to capture Salinger's first book of stories. Now and then, says Hotchner, he and Salinger would go for a drink "at Chumley's after a game.... We'd sit there and Jerry ... would arrogantly condemn all the well-known writers from Dreiser to Hemingway. In fact, he was quite convinced that no really good American writers existed after Melville— that is, until the advent of J. D. Salinger. I used to listen to his angry discourses, utterly fascinated with his opinionatedness and with the furious belief he had in his own literary destiny."[6]

At first Hotchner guessed that Salinger's anger had to do with poverty, but then he "found out that Jerry lived in a luxurious Park Avenue apartment with his parents." He also found out, he says, that Salinger had had a nervous breakdown during the war. Maybe this accounted for his vehemence. Maybe, like everybody else, he was just insecure:

I never felt that he was a friend, he was too remote for friendship, but on a few occasions he invited me along on one of his night-clubbing sprees—he particularly liked the Blue Angel [on East Fifty-fifth Street] and the Ruban Bleu [on East Fifty-sixth street], two of the clubs that featured young, un-proved talent. On these occasions, we stayed up late drinking beer and enjoy-ing the endless parade of beginning performers, some of whom were destined to have successful careers. In between the acts, Jerry talked, mostly about writing and writers, but sometimes he took on institutions, like the prep schools that had dismissed him, country clubs, writing classes that duped untalented boobs into thinking that one could learn to be a writer in the classroom, and so forth.[7]

Luckily, it was evident to Hotchner that Salinger was not just an-other late-night literary bore: ". . . he was an original, and I found his intellectual flailings enormously attractive, peppered as they were with sardonic wit and a myopic sense of humor." Of Hotchner's Greenwich Village group, only Salinger, he thought, "had complete confidence in his destiny as a writer—a writer he was and a writer he would always be—and what's more an *important* writer."

Something of how Salinger himself might have defined this "destiny" can be discovered from the long story that claimed most of his attention during these postmarriage Greenwich Village months, and that marked the end of his (for him) long silence. *The Inverted Forest* was described as a "novel" in the December 1947 issue of *Cosmopolitan;* it's about thirty thousand words long and was published as part of a new "experimental" policy by *Cosmopolitan*'s editor, Arthur Gordon: Gordon ". . . printed it as a kind of separate supplement to the magazine, with a cover page heralding it as one of the most distinguished pieces of fiction the magazine had ever given its readers." Unluckily, few of these readers seem to have understood the story. "Gordon was swamped with letters of protest, and from that point on . . . he refused to publish anything in which the story-line was not clear-cut and definite."[8]

The hero of *The Inverted Forest* is a 1930s poet called Raymond Ford, the first of a new species of Salinger hero—the literary saint. Ford's first book, *The Cowardly Morning,* had been a spectacular success, winning all the prizes (the Rice Fellowship twice, the Annual Strauss three times) and deluged with critical acclaim. Three full-length critical studies are being written about Ford's single incandescent volume, and it seems that anyone brave enough to get into close contact with this poet's work is likely to catch fire:

. . . all the while she was getting dressed she felt Ray Ford's poems standing upright all over the room. She even kept an eye on them in her dressing-table mirror, lest they escape into their natural, vertical ascent.[9]

Ray Ford, then, is a genius. A genius poet, it is explained, is one who "discovers" his poems; the nongenius merely "invents." And being a genius, Ford cannot help also being "a gigantic psychotic . . . up to his ears in psychosis"; "a man just can't reach the kind of poetry Ford's reaching" and remain any sort of ordinary Joe. This is the story's voice-of-reason character warning the entranced Corinne that she ought not to get herself romantically involved with Ford: If Ford wrote *verse*, it would be different; if he merely had *talent*, it would be different. Genius poets, though, are not built for personal relationships; they work "under pressure of dead-weight beauty" and nothing else really matters to them. But surely, Corinne protests, poets are "supposed to know more about these things"—i.e., personal relationships—"than anyone else." Not so, says voice of reason: "He's cold. I don't care how *tender* you find him. Or how kind. He's cold. He's cold as ice."

Corinne takes no notice of all this and marries Ford; he agrees to this arrangement because he "can't think of any reason why he shouldn't." Corinne is rich, social, warmhearted, and she tries to make a life in "her world" for the poet Ford, who is, by the way, half blind from too much reading of great works of the past. She gives him a study to work in; she introduces him to some of his more intelligent admirers. Ford goes along with all this for a time in his icy, detached way, and then he disappears. He has run off with a dopey young thing who thinks he looks like a movie star, doesn't like his poetry much, lets him drink a lot, and—simply by being so unsuitable—protects him from the smart social world that Corinne has attempted to provide for him.

With his new companion, Ford can lose himself in the "inverted forest" of his imagination; he can go underground, he can become a "recluse." At the climax of the tale, Ford tries to explain to Corinne why he has made this choice. Bunny, his new girl, reminds him of his mother—a drunkard, a slob, an ignoramus. Just like his mother, though, she is prepared to be Ford's keeper. She looks after him, tells him what to do, and—what matters most—she lets him play his private games. She lets him be a child. That is to say, she makes no attempt to penetrate or appropriate his mystery. The Corinne type is forever trying to turn him into something presentable, into a grown-up.

It is hard not to read Raymond Ford as a melodramatic projection of Salinger's own guilts and determinations at this time; indeed, as a defiant apologia addressed to the wife he himself had broken with a year before. It is also, of course, a foreshadowing of Salinger's own career in relation to the smart literary-social world that Corinne is made to represent. Raymond Ford is the first of Salinger's fictional great poets ("This man is Coleridge and Blake and Rilke all in one, and more"); from now on there will be a steady procession of dead, magically gifted artists in his work. When he wrote *The Inverted Forest*, though, he was toiling in a world of letters—the world of *Cosmopolitan* and *Collier's*— for which a Raymond Ford would have had nothing but contempt. Salinger no doubt shared this contempt, but his portrayal of Ford's highbrow literary milieu makes one want to look the other way—it is entirely guessed at, a magazine writer's fantasy of literary martyrdom. Both Corinne and the voice-of-reason character work for big-circulation magazines.

As if to demonstrate that his destiny had summoned him to higher planes, Salinger's relations with the slicks soon became even more edgy and suspicious than they had been in the past. Professionalism was no longer to be prized: It involved too many entanglements and compromises and in any case could hardly be squared with the ethereal commitments of a Raymond Ford. From this point on, Salinger begins quarreling with editors: Did they not invariably turn out to be agents of commercial exploitation? The sanctity of the artist was now set in fierce opposition to the parasitic opportunism of all literary middlemen.

In 1948, Salinger made his last appearance in the slicks, and engaged in several bitter quarrels. Not without reason, although his responses always seem a shade more venomous than the events themselves deserve. For *Cosmopolitan* he wrote a story called "Scratchy Needle on a Phonograph Record" (an unconvincing tear-jerker about jazz and racial prejudice down South). He gave it to Hotchner, who had just joined the magazine in an editorial capacity: "With his usual arrogance, Jerry attached a note to the story that said, if published not a word could be changed or deleted." Hotchner did his best, he says, to do what he was told—"I checked the galleys carefully"—but he forgot to check that the story's title was untampered with. When it came out, he discovered that Arthur Gordon, the no longer experimental editor-in-chief, had altered it to "Blue Melody." So far as Salinger was concerned, Hotchner was to blame: "[He] was furious. Never spoke to me again."[10]

There was another unpleasant run-in with the magazine *Good Housekeeping*, which had accepted Salinger's Vienna story (the one with the concentration camp plot twist). The editor, Herbert Mayes, didn't like Salinger's original title, "Wien, Wien," and fastened instead on a sentence in the story that read "Probably for every man there is one city that sooner or later turns into a girl" and decided that "A Girl I Knew" would be a more "appropriate" title. "The blurb we used was a line taken direct from the story. I don't know what upset Salinger but he protested vehemently and ordered his agent, Dorothy Olding, never again to show me any of his manuscripts."[11] Mayes's complacent manner here ("I don't know what upset Salinger") gives some idea of what the author in those days, and in those places, was up against. On the other hand, it is hard to believe that Salinger could have been all that surprised. He had had titles changed before and most of his *Collier's* and *Saturday Evening Post* contributions were beribboned with arch drawings and slick little come-on headings and subheadings. But in the past he had always managed to avoid a final showdown.

Not so in 1948. The difference is not just that Salinger, postwar, had acquired a new, more "trembling" *gravitas*. Perhaps just as important, he now had somewhere else to go. It was in this year that he was finally taken up by *The New Yorker*. In January 1948, "A Perfect Day for Bananafish"; in March "Uncle Wiggily in Connecticut"; in June, "Just Before the War with the Eskimos"—a truly impressive run of acceptances after nearly ten years of trying. And each of these stories is tighter, more laconic and oblique than anything he'd had in print before.

Salinger had never really had an editor, in the sense of a trusted adviser, an intelligent line-by-line consultant who could moderate his tendency to self-indulge. Without access to the magazine's files, we cannot know what was done to these manuscripts by *The New Yorker*'s editors. We can guess that quite a lot was done. We can also guess that it must have been done (if 'twere done) with considerable sensitivity, that there was nothing crude or high-handed to fight against, and that no story was altered or cut without detailed consultation. We might learn a lot about Salinger's education as a writer if we could get a look at the edited manuscripts of these first *New Yorker* stories. It can be no accident that the slacknesses and vulgarities that disfigured even Salinger's best stories of the past decade contrived a sudden disappearance in this year. Only a month separates the publication of *The Inverted Forest* from that of "A Perfect Day for Bananafish," but a reader at the time who chanced upon both works would have found it hard to believe that they were by the same writer. *The Inverted Forest* is rambling, narcissistic, wasteful of its own bewildered energy. "Bananafish" is spare, teasingly mysterious, withheld. Salinger, it seems, had at last entered a world in which his own fastidiousness would be honored, and perhaps surpassed, by that of his editorial attendants. *The New Yorker* was private, punctilious, and loyal; it was also metropolitan, nonacademic—in some respects, its values could be seen as regimental. Salinger had had his eye on it for years, an eye often thwarted and resentful but transfixed, finally, by the belief that he would eventually "belong." In 1948, it was the certainty that he had won secure access to this high ground that finally emboldened him to get out of the swamps represented by the slicks. He would not publish in these low places again and he would do his utmost, later on, to pretend that he had never published there at all.

From *The New Yorker*'s point of view, here was a new writer who, for all his faults, was in many respects coming to them ready-made, a kind of veteran apprentice. The best of Salinger's early stories were indeed bristling with promise—tight, energetic dialogue; a laconic way with minor characters; a hard-boiled urban wit; and, best of all, a genuine storyteller's gift for pace and timing. Few of these early pieces have anything lumpish or pretentious in them (indeed, *The Inverted Forest* is the first thing Salinger has published that seems to be straining, all the way through, for some highbrow "significance"). The slicks had, it is true, forced upon Salinger some formulaic plot lines, and they had certainly licensed his tendency to sentimentalize. But they had also taught him to handle the mechanics of narrative with a technician's self-assurance. *The New Yorker* could see this, but it could also see that this fluency needed to be contained and redirected. Again, this is speculative. My companion is already muttering about how great it would be to "break into those *New Yorker* files." The only thing we know for certain is that something happened in 1948 to transform a high-grade magazine professional into an artist whom even Raymond Ford might have been willing to call "serious."

3

In January 1947, Salinger had moved out of the city to Tarrytown, in Westchester County, to a small apartment over a suburban garage. It was there, we must assume, that he completed *The Inverted Forest*. Later in the year, he moved again—to a barn studio in Stamford, Connecticut. He stayed there for the winter of 1947–48, spent the summer of 1948 in Wisconsin (there seems to have been some girlfriend angle here), and then returned to Stamford for the winter. It was probably at this point that he resumed work on his Holden Caulfield novel, the book he had found hard to face during the three unsteady years since World War II.

In this latest version, Salinger gives Holden a new older brother—not Vincent anymore but a writer called D.B. This brother had once been a "regular writer" but had gone out to Hollywood to be "a prostitute." It seems pretty clear that D.B. is, for Salinger, some final exorcising gesture. For years Salinger had both yearned for and despised the movies. More than once he had cold-bloodedly written material that had a movie potential, and yet his early stories are also full of characters who are to be pitied for their susceptibility to screen versions of how life should be. Salinger himself, it is evident from early on, had a fan's encyclopedic grasp of cine lore. To this day, his favorite home entertainment (we've been told) is playing old films from the 1940s, of which he has a connoisseur's collection.

It was in 1948 that he had his first direct authorial dealings with the medium. Darryl Zanuck bought the screen rights of "Uncle Wiggily in Connecticut" and, in 1949, turned it into a weepie of the year called *My Foolish Heart*. The movie was a big success. Its theme song won an Oscar, and is still a nightclub standard: "The night is like a lovely tune/Beware, my foolish heart." Susan Hayward got an Oscar nomination for her playing of the female lead, a poignantly bereft Eloise, whose lover (Dana Andrews) dies nobly in a plane crash shortly after penning an overdue marriage proposal. Eloise is pregnant, but Dana doesn't—didn't—know it. After his death she seduces her best friend's fiancé into marriage so as to give her child a father. Ought she to tell her new hubby about Dana?

It will be seen from this brief précis that for Salinger, there could have been scant triumph. The film of "Uncle Wiggily" was a travesty, even by Hollywood criteria. Julius and Philip Epstein's shamelessly lachrymose screenplay is barely polite to the original. Salinger joked bravely that if Hollywood filmed "Bananafish," Edward G. Robinson would no doubt get the part of Sibyl. But he was furious—not just at Hollywood, one suspects, but at himself for having let all this happen. The last straw came when Sam Goldwyn invited him out to the West Coast to pen a story of young love in a naval academy.

Holden Caulfield's rage against the movies might seem excessive for a boy of sixteen if it is not kept in mind that *My Foolish Heart* opened at Radio City Music Hall in January 1950, a month in which Salinger would have been about halfway through the novel he'd been planning for ten years. Holden himself, it will be recalled, goes to a movie at Radio City around Christmastime, and if Salinger did any field research he would have seen *My Foolish Heart* billed as a forthcoming feature—and billed also as based on "a story by J. D. Salinger." The character of D.B.—although barely a character since he never actually appears—

surely embodies that part of Salinger which had drifted perilously close to selling out.

Before going to Hollywood, D.B. had been well known for a story called "The Secret Goldfish." Salinger himself had recently caused a minor stir in the New York literary world with his mysterious "A Perfect Day for Bananafish." In 1949, "Bananafish" appeared in *The New Yorker's 55 Short Stories 1940–50*. The anthology's time span was almost precisely that of Salinger's own literary career. Since much of that career had been spent trying, and failing, to get into *The New Yorker*, it was no small victory to find himself selected as one of the magazine's elite. He was more convincingly armored now against Hollywood's enticements than he had been a couple of years earlier—all the more reason for him to believe that he should have handled the *Foolish Heart* fiasco more determinedly. But then, those negotiations had been handled by an earlier Salinger, now dead.

Another Caulfield obsession is with education, a subject to which the author had devoted long years of uneasiness and which, it can plausibly be said, is near the heart of everything Salinger has written since *The Catcher in the Rye*. In 1949, Salinger the failed student had his first—and last—experience of teaching. He agreed to spend a day at Sarah Lawrence College, addressing a short story writing class. "I enjoyed the day," he said later, "but it isn't something I'd ever want to do again. I got very oracular and literary. I found myself labeling all the writers I respect. . . . A writer when he's asked to discuss his craft ought to get up and call out in a loud voice just the *names* of the writers he *loves*." The names Salinger ought to have called out at Sarah Lawrence were, he says, as follows: Kafka, Flaubert, Tolstoy, Chekhov, Dostoevsky, Proust, O'Casey, Rilke, Lorca, Keats, Rimbaud, Burns, E. Brontë, Henry James, Blake, Coleridge. Only one American—but then Salinger would name no living writers: "I don't think it right."[12]

Also in this same year book publishers were beginning to make overtures. Salinger's *New Yorker* stories were getting talked about; indeed one *New Yorker* reader of the time recalls that "the magazine was going through one of its dull periods and Salinger's stories stood out marvelously—they offered something new, exciting, strange. It would be hard to overstate the sense we all had then that Salinger's was *the* new voice. Each new story by him was viewed as an event."

Robert Giroux, then working as an editor at Harcourt Brace, confirms this recollection: From the book publishers' point of view, Salinger was suddenly the writer everyone wanted to get hold of:

I wrote him in care of the magazine to the effect that I was sure every publisher had written to ask him if he were writing a novel and that I would be happy to publish his stories. No reply. Months later, the receptionist rang my desk to say that Mr. Salinger would like to see me. A tall, sad-looking man with a long face and deep-set black eyes walked in, saying, "It's not my stories that should be published first, but the novel I'm working on." I said, "Do you want to sit behind this desk? You sound just like a publisher."

He said, "No, you can do the stories later if you want, but I think my novel about this kid in New York during the Christmas holidays should come out first."[13]

Giroux asked to see the book, and said, "I know I want to publish you so let's shake hands on it," and they did. At the time of this meeting, Salinger already knew that his pre-*New Yorker* stories must be regarded as apprentice work, that each of them was in its way tainted by his association with the slicks. This being so, he had by no means enough *New Yorker* work for a collection. He was anxious now to separate the new work from the old. He knew that if, say, "Bananafish" had been written for the *Saturday Evening Post* or even *Cosmopolitan*, it is probable that Seymour Glass would have delivered an explanatory speech. A slicks editor would never have allowed a guy to kill himself, just like that. Also, Seymour's encounter with Sibyl on the beach would surely have been scrutinized for pedophiliac impropriety. When Seymour kisses the arch of Sibyl's foot, she does after all run off from him "without regret." *Post* readers had strong views about what little girls should say to any strange men they might encounter on the beach. After the publication of "Bananafish" Salinger was no doubt often

asked of Seymour's suicide "But why?" From now on, he wouldn't
need to answer dumb questions of this sort. Thanks to *The New Yorker*
he was beginning to learn the pleasures of reader manipulation, of
having a sophisticated readership that had been trained in the enjoyment of inconsequential sorrow. He was learning how to leave things
out, to flatter and deceive.

Chapter 8

J D. Salinger was now a public figure. Not *very* public yet, but public enough for him to be talked about by a lot of people he had never met, to have an identity in many others' minds that was outside his immediate control. From my biographer-companion's point of view, this was a lucky break: It meant that our subject could now be got at from several fresh angles. And since Salinger's "problem" later on would be centered on matters of privacy versus publicity, it was something of a relief to be able to begin tracing the buildup of this tension. In short, my sleuthing alter ego was in no mood to go soft on the agonies of stardom. "We are all talked about by people we have never met, even if they're only the postman and the paperboy. And none of us has any immediate control over how he seems to others." "But surely there is a distinction between the village gossip sort of fictional identities most of us have to live with and the 'image' that attaches itself to personalities who have voluntarily 'gone public'?" "Well, maybe there is, but I'm glad you use the word 'voluntarily.'"

I tried him with a personalized anecdote, although as we have seen these were never his strong suit. "Look. The first time we had our picture in the papers, along with a 'profile' that was full of quite outra-

geous lies and misquotations, I skulked in the house for days afterward
in a turmoil of embarrassment and shame. O mirror, I have lost my
privacy: If I go out on the street, people will Know Who I Am. What
I mean is: You can't be certain how you will feel about these things until
they happen." "And what did happen?" "Absolutely nothing. I could
hardly believe it, when I eventually *did* slink out of doors, how just the
same everything had managed to remain." "Bad luck." "No, no. I was
also surprised at how relieved I was. I'd always thought I wanted to be
famous." "And you think that little fable will persuade me that you
didn't, that you don't?"

He also couldn't see what all this had to do with Salinger. There was
nothing, he insisted, in our subject's early life to suggest that he was
unusually sensitive in the matter of self-advertisement. Indeed, the boy
Salinger was heavily attracted for a time to the idea of stardom as
enjoyed by others: He wanted to go to Hollywood; he wanted to be
on Broadway. And all of the time, he wanted his distinctiveness to be
acknowledged. Part of his excitement, when he first started publishing
in the slicks, was to do with these magazines' gigantic circulations. And
was there not also something rancorous, akin perhaps to envy, in his
attitude to literary reputations that in his view were "inflated," as if
others had been wrongly given what ought to have been his?

"But he *was* touchy, almost from the start." Yes, but most of his
touchiness expressed itself in backstage grumblings and occasional
flare-ups, betokening self-importance rather than any rage for anonymity. If anything, his youthful angers were more to do with his sense of
being undervalued than with any shrinking from unwanted plaudits.
Schoolmasters had failed to see his point, or had stupidly misrepresented him, foreshadowing in this the obtuse critics and journalists who
were to plague him later on. The only hint really of what was to come
can be detected in Salinger's neurotically protective view of his own
fiction, of the characters he—Jerome Salinger—had given life. One
might have predicted trouble here. After all, publication and literary
fame don't just involve a surrender of personal anonymity: They con-
spire also to betray that sometimes sacred-seeming pact between an

author and the words that he believes "belong" to him. "Perhaps *that*'s what I meant." Perhaps it was.

But we were jumping ahead. In 1949, Salinger had begun to make an impact, but the impact was limited to smart literary circles in New York. He himself would have been aware that worse, or better, was to come, and very soon. As we have seen, his Holden Caulfield novel had been put on ice. It had been impossible for him to work on it until he had made an effort to reach for that trembling melody which would do justice to the war-damaged and the dead. Seymour Glass is a war victim recently discharged from a military hospital and still on the brink. In "Uncle Wiggily in Connecticut" it is Seymour's brother, Walter, who is killed in a freak wartime accident in the Pacific. In "Just Before the War with the Eskimos" everyone is afflicted by postwar neurasthenia. It is as if they are waiting for the Next One. Franklin looks out of his apartment window and imagines that all the "goddam fools" down in the street are on their way to the nearest draft board: "We're gonna fight the Eskimos next. Know that?" The most rawly autobiographical of all his *New Yorker* stories, "For Esmé—with Love and Squalor" (published in April 1950 but probably written many months earlier) is Salinger's last published piece to have war damage lurking at its center. It had taken him five years to get to the point where he could decently honor Gladwaller's pre-Europe pledge of silence. Salinger would never again write directly about war.

"For Esmé," indeed, is the only Salinger story to be published between April 1949 and July 1951, the month in which his Holden Caulfield book was finally published as *The Catcher in the Rye.* From summer 1949 to summer 1950 he seems to have worked flat out on the novel, although still professing himself worried that he might be a dash man, not a miler. At first he found it hard to settle. The Stamford retreat seems to have been available only in winter, and New York was full of distractions. "I [Gavin Douglas] remember Jerry telling me that a writer's worst enemy is other writers, because they'll destroy your work for you."[1] Eventually he moved to a rented house in Westport, Connecticut; for "company and distraction" he had a large black dog called Benny, which people said looked just like him. ("You don't have to take time to explain to a dog, even in words of one syllable, that there are times when a man *needs* to be at his typewriter."[2]) He liked West-port, and it was probably there that *The Catcher in the Rye* was finished, although there is a hard to confirm story that the major effort on the book took place in a "hot furnished room on 3rd Avenue, with the El running nearby. He locked himself in there and ordered sandwiches and lima beans while he got the book out of himself."[3] We will be coming to this witness again shortly.

Much more reliably, Robert Giroux recalls that Salinger took him up on his handshake and sent the manuscript of *The Catcher* to Harcourt Brace a year after their first meeting.

I thought it a remarkable book and considered myself lucky to be its editor. I was sure it would do well, but I must confess that the thought of a best-seller never crossed my mind. I told my boss, Eugene Reynal, the whole Salinger story, including the handshake, and said, "In a way, we already have a con-tract." I thought he would OK it on that basis alone, but he ignored this. I didn't realize what big trouble I was in until, after he'd read it, he said, "Is Holden Caulfield supposed to be crazy?" He also told me he'd given the typescript to one of our textbook editors to read. I said *"Textbook,* what has that to do with it?" "It's about a preppie, isn't it?" The textbook editor's report was negative, and that settled that.[4]

Salinger himself reported to a friend that he had been taken out to lunch by Giroux, along with Dan Wickenden (also of Harcourt Brace) and that "those bastards" had told him that they wanted him to rewrite the book. He had kept his temper throughout lunch, but immediately afterward he had telephoned Harcourt Brace and told them to give him back his manuscript.[5]

Whatever the detail, this was not the sort of episode to bolster Salin-ger's already fragile confidence in publishers, and when the book was finally accepted by the Boston firm of Little, Brown, he was already in a defensive mood. Relations speedily turned sour. Salinger didn't take to Little, Brown's New York editor, John Woodburn, and blamed him for some of the more vulgar aspects of the book's prepublication buildup. For example, just after *The Catcher in the Rye* was set in galleys, Woodburn telephoned Salinger in Westport to tell him that the Book-of-the-Month Club had taken the book as its main midsummer selection for 1951. Salinger's response to this was simply to wonder if publication would have to be delayed. Woodburn's crime was to pass on the story to the literary press, so that before the novel had a chance to make its way the author was already being built up as an oddball. The New York *Herald Tribune*'s coverage was typical:

Shortly before his "Catcher in the Rye" appeared, Jerome David Salinger not only asked his publisher's office to send him no reviews of his novel but actually made them promise not to. "That," said a friend of his the other day, "will give you an idea of the kind of guy he is," together with the Salinger reaction to his publisher's phone-call informing him that the Book-of-the-Month Club had chosen "Catcher" as its midsummer selection.

"That's good, is it?" said Mr. Salinger. Later he asked that there be no special publicity to-do about him "because I might get to believe it." As a matter of fact, he was inclined to be annoyed by the picture of him that filled the back of the book's jacket. Too big, he said.[6]

One story that didn't get into the press is told by Angus Cameron, then chief editor at Little, Brown. He recalls being telephoned by a rather panicky John Woodburn shortly before *The Catcher*'s publication. Salinger, it appeared, was insisting that no advance galleys, indeed no review copies, of the book should be sent out to the press. He wanted no publicity of any sort, and he was also demanding that his photograph be removed from the back cover. Cameron had to rush down to New York to reason with him: "Do you want this book published," he asked, "or just printed?" In the end, Salinger gave way, but with considerable reluctance. And later he did have the photograph removed.[7]

In spite of these annoyances, Salinger did cooperate with the Book-of-the-Month Club to the extent of allowing himself to be interviewed for its subscribers' journal, *BOMC News*. But then the interviewer was a *New Yorker* friend, the novelist and editor William Maxwell, and Salinger no doubt felt that he could depend on him not to pull any journalistic stunts. It was as writer to writer that he was able to confide:

I think writing is a hard life. But it's brought me enough happiness that I don't think I'd ever deliberately dissuade anybody (if he had talent) from taking it up. The compensations are few, but when they come, if they come, they're very beautiful.[8]

2

By the time *The Catcher in the Rye* was published, Salinger had left for Britain, to avoid any further involvement in the marketing of his imagined friend: The prospect of seeing Holden anatomized in the public prints must have been daunting indeed for the parent-author who had nurtured the boy's delicate sensitivity for a decade; it was a kind of separation. In Britain, Salinger did all the usual touristy things: Shakespeare country, Wordsworth country, Brontë country, and so on. He visited Dublin and the Hebrides. The whole adventure lasted two months—long enough, he believed, for him to make sure of missing the worst of whatever was in store for him, *and* Holden Caulfield.

Meanwhile, back in New York, *The Catcher in the Rye* was published on July 16. The *New York Times* reviewed it on the day of publication, declaring it "an unusually brilliant first novel. . . . You'll look a long time before you meet another youngster like Holden Caulfield." The *San Francisco Chronicle* called the book "literature of a very high order. It really is," and the *Philadelphia Enquirer* was in no doubt that "this year will produce no book quite as explosive. . . . Here, at last, is a fresh and vigorous fiction talent, notable in its own right, without debt to the influence of the twenties, thirties, or what have you. And that is real news." *Time* magazine agreed: "The prize catch in *The Catcher in the Rye* is novelist Salinger himself. He can understand an adolescent mind without displaying one." In most of the newspaper reviews, there was a note of genuine astonishment. The weeklies and monthlies were more restrained, but in the main no less admiring of the book's originality: *Harper's* called it "the most distinguished first novel, the most truly new novel in style and accent, of the year," and this more or less set the tone.

There were a few negative reactions. The *Christian Science Monitor* expressed fears that "a book like this given wide circulation may multiply his [Holden's] kind—as too easily happens when immorality and perversion are recounted by writers of talent whose work is countenanced in the name of good intentions." The *New York Herald Tribune* complained of the book's "offensive language. . . . There is probably not one phrase in the book that Holden Caulfield would not have used, but when they are piled upon each other in cumulative monotony, the ear refuses to believe." And Ernest Jones, Freud's pupil and biographer, wrote in *The Nation* that Salinger had merely recorded "what every sixteen-year-old since Rousseau has felt" and that the book as a whole was "predictable and boring."

Such grumbles, though, were either too obscurely positioned or appeared too late to impede the book's immediate success. By October it reached fourth place in the Sunday *Times* best-seller list and altogether it lingered on the list for seven months. Over the year, its sales were far outstripped by James Jones's *From Here to Eternity*, Herman Wouk's *The Caine Mutiny*, and Nicholas Monsarrat's *The Cruel Sea*, but for a short novel not about the war by a relatively unknown author, it could be counted a considerable triumph.

By the time the most prominent reviews were coming out, Salinger was homeward bound, on the *Mauretania* (we have no evidence that he has ever gone anywhere by plane). He was by this date—mid-July— in flight from the British publication of his book, scheduled by Hamish Hamilton for August. Salinger had checked the proofs in London before setting off on his trip to the north of England. Salinger's relations with Hamish Hamilton and with his chief editor, Roger Machell, were to be important to all three in years to come, and from the beginning seem to have had a rather fragile aspect, with each side, British and American, almost nervously respectful of the other. Hamilton was the English publisher of *New Yorker* writers such as James Thurber, John Collier, and Mollie Panter-Downes, and he prided himself on his transatlantic vigilance; indeed, he was half American by birth. He had founded his imprint in 1931 partly in order to "contribute something to the cause of Anglo-American understanding in the face of the growing menace of German aggression." Hamilton first wrote to Salinger in August 1950 after reading "For Esmé—with Love and Squalor" in a British magazine called *World Review*. This was "much the most impressive story" Hamilton had read "in recent years" and he expected to be "haunted by it . . . for a long time to come." He wanted to know about the British rights to Salinger's short stories. He ended up instead with *The Catcher in the Rye*.

In March 1951, Hamilton and his wife, Yvonne, met Salinger for the first time in New York. Perhaps because Little, Brown had by then fallen darkly out of favor, Salinger seems to have welcomed this smooth, *New Yorker*-oriented Briton as *The Catcher in the Rye*'s "real" publisher—as a fitter custodian, certainly, than the garrulous John Woodburn. The two of them struck up a friendship, and on his return to England, Hamilton wrote flatteringly to his new author: "At the risk of embarrassing you I must tell you that Yvonne revealed to me on our return—and has since said the same to others—that you were much the most interesting and fascinating new friend we had made in America this trip." He also sent Salinger a parcel of books just published by himself: Martin Turnell on French novelists and Enid Starkie's life of Rimbaud, together with Readers Library editions of Jane Austen and Turgenev. Salinger was delighted by this gesture—as if this were how publishers *ought* to behave.

The pair met again in London two months later, when Salinger was fleeing his American debut. Salinger presented Hamilton with an inscribed copy of one of Holden Caulfield's favorite books, Isak Dinesen's *Out of Africa*, and was taken to the theater to see the "Oliviers in the two Cleopatra plays, Shaw and Shakespeare." At supper afterward, Salinger was introduced to the Oliviers, a meeting which for Salinger presented a small art versus life embarrassment. He knew, after all (as Olivier did not) that the esteemed actor had a walk-on part in *Catcher in the Rye:* "I just don't see what's so marvelous about Sir Laurence Olivier, that's all," says Holden, after D.B. takes him to see *Hamlet*. "He has a terrific voice, and he's a helluva handsome guy, and he's very nice to watch when he's walking or dueling or something," but he is not Holden's idea of how Hamlet should be played. "He was too much like a goddam general, instead of a sad, screwed-up type guy." Hamish Hamilton, of course, *had* read this paragraph, but may have forgotten it. In any event, no one mentioned it. But Salinger continued to brood on the matter for some weeks afterward. What if Olivier did get to read the book: Would he not think Salinger something of a hypocrite, a phony, to have sat there being friendly over supper? In a long letter to Hamish Hamilton, he goes to great pains to separate *his* view of Olivier from the view of Holden as expressed in the book, and asks Hamilton to convey this explanation to the actor. Hamilton seems to have obliged, because eventually Olivier did write Salinger a reassuring note (and three years afterward asked if he could adapt "For Esmé" as a radio play, with him playing Sergeant X. Salinger said no.)

3

Armed with an advance copy of the British *Catcher* (no photograph, no biography, but with a rather "cute" illustration on the cover), Salinger arrived in the United States in late July. He decided almost immediately to quit his Westport home. A best-selling writer now, he believed it would be easier to recapture some obscurity back in New York. After a couple of weeks' search, he rented an apartment at 300 East Fifty-seventh Street, and settled down to start work again. Before starting, he had to assimilate the reviews of *The Catcher in the Rye,* which he seems to have studied with a fierce attentiveness. In a letter to Hamish

Hamilton describing the book's American reception, he manages to sound both angry and contemptuous.

And, on the face of it, he sounds remarkably unfair, as if he couldn't bear to admit that a reviewer might have been equal to this most rare and delicate of challenges. But then we are not sure which reviews he read, and it is true that as the first wave of enthusiasm for the book began to settle, Salinger did have to contend with some downright unpleasant assaults from the special-interest monthlies: *Catholic World,* for instance, denounced *The Catcher* for its "formidably excessive use of amateur swearing and coarse language," and *Commentary* used the occasion to launch an attack on *The New Yorker.* On the book itself, William Poster wrote:

The ennui, heartburn, and weary revulsion of *The Catcher in the Rye* are the inevitable actions, not of an adolescent, however disenchanted, but of a well-paid satirist with a highly developed technique, no point of view, and no target to aim at but himself.

But this was characteristic of the magazine Salinger wrote for; *The New Yorker* had "run down," says Poster, "because it cannot be recharged from the battery of some viable, positive approach to culture, morals, religion or politics." A *New Yorker* parodist could not have put it better.

By the end of August, the British reviews began to trickle in. Hamish Hamilton had clearly been nervous about the book's seeming "too American," and on the blurb somewhat too patiently explained, "Although the dialogue is distinctly American in vernacular and cadence, it is so masterly that English readers will not find it in the least difficult." Only the *Times Literary Supplement* seemed bothered on this score, taking exception to "the endless stream of blasphemy and obscenity." Although "credible," the language of the book "palls after the first chapter." The *Punch* reviewer made some self-satisfied points about the difference between American and British taste. He found *The Catcher* essentially a "sentimental" book but allowed that this "may be merely the reaction of a corrupt European who prefers a soft surface and a hard core." The *Spectator* called it "intelligent, humorous, acute and sympathetic in observation" but "too formless to do quite the sort of thing it was evidently intended to do."

Elsewhere, the reception was enthusiastic. Marghanita Laski in *The Observer* and L. P. Hartley in the *Sunday Times* were charmed, although each of them found aspects of the book "repellent," as did the *Listener* and *New Statesman* critics. Jocelyn Brooke in the *Statesman* called *The Catcher* an "odd, tragic and at times appallingly funny book, with a taste of its own" and in the *Listener* John Russell wrote of Salinger's "carefully modulated, but wholly contemporary *parlando*. His is an art which denies art; but the wit, the conversational ease and the cunning ellipses of his method bespeak an attention to rhythm and to the details of narrative which [Henry James and Edith Wharton] would have been the first to recognise."

Altogether, the British reviews ought to have been more offensive to Salinger than the American; in Britain, even the most favorable notices were delivered with an air of condescension. And in Britain there was not the consolation of high sales: The book sold modestly at first. But Salinger's Anglophilia seems to have been important to him at this stage: a newly acquired style of outsiderism which he could use to good distancing effect back home. Certainly there were no complaints about his British publication; indeed, his praise of Hamish Hamilton is almost as excessive as his blasts against poor Little, Brown. Hamilton, all in all, was being given a lot to live up to.

4

The fact is, I feel tremendously relieved that the season for success of *The Catcher in the Rye* is over. I enjoyed a small part of it, but most of it I found hectic and professionally and personally demoralising. Let's say I'm getting good and sick of bumping into that blown-up photograph of my face on the back of the dust-jacket. I look forward to the day when I see it flapping against a lamp-post in a cold, wet Lexington Avenue wind, in company with, say, the editorial page of the *Daily Mirror.* [9]

When he said this in February 1952, Salinger had no idea how long or how spectacular *The Catcher in the Rye*'s real season for success would eventually turn out to be. Another five years would pass before the academics began to take any notice of the book and almost a decade before its "cult" status was announced. In 1968 it was declared one of America's twenty-five leading best sellers since the year 1895. Today, it is still clocking up annual sales worldwide of some quarter of a million copies.

But in 1951, *The Catcher* seemed merely the book of the moment. Salinger believed that the fuss would last only until the next season's new celebrity appeared. In the meantime, he lingered in New York, part enjoying, part hating his new fame. He plans a trip to Florida and Mexico, he falls in love unsatisfactorily, he goes to parties, and then wishes that he hadn't. The sense we get from these three months or so—December 1951 until around March 1952—is of an irritated restlessness, a not knowing what to do with the new social identity his book has thrust upon him. He discovered during these months that the life of the New York literary celebrity was not to be sustained for very long. He had already begun to exhibit symptoms of that "perfection complex" which he would later embody in the character of Seymour Glass. The perfection of the text should be paralleled by the perfection of the life, but perfecting a famous life is different from perfecting a life that the world takes little notice of. He also seems to have discovered a way out, a route that was both escapist and ennobling. But we will come to that.

Whatever happened, there was always *The New Yorker*, he might well have thought in 1951. But there were upheavals in that department too. In December, Harold Ross, the magazine's founding editor, died. He was succeeded by William Shawn. (Salinger's friend and fiction editor, Gus Lobrano, had been hoping *he* would get the job and, according to Brendan Gill, "never forgave Shawn or anybody else" when he didn't.[10]) Salinger had not known Ross well—his own dealings at the magazine had been chiefly with Lobrano or William Maxwell—but he respected him as head, indeed progenitor, of the family. He attended Ross's funeral and hated it. In his account to Hamish Hamilton Salinger makes a point of deriding the Yale University chaplain who officiated at the service. But E. B. White's obituary in the magazine in part made up for this. When White's measured, heartfelt piece appeared, Salinger wrote to thank him for it. White replied (to "Mr. Salinger"): "I felt worried, as well as sick, attempting to say anything about Ross in his own magazine. A letter like yours helps relieve the worry."[11] Years later, in 1960, when James Thurber's book on Ross appeared, Salinger wrote a long open-letter essay in the editor's defense: It was some thirty pages long and was turned down by both *Partisan* and *Saturday Review*, which seems odd. The essay is now lost.

Ross's successor, William Shawn, was closer than the rough-edged Ross could ever have been to the sort of editor-guru figure Salinger so evidently needed, or believed he needed. The fantasy of a wise, all-seeing elder brother is common to all of Salinger's turbulent young heroes, and Shawn was almost miraculously well equipped for such a role in Salinger's own life. He was twelve years older; he was from Chicago; he was a magazine professional; he had not attended an Ivy League college; he played jazz piano. More than all this, though, he was renowned for his personal reticence; in nearly twenty years he had written only one signed piece for the magazine, and even that was signed with his initials—and for his total devotion to the idea of a publication that would stylishly eschew the "shoddy, shabby, cynical, petty, sensational, gossipy, exploitative, opportunistic, coarse, pedestrian or banal."[12] Students of Shawn's personality speak of his courtesy, his considerateness, his loyalty, but they speak of such things with trepidation because of the man's notorious "passion for privacy." "He is today," said Brendan Gill in 1975, "one of the best-known unknown men in the country."[13] By 1975, of course, Salinger was himself a sturdy contender for this same very American award.

Ross's death, oddly enough, coincided with Salinger's first rejection by *The New Yorker* since he had been taken up some three years earlier. He had spent some of his time since returning to the United States in August 1951 working on a facetious, mystical, and flailingly symbolic yarn called "De Daumier-Smith's Blue Period." Salinger's response was to set the story to one side; if the family rejected a piece of work, there might well be something wrong with it. In the end the story did appear in the British magazine *World Review*, the periodical in which Hamish Hamilton had first spotted a reprint of "For Esmé." But Salinger did not submit it elsewhere in America.

During January and February 1952, Salinger was now and then to be witnessed "on the town." His English editor, Roger Machell, was in New York, and he took Salinger—or Salinger took him—to a few literary parties. Here *The Catcher in the Rye*'s celebrity could be measured at first hand. Salinger anecdotes of the period present the young author as veering uneasily between extremes of social clumsiness: sometimes arrogant and quarrelsome, sometimes too full-heartedly anxious to be liked. His own references to the cocktail party scene are usually to do with how much too much he'd had to drink.

One rather touching story might stand as evocative of his unease during these social months of early 1952. The narrator is the wife of a New York editor, and she would rather not be named:

I met Jerry Salinger at a party given, I think, by or for his English publisher. I had heard of him, and liked the book, but I was not prepared for the extraordinary impact of his physical presence. There was a kind of black aura about him. He was dressed in black; he had black hair, dark eyes, and he was of course extremely tall. I was kind of spellbound. But I was married, and I was pregnant. We talked, and we liked each other very much, I thought. Then it was time for us to leave—I had gone to the party with my husband and with another couple, two friends of ours—and I went upstairs to where the coats were. I was just getting my coat when Jerry came into the room. He came over to me and said that we ought to run away together. I said, "But I'm pregnant." And he said, "That doesn't matter. We can still run away." He really seemed to mean it. I can't say I wasn't flattered, and even a bit tempted maybe.

She extricated herself and went back downstairs. Later on when she, her husband, and their two friends were leaving, she saw Salinger standing on his own. She felt sorry for him, and suggested that he might like to go with them for supper or a drink. He said, "Why don't you all come back to my place?"

When we got there—it was this small apartment on East Fifty-seventh Street—he was very friendly and talkative and serving drinks. But then the conversation got around to colleges. My husband and his friend had both been to Harvard and they asked Jerry where he had been to college. All of a sudden, Jerry's mood changed. He became furious, and started denouncing the two men as leeches and parasites, people who lived off the arts. And then he got into a long thing about the twelve stages of enlightenment. My husband, I think he said, was at the first stage, the very lowest, and I was around stage four. As for Jerry, he said that for him the act of writing was inseparable from the quest for enlightenment, that he intended devoting his life to one great work, and that the work would be his life—there would be no separation. Well, eventually we were able to get away—after he had raged on like this for maybe two hours. We went out into the street and got a cab. And then, I remember looking back out of the cab window. Jerry was there on the sidewalk. He had followed us out into the street. I thought he was calling out to us, but I couldn't catch what he was trying to say. That was the last time I ever saw Jerry Salinger.

On the following day her husband got a call from Roger Machell saying that Salinger felt bad about what had happened.

The preoccupation with enlightenment that is talked of here seems to have taken hold in these same months of 1952. Suddenly our hero is talking a new language. *The Catcher in the Rye* does, it is true, set up a vague opposition between organized and "true" religious feeling: Holden Caulfield feels bad about blowing smoke in nuns' faces, and so on. There are also moments in some of the stories which—with hindsight—critics have been keen to label Zen. And we do know that Salinger liked to listen to church music on occasion. But there has been no God talk in his work. The little girls who offer hope to his disaffected, damaged heroes are authentic little girls, entirely secular, their portraits based on fond and detailed observation. And the yearning for childlikeness that has run throughout his fiction from the beginning has seemed all the more potently sorrowful because its imagined outcome is a kind of blank: flight, early death, or madness. A skilled missionary might have perceived in all this Salinger's susceptibility to swift conversion, but even such as he would have had to reckon with his victim's loathing for educators and persuaders.

And yet for some years, Salinger has needed to set his gaze on some high purpose, and his dedication to his craft has often had a monkish tinge. Up until 1952, the order he aimed to belong to was an order based on talent and on the disciplines of art. From now on, though, he will speak of "talent" as if it were the same thing as "enlightenment," and will seek in the curricula of holy men a way of dissolving what has all along been for him an irritating, hard to manage separation between art and life, between, that is to say, his art, his life.

The author Leila Hadley remembers Salinger around this time. She met him first in 1951 and then again after a two-year interval:

I was introduced to Jerry by Sid Perelman. Jerry was a great friend of Sid's in those days—they used to have lunch together quite a bit. I had liked some of Jerry's stories and I think Sid must have told him this. Anyway, Jerry called me and we went on a few dates. It was just before *The Catcher in the Rye* appeared, and I remember him talking about Holden Caulfield as if he were a real person—quoting his opinions. Jerry was not easy to be with—he was always pulling me up for something I had said. He had this huge distrust of clichés. If I said I liked walking in the rain, he would tell me that was just a cliché—that nobody *really* liked walking in the rain. Certainly he didn't. If I saw a painting I liked in a museum or an art gallery, I would maybe say, "I'd like to own that." He'd tell me that I shouldn't be so acquisitive, that possessions didn't matter. He was very like that character of his in *The Inverted Forest*—Raymond Ford. He didn't speak much; he didn't speak unless he had to speak.

I was about to go on a world cruise, and he said he thought travel was pointless, that inner travel was what mattered. I think he liked putting me

down. There was something sadistic about it. But he did have this extraordinary presence—very tall, with a sort of darkness surrounding him. His face
was like an El Greco. It wasn't a sexual power, it was a mental power. You
felt he had the power to imprison someone mentally. It was as if one's mind
were at risk, rather than one's virtue. He never talked about himself and he
resented any personal questions—about his family, or his background. His
room on East Fifty-seventh Street was extremely bare. There was just a lamp
and an artist's drawing board. He used to do rather good sketches, and when
I read "De Daumier-Smith's Blue Period," I was sure he had based the hero
on himself. On the wall of his apartment there was a picture of himself in
uniform.[14]

When Leila Hadley returned from her world cruise two years later, she
was married. She saw Salinger twice more, and then lost touch with
him:

This time he wrote out a list of the ten best books on Zen for me to read. I
remember buying *Zen and the Art of Archery*, which had just come out. I
thought maybe he would be interested in my visit to the Far East, but he
wasn't. He knew that I intended to write a travel book, and he was scathing
about that: he said he was against all descriptive writing. He couldn't see the
separateness of things, he said, so why bother to describe them?[15]

In March 1952, Salinger finally set off on his trip to Florida and
Mexico, but we know nothing of what happened there. In his letters
before setting off, he hints that something momentous has made an
appearance in his life, and on his return he urges Hamish Hamilton to
consider publishing a British edition of *The Gospels of Sri Ramakrishna*.
He even sends Hamilton a copy, and seems confident that his superior
new friend will like nothing better than to rush it into print.

The book is actually more than a thousand pages long and is a kind
of single-volume study course in world religions, or in how to assimilate world religions to the omniscience of a wayward Hindu mystic (if
"wayward" can be used without tautology of any mystic). Ramakrishna believed that no religion, no quest for God or Om or Allah

could be thought of as "untrue," and he had offered hospitality to Christian, Muslim, and Buddhist teachings in the course of his own search for enlightenment. A respectful reading of Ramakrishna's gospel would take several months—the glossary alone supplies almost a thousand razor-thin definitions—and it is possible that Salinger had been dipping into it for years. The book was first published in America in 1942 by the Ramakrishna Center in New York, and the center was just around the corner from his parents' Park Avenue apartment. There is also a report that his interest in Oriental mysticism has its origins in his mysterious first marriage. Salinger told Leila Hadley in 1951 that there was still a "bond" between him and his French wife. "They were capable of going into trances and meeting each other, having conversations, even though they were miles apart, that they had the same dreams. Telepathically, the marriage still went on."

Sri Ramakrishna's own biographical outline would have had much appeal for Salinger. "At the age of sixteen he went to Calcutta but was disgusted by the materialistic ideals of the people of the great metropolis. Refusing to direct his attention to secular studies, he became a priest in the Dakshineswar temple, where God is worshipped as the Mother of the Universe. By dint of intense prayer and longing, and practically without the help of any teacher, he obtained the vision of God."[16] And thus it might have been for Holden Caulfield, after *his* sixteen-year-old encounter with the great metropolis.

Ramakrishna did not fall into a contemplative silence or go mad, although some of his contemporaries were none too certain about *that*. He talked and talked, and his words were faithfully transcribed by his disciple M. Although Ramakrishna's gospels are praised for their worldly flexibility, in the main they are aimed at the reader who is "possessed of a strong spirit of renunciation." And on the matter of renunciation the master is severe indeed: "A man may live in a mountain cave, smear his body with ashes, observe fasts, and practise austere discipline, but if his mind dwells on worldly objects, on 'woman and gold,' I say, 'Shame on him!' 'Woman and gold' are the most fearsome enemies of the enlightened way, and woman rather more than gold, since 'it is woman that creates the need for gold. For woman one man becomes the slave of another, and so loses his freedom. Then he cannot act as he likes.' "

The faithful disciple M one day confesses that he has been enjoying sexual intercourse with his wife, even though their intention was not procreative. Hearing this, the master almost spins out of control:

Aren't you ashamed of yourself? You have children, and still you enjoy intercourse with your wife. Don't you hate yourself for thus leading an animal life? Don't you hate yourself for dallying with a body which contains only blood, phlegm, filth and excreta?[17]

The hapless M is further reminded that if he can get a grip on himself and control his "seminal fluid" for twelve years, he will develop special powers of memory and understanding—indeed, he will grow "a new inner nerve of memory."

When Ramakrishna died in 1886 at age fifty, he left behind him a team of trained disciples, and the most energetic of these was Swami Vivekananda. It was Vivekananda who, toward the end of the nineteenth century, carried to the West the master's vision of a "universal religion" and then organized a Ramakrishna movement in America. And later on it was Vivekananda whom Salinger had Seymour Glass describe as "one of the most exciting, original and best-equipped giants of this century." Seymour would give ten years of his life, he says, if he could shake the swami's hand or at least say "a brisk, respectful hello to him on some busy street in Calcutta or elsewhere."

Sensibly, Vivekananda does not emphasize the "woman and gold" aspect of his master's teachings. In his several works on yoga, his whole approach is cunningly tailored to appeal to the requirements of his Western audience, an audience trapped in the habits of rationalism and material self-advancement. He is always consolingly antiintellectual, preaching that "when you step beyond thought and intellect and all reasoning, then you have made the first step towards God: and that is the beginning of life."[18]

For Salinger, there was something in the tone of these Eastern teachers that reminded him of Gladwaller addressing the child Mattie, telling her to hold on to her innocence. "Childlikeness" has so far in his work been the exclusive property of children, although there have been hints that a Raymond Ford-like dedication to high art might keep some areas of innocence intact, even within adulthood. Holden Caulfield, of course, doesn't want to join the grown-up world at all; he can't see a way into modern American life that won't mean having to turn himself into one of the phonies he detests. Until 1952, Salinger has not had much to offer in the way of consolation or advice for his "young folks," except mutely to encourage them in their fantasies of flight, or stasis. The fear of growing up has been seen as something like the fear of death. Teachers and intellectuals have been the agents of corruption. Now, with the help of Vivekananda, Salinger can offer innocence a book of rules: You don't have to grow up if you don't want to; you don't even have to die.

In *The New Yorker* of January 31, 1953, Salinger published a story called "Teddy" and it is our first chance to meet him in his new Orientalized persona. The story is a direct challenge to our narrow rationalistic habits of curiosity. We, the readers, are given the role of a rather sluggish M to Teddy's inspired Ramakrishna. And Teddy is but ten years old. Our representative within the tale is a plodding academic, his head so full of "logic" that he finds himself both baffled and irritated by the strange pronouncements of the boy mystic he is trying to interrogate. Nicholson stands for all the teachers and critics Salinger has ever known; he is the enemy:

He was dressed, for the most part, in Eastern seaboard regimentals: a turf haircut on top, run-down brogues on the bottom, with a somewhat mixed uniform in between—buff-colored woolen socks, charcoal-gray trousers, a button-down collar shirt, no necktie, and a herringbone jacket that looked as though it had been properly aged in some of the more popular postgraduate seminars at Yale, or Harvard, or Princeton. "Oh God, what a divine day," he said appreciatively, squinting up at the sun.[19]

Teddy, we are meant to understand, is further along the path of spiritual advancement than his author, J. D. Salinger. In his last "appearance" on this globe Teddy had been an Indian, no less. His reincarnation as an American he sees as a kind of punishment for having fallen short of Oriental standards: "I met a lady, and I sort of stopped meditating. . . . But I wouldn't have had to get incarnated in an *American* body if I hadn't met that lady. I mean it's very hard to meditate and live a spiritual life in America. People think you're a freak if you try to."

Leaving aside the story's trick ending (like the ending of "Banana-fish," a seminar talking point for years to come), and also leaving aside the splendidly handled ocean-liner setting, we are left in "Teddy" with something very like a new convert's testimony, as if Salinger couldn't wait to get his new perceptions into print. Thus we are given a brisk run-through of Teddy's views on the matters that we know were closest to his author's heart. Education, the boy says, should be based on meditation, not reason; poetry should be austere and Japanese-like, not centered on the poet's ego; love should be nonpossessive and unsentimental; people should "know who they are":

You know that apple Adam ate in the Garden of Eden, referred to in the Bible? . . . You know what was in that apple? Logic. Logic and intellectual stuff. That was all that was in it. So—this is my point—what you have to do is vomit it up if you want to see things as they really are.

Teddy's aim now is to reach that point of spiritual advancement at which he will be permitted to die, to go "straight to Brahma and never again have to come back to Earth."

On his very first encounter with Sri Ramakrishna, the disciple M asks: "How, sir, may we fix our minds on God?" The master's pronouncement is as follows:

Repeat God's name and sing His glories, and keep holy company; and now and then visit God's devotees and holy men. The mind cannot dwell on God if it is immersed day and night in worldliness, in worldly duties and responsibilities; it is most necessary to go into solitude now and then and think of God. To fix the mind on God is very difficult, in the beginning, unless one practices meditation in solitude. When a tree is young it should be fenced all around; otherwise it may be destroyed by cattle.

To meditate, you should withdraw within yourself or retire to a secluded corner or in the forest. . . . To get butter from milk you must let it set into curd in a secluded spot: if it is too much disturbed, milk won't set into curd. Next, you must put aside all other duties, sit in a quiet spot, and churn the curd. Only then do you get butter. Further, by meditating on God in solitude the mind acquires knowledge, dispassion and devotion. But the very same mind goes downward if it dwells in the world. In the world, there is only one thought: "woman and gold."[20]

In the winter of 1952–53, as if in obedience to the master's text, Salinger set off for New England in search of a retreat. The place he settled on was a cottage in the small New Hampshire town of Cornish, just across the Connecticut River from Windsor, Vermont. The cottage was set in ninety acres and had "spectacular" views (according to the people who sold it to him), but it was a "kind of home-made house . . . no furnace, no electricity, no running water." This primitive aspect appealed to Salinger. "He seemed to have a city boy's romantic ideas about life in the country. I think he thought he could just chop wood and get along there—and I guess he did, that first winter. He got along without heat, and carried water from the spring."[21] The cottage itself had a living room clear to the roof, and a tiny aerie above and behind the fireplace that Salinger at first used as a study. He moved in on New Year's Day 1953—his birthday. He was now thirty-four, and for the first time he had a home—a "secluded corner"—he could call his own.

Chapter 9

1

Biographers like to pretend that they are capable of "exploring" their subjects' inner lives, but in truth they tend to have little patience for sustained episodes of self-sufficiency: a happy marriage, a lengthy convalescence, an unbroken regimen of silent toil, even a year or two in prison usually constitute bad news. Something can be made out of such plateaus if there are documents, but even with documents no life is more forbidding than a life that has been tamed, or set in order, or that is running to a hidden plan. And when, as in the case of J. D. Salinger, the inner life becomes virtually indistinguishable from any life that we might sensibly call "outer," then even the most intrepid chronicler knows himself to be facing an impasse. When Salinger embraced Eastern religion he was not just in retreat from a corrupt America; he was also imposing on his biographical pursuers a troublesome narrative longueur. After all, you can't eavesdrop on a man at prayer, nor (if you are us) can you bury your post-sixties skepticism to the extent of pretending solemnly to fathom what *might have* come to pass between this eager convert and his new Easternized idea of God.

But then again, our interest was in Salinger the writer, the externalizer. We would simply have to wait and see what happened to the work, post-Ramakrishna. "Teddy" did not encourage optimism. Rather like Salinger's own life, it was in flight from realism—a bad sign because we already knew from this writer's early work that he has a tendency to preach. We also knew that "the work" has always been for Salinger near sacred, and that ever since he linked up with *The New Yorker*, his protective attitude to what he writes has steadily hardened into a position. He is already known in literary circles as a writer to be handled with great care. Now, post-Ramakrishna, his natural prickliness can be thought of as vocational. When critics fail to grasp what he is up to, or when Ivy League intellectuals wax superior about his low-grade education, he can now answer them with the scornful radiance of the otherwise-impelled.

It would be a few years before Oriental mysticism became a fashion in the United States, and it is impossible to calculate how much Salinger's example had to do with directing future styles of hippiedom. Later on, he would angrily dissociate himself from the faddists of the 1960s. In 1953, Zen was just beginning to make its mark: Suzuki's introductory texts had, after all, been in print since 1949. And the American psyche was getting ready to somehow settle with Japan; that is to say, James Michener had already begun work on *Sayonara*. Even so, most literary city slickers would have found Salinger's new Easternism both dotty and intimidating.

Hamish Hamilton, certainly, was not overjoyed to be in receipt of Ramakrishna's weighty text. After six months Salinger had to prod him into a response, and Hamilton confessed: "I feel terribly guilty about the Ramakrishna book. I am usually meticulous about acknowledging letters, and even more so books, but in this case I seem to have slipped up. I received it safely and read much of it with enjoyment, though some I confess defeated me." Luckily, another British publisher was talking of bringing out an abridged edition and may thus "have pretty well spoilt the market for the complete book."[1]

Salinger was evidently prepared to overlook this lapse. For the next year he persistently pressed Hamilton to take an interest in the handful of American writers he considered to be not beyond the pale: Peter de

Vries, S. J. Perelman, William Maxwell, and Eudora Welty. And he was now definite in his readiness to bring out a volume of short stories—indeed, arrangements for this publication were made well before he moved to Cornish. *Nine Stories* appeared in the United States in April 1953 and from Hamish Hamilton in Britain two months later. The ninth story in the book was "Teddy."

Aside from a glowing full-page welcome from Eudora Welty in *The New York Times Book Review,* the principal reviews, though almost unanimously favorable, had a curiously grudging edge. There was an acknowledgment of Salinger's "surface brilliance," but also a suspicion that there was something *too* brilliant going on here, that there must surely be a secret emptiness. "He is extremely deft, sometimes over-sophisticated, in his surface technique," said Seymour Krim, in *Commonweal;* and Gene Baro took this reservation a step further in the *New York Herald Tribune:* "Salinger's vision tempers an all-embracing sentimentality with a personal sophistication, so that these stories run to a kind of intellectual and emotional chic." In Britain, the *Times Literary Supplement* spoke of "a writer trapped by his own cleverness."

Salinger from very early on said that he would rather be called lousy than promising, and these were just the sort of notices that he despised—condescending, unspecific, and somehow managing to suggest that "brilliance" was an everyday, to-be-taken-for-granted item of fictioneer's equipment. After *The Catcher in the Rye*'s beautifully sustained pretense of artlessness, reviewers perhaps felt cheated by the evident shrewdness of Salinger's craftsmanship in these nine tales. The invisible author is almost rudely self-confident, even in his most oblique effects, and in stories like "The Laughing Man" and "Pretty Mouth and Green My Eyes" there is a strong charge of sheer narrative enjoyment—Salinger has been having a good time. Reviewers often feel that authors of this stamp invite deflation.

Commercially, though, the book was a success—remarkably so for a volume of short stories. Boosted by the paperback appearance of *The Catcher in the Rye* (and the appearance with it of the beginnings of a campus readership), *Nine Stories* rose to ninth position on the *New York*

Times best-seller list and stayed in the top twenty for three months.

In Britain, Salinger's book of stories was published under the title *For Esmé—with Love and Squalor, and Other Stories,* a type of formulation that Salinger had specifically refused to countenance a few months earlier. In November 1952, Hamilton had written to Salinger putting the view that the title *Nine Stories* "would be about as big a handicap as could be provided for any book at birth, and we sincerely hope you weren't serious."[2] Hamilton himself has no recollection of what happened next but by May 1953 Salinger seems to have succumbed to his publisher's objections—an act of breathtaking compliance and not to be repeated.

In Britain the book was respectfully reviewed, but sold few copies of its first printing: The booksellers' subscription was a mere one thousand. It would be another five years before *The Catcher in the Rye* appeared in a British paperback edition. (Commercial note: *Nine Stories* was also sold to Denmark and Germany, where *The Catcher in the Rye* had already been translated. *The Catcher,* by 1954, was available also in France, Israel, Italy, Japan, the Netherlands, Sweden, and Switzerland, although its peak as an international best seller would come in the early to mid-sixties; by 1970 it was translated into thirty languages. *Nine Stories* never enjoyed this breadth of distribution, although individual stories, particularly "Bananafish" and "For Esmé," have appeared around the world in magazines and anthologies.)

There are no Caulfields in *Nine Stories,* no Gladwallers. Seymour Glass makes his debut, and so too (although the connection is not stressed) do Walter Glass and Boo Boo Tannenbaum (one of the Glass sisters). Apart from "For Esmé"—which, oddly, considering its popularity, is the one piece that has a lingeringly "early" feel to it—the collection is fairly thoroughly cleansed of penetrable autobiography. It is as if Salinger knew that in his later stories for the slicks there had been elements of straight confession. "The Laughing Man" is located in Salinger's own childhood corner of New York, and "De Daumier-Smith's Blue Period" reads as if it is at least partly drawn from life, but even in these there is no sense of a writer enthralled by the detail of his own experience. Nor is there any strained inventiveness. From *The New Yorker* Salinger learned how to move with poise between these once-damaging extremes. In *Nine Stories* this stylistic self-assurance is liberating: It makes for a new economy and self-denial.

Although Salinger's work has for a time become less autobiographical, his biography in 1953 begins to read like a sequel to his novel. His first few months in his new country home can almost be read as an endearing imitation of the kind of grown-up life Holden Caulfield had envisaged for himself. Holden had said he would "drive up to Massachusetts and Vermont, and all around there, see. It's beautiful as hell up there. It really is. . . ." He would live by a brook, he said, and "chop all our own wood in the winter time." Or he would maybe pretend to be a deaf-mute and "build me a little cabin . . . right near the woods, but not right in them. . . . I'd cook all my own food, and later on, if I wanted to get married or something, I'd meet this beautiful girl that was also a deaf-mute, and we'd get married."

Space, solitude, and silence—these were the recurring elements of Holden's dream. And if he *did* anything at all, it would be priestly-pastoral, and only for the young:

Anyway, I keep picturing all these little kids playing some game in this big field of rye and all. Thousands of little kids, and nobody's around—nobody big, I mean—except me. And I'm standing on the edge of some crazy cliff. What I have to do, I have to catch everybody if they start to go over the cliff—I mean if they're running and they don't look where they're going I have to come out from somewhere and *catch* them. That's all I'd do all day. I'd just be the catcher in the rye.[3]

Within weeks of setting up house in Cornish, Salinger had gathered around him not "thousands of little kids" but certainly a small collection of child friends. He would meet them in a Windsor coffee shop, a haunt popular with teenage (fifteen- to sixteen-year-old) kids from Windsor High School. One of them recalls:

He used to be a ball of fun. . . . He had a great sense of humor—very dry. We used to love it when he came in and I think he enjoyed it too. He was forever entertaining the high school kids—he bought us meals and drinks. He was very interested in the basketball and football games—especially basketball. After the Spa, we used to pile into his jeep and go up to his house. It was always open house up there. No matter what time, it didn't matter. He was always glad to see everybody.

Salinger would sometimes drive his young friends to out-of-town basketball games or, *in loco parentis*, chaperone the girls to college dances. Another friend remembers:

He was just like one of the gang, except that he never did anything silly the way the rest of us did. He always knew who was going with whom, and if anybody was having trouble at school, and we all looked up to him, especially the renegades. He'd play whatever record we asked for on his hi-fi . . . and when we started to leave he'd always want to play just one more. He seemed to love having us around, but I'd sit there and wonder, Why is he doing this? Finally I decided that he was writing another book about teenagers and we were his guinea pigs. I don't mean he was looking down his nose at us, or had us on a pin or anything like that. He was very sincere. There's nothing phony about him.[4]

In the fall of 1953, one of the Windsor High School group, a girl called Shirley Blaney, asked Salinger if she and a friend could interview him for a high school page that came out weekly in the *Claremont Daily Eagle*. Salinger agreed. As *Life* magazine later described it:

While Salinger ate his lunch and the two girls drank Cokes in one of the Spa's wooden booths, journalistic history was made. Shirley Blaney and the *Daily Eagle*, without quite knowing what they were doing, pulled off one of the great scoops of literary history.[5]

It appears, however, that the *Daily Eagle* did know what it was doing. Four days later, on November 13, 1953, the Salinger interview appeared, not on the high school page, but as an *Eagle* scoop. It was the last interview Salinger has ever given to anyone.[6] From the day of its publication he began to distance himself from his high school chums, as if they had all somehow betrayed him, let him down. According to *Life:* "The next time a carload of them drove up to Salinger's home, he did not seem to be at home, although the Jeep was parked across the road." When they tried again, they found the house "totally hidden behind a solid, impenetrable, man-tall, woven wood fence."

Before the *Eagle* interview, Salinger had made no attempt to hide away in Cornish. It was as if he believed that the town itself was his retreat, that his neighbors could be seen as trusty allies. He was not yet famous enough for these supposed loyalties to be put to any sort of final test; for the moment it was sufficient that literary New York was escaped. There was no great risk at this time in attending—as he did—the odd local cocktail party, or in dropping by the house of the artist who lived at the bottom of his road. Indeed, the artist—Bertram Yeaton—was quite useful. Salinger didn't have a telephone, and if his publisher or agent wished to contact him, they would phone Yeaton's house and leave a message.

This kind of small-town togetherness seems to have delighted Salinger at first. He consulted with local agriculturists about how to get the best from his corn crop, or how to put in rosebushes. And he bought a chain saw to clear some of his woody acres. Now and then, he would even give small cocktail gatherings himself, entertaining some of the local teachers and retired military officers with advice on Zen and yoga, and demonstrating the lotus position to anyone who cared to learn. On one occasion, "a young woman who made it promptly got a leg cramp and it took the combined efforts of all the guests to get her untangled again."

It was at one of these local get-togethers that Salinger met a nineteen-year-old Radcliffe student named Claire Douglas. Claire was the daughter of a well-known British art critic, Robert Langton Douglas, who had moved his family to New York in 1940 to avoid the London blitz. Douglas was something of a character, renowned for his several marriages and love affairs. He was sixty-three years old when he married Claire's mother, Jean Stewart, in 1928, and already had several children by his two earlier marriages. Claire was born in 1933. During the last years of his life, Douglas worked as a cataloguer-writer for Duveen's in New York, and after he died in 1951, Claire's mother married his employer, Edward Fowles.

Even in this brief curriculum, there was much that Salinger would have found intriguing. Almost by accident, Claire had links with *The New Yorker:* Her family lived in the same East Sixty-sixth Street apartment block as *The New Yorker* writer Francis Steegmuller (indeed, the party at which they met was given by Steegmuller's friends), and Joseph Duveen was the subject of a new biography by S. N. Behrman (the book originally appeared in serial form as a *New Yorker* profile). Also Claire's huge family of half brothers and half sisters would have appealed to him. One of her half brothers was the celebrated British air ace Sholto Douglas; among the others there was said to be a nun, an airline pilot, a professor of economics, and a bohemian poet photographer.

And Claire herself had some distinctive claims on Salinger's attention. She was only nineteen when they met, but all accounts of her suggest that she looked younger. At Shipley School and at Radcliffe her passion was for poetry and theater. Her class prediction imagines her as the "Sarah Bernhardt of her generation." Also her "Why Can't I?" rejoinder in the college yearbook had a splendidly Vedantic ring: "Why can't I live nine lives?"

2

According to one account, Claire Douglas, at the time of her meeting with Salinger, was already involved with a Harvard Business School graduate (he need be known here only as C.M.) and sometime in 1954 she married him. The marriage lasted but a few months, and after the separation Claire went to live with Salinger in Cornish: Her marriage, it seems, had merely interrupted their romance.[7] If all this is true, then the interruption must have been painful for Salinger, his loved one married to a Harvard man. It seems that it was during the months of Claire's marriage to C.M. that Salinger worked on his long story "Franny," a story that takes on an extra venom if it is seen against the background of his relationship with Claire.

It is almost certainly "Franny" that Salinger speaks of when he writes to Roger Machell in January 1954 about a long story he is working on. Machell had wanted Salinger to drive down to New York for a dinner party, but Salinger pleads that even the smallest disruption of his work schedule could be ruinous. The suggestion is that this is not the first time that Machell's overtures had been rebuffed. But then Machell had already learned that Salinger was unlike most of his other authors; he also knew that an important change had taken place since their first meeting in 1951. "I would say he's basically emotional rather than intellectual. The conveniences of life mean nothing to him. He doesn't care about such things as food, wine, etc. When he came over to England he always made it clear he wanted to be left alone. When he's not pounding the typewriter, he's contemplating the Infinite. He's a profoundly serious guy possessed by a search for God."[8]

Machell said this in 1961, but he could as easily have said it 1954. Salinger's pounding of the typewriter and his search for God were now inseparable disciplines, and to be "intellectual" was not a discipline at all. In "Franny," a brightly tense young girl student spends a football weekend with her Ivy League boyfriend, Lane Coutell. According to the testimony of Claire's half brother Gavin, Franny was quite clearly drawn from life—Salinger, it seems, had carefully scattered a few blatant (to those who knew Claire) clues: "The navy blue bag with the white leather binding," for example, was the very bag that Claire had with her when she had gone off to spend a weekend with C.M.

C.M. in the tale, however, is not represented as a business school graduate but as something far worse—a literary academic, a sterile, patronizing "section man" who thinks Flaubert was "neurotically attracted to the *mot juste*," was a "word-squeezer" who lacked "tes-

ticularity." Lane had been given an A for a paper based on this percep-
tion, and was still basking in the triumph. The really "good boys"—
boys like Shakespeare, Tolstoy, Dostoevsky—he believed "just *wrote.*
Know what I mean?" and had none of Flaubert's emasculated scruples.
Franny, in the story, is equipped with just the kind of contempt that
this approach would have aroused, had been arousing for some years,
in Salinger. She knows Coutell's type from her own college: ". . . the
English Department has about ten little section men running around
ruining things for people," and she is "so sick of pedants and conceited
little tearer-downers I could scream."

The story's essential oppositions are declared right from the start: art
versus academia, truth versus reason. Lane, of course, is baffled by his
girlfriend's vehemence, and irritated too that a promising-looking
weekend is in danger of collapse. With malign exactness, Salinger
captures Lane's gradually deepening dismay as he realizes that Franny
is not going to play his game. He has taken her to a fancy restaurant
and she orders a chicken sandwich. "But I can't just work up an
appetite because you want me to." He suggests that they have drinks
later on with a mutual friend named Wally Campbell, but Franny can't
remember who he is. "It's just that for four solid years I've kept seeing
Wally Campbells wherever I go." And she is not just contemptuous of
Campbell's intellectual pretensions. She also despises the whole milieu
in which those pretensions are allowed to flourish. Lane strikes back.
"You're making one *hell*uva sweeping generalization," he declares, and
goes on to point out that at Franny's college, "You've got two of the
best men in the country in your goddam English Department. Manlius.
Esposito. God, I wish we had them *here.* At least, they're poets, for
Chrissake."

Franny's reply to this is really a restatement of the Raymond Ford
distinction between versifiers (who invent) and real poets (who discover): "They're not. That's partly what's so awful. I mean they're not
real poets. They're just people that write poems that get published and
anthologized all over the place, but they're not *poets.*" Coutell is scan-
dalized: Does a poet have to be dead, he asks, or bohemian before he

can be accepted as a "real poet"? "What do you want—some bastard with wavy hair?" Franny replies:

"I know this much, is all. If you're a poet, you do something beautiful. I mean you're supposed to *leave* something beautiful after you get off the page and everything. The ones you're talking about don't leave a single, solitary thing beautiful." We know that Salinger himself has had ambitions as a poet, and in *The Inverted Forest* he has granted an insight into the kind of poetry he values. Gavin Douglas has testified that throughout the 1950s Salinger was writing or translating haiku and had composed other poems that were "too far out or far too personal" for publication. "He doesn't want to be thought of as an intellectual New York sort of poet."

In 1954, when Salinger was writing "Franny," American poetry was indeed firmly based in the academies, and it was pleased to be there: Cerebral complexity and an attachment to traditional forms were still the principal requirements and T. S. Eliot was the model. A poet of the Salinger/Raymond Ford disposition would certainly have felt himself to be out of the fashionable mainstream. Indeed, it is surely no accident that the only two lines of Raymond Ford's that we're allowed to see are offered as a kind of riposte to Eliot's sterile vision:

> Not wasteland, but a great inverted forest
> with all foliage underground.

The poets Franny yearns for would be the ones who "discovered" this mysterious, subterranean source of fecundity, but such a discovery is most unlikely in a society dominated by the teachable, by the English departments that, in 1954, were at the peak of their influence. This was, in Randall Jarrell's diagnosis, the "age of criticism" and such poets as there were had come to depend on the universities for their livelihood and their prestige. A criticism that was geared to a quasi-scientific reverence for "difficulty" could only engender a poetry that was written to be taught—precisely the sort of "terribly fascinating, syntax" poetry that Franny and her author loathed.

Although offered as a story of religious affirmation, "Franny" is actually a cold-eyed polemic against academia, Salinger's enemy, and his obsession, for some fifteen years. Franny herself seeks, and has partly found, an "alternative education" in the yogalike disciplines recommended in the little green book she carries in her handbag, but it is made clear that she has been *forced* into this position by the world of Lane Coutell. Like Holden Caulfield, Franny feels that she might well be driven mad by the stupidity and self-interest of others.

All I know is I'm losing my mind. I'm just sick of ego, ego, ego. My own and everybody else's. I'm sick of everybody that wants to *get* somewhere, do something distinguished and all, be somebody interesting. It's disgusting—it is, it *is*. I don't care what anybody says.[9]

Unlike Holden, though, she has discovered a way out—or forward, as she believes—in the discipline of prayer; incessant prayer, as in *bhaktiyoga*, which Ramakrishna prescribes as the "religion for this age." "What is *bhaktiyoga*? It is to keep the mind on God by chanting His name and glories." If you do this, says Franny, "eventually what happens, the prayer becomes self-active."

Something *happens* after a while. I don't know what, but something happens, and the words get synchronized with the person's heartbeats, and then you're actually praying without ceasing.[10]

Lane's response is to warn against the dangers of "heart trouble."

But then Lane, we are meant to register, is supremely a product of the times. In 1953, the editors of *Partisan Review* had offered a description of the "ideal reader." Such a paragon, they said, would be "aware of the major tendencies in contemporary criticism . . . concerned with the structure and fate of society . . . and informed or (wishing) to become informed about new currents in psychoanalysis and other humanistic sciences."[11] Lane Coutell, it could be said, entirely fits the bill. He believes in "tendencies in contemporary criticism," in psychoanalysis, and he is scornful of mysticism ("You actually believe that stuff, or what?"). Although he doesn't say so, we can be sure he believes himself to be "concerned with the structure and face of modern society."

How many of these affiliations were shared by Claire Douglas's C.M. cannot be known (Gavin Douglas said he "wasn't a bad guy, I rather liked him, but he was a jerk"). Nor can we judge the effectiveness of "Franny" as an instrument in Salinger's courtship of Claire. The record merely states that "Franny" was published in *The New Yorker* on January 29, 1955, and Salinger was married to Claire Douglas on February 17. The wedding took place in Barnard, Vermont, and shortly afterward Salinger's Cornish neighbors jocularly elected him Town Hargreave. This title, it seems, is given to the community's "most recently married man" and the idea was that if "anybody's hogs got loose, it was the Hargreave's job to round them up and bring them back." Salinger, apparently, was not amused.

With his new wife he was all the more disposed to keep his distance from the neighbors; indeed, some Cornish residents have said that his concern for privacy was not thought to be all that remarkable until after he got married. For the first year of his marriage, he and Claire set about devising a life of uncompromising purity: According to Gavin, they would grow their own food but would not kill even the tiniest of creatures. Salinger himself had a pioneer-style idealism as he set about controlling his domain:

He wanted to be self-sufficient. He had this vegetable garden, and Maxwell and all the others would send him things to grow. It was a primitive sort of life—you can call it Zen or whatever you like. Once he took me to the ruins of an old farmhouse on his property that he said had been built about revolutionary times. He showed me the old well and said that's where they'd gotten the water. Then he showed me the barn where they'd kept their cattle. He said, "They're gone. They couldn't make it. But I'm here now. And I'm going to make the land profitable." It was an affirmation, see, a statement of belief in humanity. He takes that self-sufficiency very hard.[12]

Throughout the spring and summer of 1955 Salinger worked on a twenty-thousand-word epithalamium entitled "Raise High the Roof Beam, Carpenters." It is the story of a wedding that turns into an elopement, and it is Salinger's first extended exploration of the fictional family that from now on will be the focus of everything he writes. The Glass family has already made a few appearances, but its full structure, genealogy, and vital statistics have never been spelled out.

Salinger's earlier family, the Caulfields, had been smaller and rather less complicated than the Glass ménage turns out to be, but the two broods have much in common. The Caulfields—although the names sometimes changed—were always a family of four: Vincent (or D.B.), the writer; Holden, the wild boy; Kenneth (or Allie), the dead seer; and Phoebe, the cute little voice of innocence. The Caulfield parents were both in the theater—until *The Catcher in the Rye*, in which Mr. Caulfield turns into a businessman who now and then invests in Broadway shows.

An unpublished story called "An Ocean Full of Bowling Balls" (written in the mid-1940s) is the most Glass-like of Salinger's early tales and it shows, in a helpfully overt manner, how he used these invented brothers and sisters as a means of exploring his own separate selves. Bound as they are (in fiction) within the "body" of a single family, these selves can be set in opposition without risking any final break. Thus, in "An Ocean Full of Bowling Balls," we have the poet-saint (Kenneth), the angry disaffiliate (Holden), the literary careerist (Vincent and/or D.B.), and the clairvoyant juvenile (Phoebe). Each of these could be said to stand for an important element in Salinger's own nature, as he perceived it at the time. The story was written at a period when Salinger was anguished about his own motives as a writer; he had detected in himself an authorial vengefulness that didn't at all fit with his artist-saint sense of vocation. In the story he tries to fathom this conflict by means of a dialogue between Vincent (in his twenties) and

Kenneth (aged twelve). Kenneth persuades Vincent to destroy a short story he has written in which one of the characters is badly used; Kenneth wishes that Vincent would stop doing this sort of thing. Later on, Kenneth is killed in a swimming accident for which Vincent blames himself.[13]

In the Glass family, Seymour takes the Kenneth role, and we already know—from "A Perfect Day for Bananafish"—that he too, by 1955, is dead. Buddy, his younger brother by two years (born in 1919, like Salinger himself), assumes the part of Vincent, the almost worldly writer figure endlessly fascinated by Seymour's loftiness of spirit. In "Raise High the Roof Beam, Carpenters," which he narrates, Buddy is remembering the day of Seymour's wedding. The bride is Muriel ("a zero in my opinion but terrific-looking"), and Buddy has been summoned to attend the ceremony. The summons and the judgment of Muriel come from the third Glass child, Boo Boo. She herself can't make it to the wedding (she is on duty with the WAVES) and more or less begs Buddy to be there. This is not easy, because Buddy is in an army hospital—the year is 1942—recovering from pleurisy.

After Boo Boo, there is Walter (whose death in the Pacific has already been reported in "Uncle Wiggily in Connecticut") and his twin brother, Waker (a Catholic priest about whom we learn very little; he is in a conscientious objector camp in Maryland). And then there are the children—Franny, now eight, and her brother Zooey, age thirteen. Franny and Zooey are on the West Coast with their parents, who are in show business, but at a somewhat lower level than the Caulfields; they are "retired Pantages Circuit vaudevillians." At the time of the wedding, Mr. Glass is "hustling talent for a motion picture studio."

All the Glass children are, or were, precocious. As the Black brothers, Seymour and Buddy had in 1927 appeared in a children's radio quiz program called *It's a Wise Child*, and since then each succeeding Glass has served time on the show. Franny and Zooey are the current stars. Seymour, oddly enough, has enjoyed considerable success in academia: A student at Columbia when he was fourteen, he is a "professor" in civilian life.

And now he is getting married. In late May 1942, Buddy is the only Glass near enough to New York to attend the wedding, so he does, perspiring and in pain. Seymour, though, fails to show up at the ceremony and Buddy gets stranded in a limousine filled with indignant, Muriel-related guests. This is a marvelously comic sequence—almost Salinger's last essay in mordant, out-of-doors social observation. None of the disgruntled guests in the limousine knows quite who Buddy is, so they are able to let rip on Seymour's terrible behavior. Muriel's mother (recently psychoanalyzed) had, it seems, already diagnosed the groom as a "latent homosexual and a schizoid." And it transpires that the night before, Seymour had met with his intended bride and told her that he was "too happy" to attend the wedding. "Does that sound like somebody *normal*? Does that sound like somebody in their right mind?"

Toward the end of the story, Buddy reads a diary of Seymour's in which there is an account of his prewedding qualms. Seymour had begged Muriel "to just go off alone with me and get married. I'm too keyed up to be with people. I feel as though I'm about to be born. Sacred, sacred day." And he goes on:

I've been reading a miscellany of Vedanta all day. Marriage partners are to serve each other. Elevate, help, teach, strengthen each other, but above all, *serve*. Raise their children honorably, lovingly, and with detachment. A child is a guest in the house, to be loved and respected—never possessed, since he belongs to God. How wonderful, how sane, how beautifully difficult, and therefore true. The joy of responsibility for the first time in my life.

Sometime after discovering Seymour's diary, Buddy learns that Seymour and Muriel had indeed managed to elope.

We never meet Seymour in the story, but we can instantly recognize him as the "saintly artist" type, redeemed from alienation and misanthropy by his attachment to Eastern divines. For Seymour "the human voice conspires to desecrate everything on earth" (there is a near-saintly deaf-mute in "Raise High the Roof Beam," who must be a kind of joke sequel to Holden Caulfield's fantasy), but Seymour is striving to transcend this sort of negative discrimination: "I'll champion indiscrimination till doomsday. . . . *Followed purely,* it's the way of the Tao, and undoubtedly the highest way." This path of indiscrimination means that Muriel's mother, an "irritating, opinionated woman," must be seen as "unimaginably brave" because "she might as well be dead, and yet she goes on living." It also seems to mean that Muriel's coldness should be worshiped as "her simplicity, her terrible honesty." But how does a "discriminating man" learn how to indiscriminate? Does he pretend, for example, that bad poetry is really good? Seymour believes that such a man "would have to dispossess himself of poetry, go *beyond* poetry."

Seymour, we learn, has had encounters with psychoanalysis and has even "more or less" promised his new wife to try again "one of these days." The diagnosis last time was that he suffered from a "perfection complex," that he found even the smallest falling short almost impossible to bear. How can *this* be squared with the Taoist path of indiscrimination? And is he not doomed always to be misread, to have his perfectionism misinterpreted as something sinister or aggressive? In "A Perfect Day for Bananafish," the child Sybil is frightened when Seymour kisses the arch of her foot. Six years earlier (according to "Raise High the Roof Beam, Carpenters") Seymour had written in his diary: "I have scars on my hands from touching certain people." At the age of twelve the boy Seymour had thrown a stone at a girl he admired and injured her quite badly; he had thrown the stone, he said, "because she looked so beautiful."

3

My companion was now looking as if he'd like to throw a stone at *me*—and not because he found my musings about Seymour Glass at all attractive. So far as he was concerned, we'd been drumming our gumshoed heels for almost a whole *chapter,* and he was in no mood for any further fancy talk. "Obviously, Seymour Glass is Salinger in thin disguise: Why not come out and say so? It's evident Salinger has a saint complex. He wants to *be* a saint. The trouble is, he doesn't have a saintly personality; quite the opposite—he is egotistical, ill tempered, unforgiving. But he wants to be a saint because saints are above the human, they are unstoppably superior. So what does he do? He stops writing about people, those imperfects, and starts writing about saints. He *invents* a saint, one that belongs to him, that *is* him: a saint who writes beautiful poetry, who has a breakdown in the war, who marries the wrong woman, who commits suicide. Well, all right, Salinger doesn't commit suicide, but he does the next best thing: He disappears, he stops living in the world, he makes himself semiposthumous. You can talk about him but you can't talk *to* him, just like Seymour Glass. But I can see from your face you think this is too unbearably crude; you prefer the delicate suggestion, the wispy probability, the gentle teasing out of parallels, and so on. But we are writing biography, not criticism, are we not?"

It was not easy to persuade an alter ego in this mood that here we had a case in which biography and criticism were one, and that in getting to the heart of Seymour and Buddy Glass we were getting closer to the heart of Salinger than we ever would by knowing what time he got up in the morning, or how many cigarettes he smoked, or any of that circumstantial stuff, which, in any case, we hadn't got. The "life" was immobilized; when Salinger wasn't praying, or growing vegetables, he was writing. There was nothing at all that we could do about that, was there?

"We could do some *scene setting*, couldn't we?" There was something almost pitiful in this entreaty. "We could go up there to Cornish and do some word pictures of the town, talk to a few ex-neighbors, or track down some of those kids he used to hang around with. I know that's against the rules, but we have already *used* quotations from those kids that we dug out of the *Time* archive. Some of them will be in their forties now . . ."

It was tempting, I agreed, but no; in our case, the rules of trespass were quite clear, and the first rule was not to go within a hundred miles of Cornish. But it was time, certainly, that my companion got one of his lucky breaks. He had been in these sulks before, as I had been in mine. Last time, it had been around the year of the publication of *The Catcher in the Rye*. Here was the most important event in Salinger's career and we had almost nothing on it apart from a few review clippings and a single interview. His movements during the early fifties were unknown to us; our "map" for these months was a taunting blank. We had written to the publisher Little, Brown for "any information" but had been told that there was nobody still at the firm who had had anything to do with Salinger. John Woodburn, his editor, was dead.

What about the British end? We wrote to Roger Machell; he was ready to talk to us, but sadly he too died a few days before our scheduled meeting. We wrote to Hamish Hamilton Ltd. several times but it was moving offices and could not track down any Salinger papers; indeed, it doubted if there were any. And Hamish Hamilton himself had long before retired to Italy. He had already given us some personal reminiscences by letter but could not be expected to have access to the office files. But then, weeks later, the office itself called in the shape of a slightly ragged-sounding secretary. "This is Hamish Hamilton. We have a package for you in reception. To do with J. D. Salinger [which she rhymed with "singer" or "gunslinger"]. The package was in our hands some twenty minutes later. It contained about thirty letters from Salinger to Hamish Hamilton and Roger Machell, dating from the beginning of their relationship in 1951 through to the somewhat bitter end in 1960, which we will be coming to in Chapter 10.

Remarkably, the letters were not photocopies; they were the yellowing originals. Once again we marveled at the lax security we trespassers had to contend with. Salinger was supposed to be elusive, we exclaimed, but so far—without resorting to subterfuge or theft or even mild persuasion—we had accumulated more than a hundred letters covering almost every month of his adult life. And now we were being given not just access to letters, but the letters themselves—the only copies, probably, unless Salinger kept carbons. Shocking, really.

And that was how we got ourselves through the early 1950s. The

letters to Hamilton were strong on dates and places. They gave us
Salinger's account of his relations with John Woodburn, his response
to the reviews of *The Catcher in the Rye*, his anxiety about the Olivier
encounter, and so on. And their tone was revealing. They were wordy
letters, but rather self-consciously affectionate; and there was a wariness
about them, a wanting to impress. Clearly, Hamish Hamilton was
thought by Salinger to be a cultivated English gent to be addressed
accordingly. But there was a pathos, too, in observing how badly
Salinger wanted to be friends, to have an older brother figure he could
trust.

By 1956, the moment of our present gloom, the relationship with
Hamilton and Machell was beginning to turn cool. Salinger's letters
were cordial enough, but more aloof and businesslike. After all, in spite
of their seeming virtues, these men were of the metropolis, book mer-
chants, and they moved in a world of deals and dinners that Salinger
had repudiated. "If he stops talking to *them*, where does that leave *us*?"
To get through the late fifties, yes, we were (I supposed) rather badly
in need of what my companion has now taken to describing as a
"Hamish Hamilton-type coup."

Chapter 10

1

In a letter written to us just before he died, Roger Machell reflected with some sorrow on the quarrel that caused Salinger to break with Hamish Hamilton, and he noted that "not even Learned Hand" had been able to effect a reconciliation. Judge Learned Hand, we discovered, had had a summer house near Cornish. He was in his eighties when Salinger met him and was revered throughout the land as a jurist of vision and integrity. Often called "the tenth justice of the Supreme Court," Hand was celebrated for his defense of free speech and the right to dissent, but was also valued as a sturdy patriot, an opponent of communism, and a man of God. In 1952 he had published a book called *The Spirit of Liberty,* a collection of his thoughts on retiring from fifty-two years on the bench. It is easy from these reflections to see how Salinger would have warmed to the idea of Hand: a great legislator, a guru, who named "detachment" and "imagination" as his first two requirements in a judge, and who furthermore believed that "the work of a judge, like a poet's, or a sculptor's, was an art."

"The spirit of liberty," wrote Hand, "is the spirit which is not too sure that it is right."

The spirit of liberty is the spirit which seeks to understand the minds of other men and women. The spirit of liberty is the spirit which weighs their interest alongside its own, without bias. The spirit of liberty remembers that not even a sparrow falls to earth unheeded. The spirit of liberty is the spirit of Him who, nearly 2000 years ago, taught mankind that lesson that it has never learned, but has never quite forgotten, that there may be a kingdom where the least shall be heard and considered side by side with the greatest.[1]

In his social aspect, Judge Hand was capable of less sonorous cadences than these; he was a gifted singer and mimic with a weakness for Gilbert and Sullivan lyrics and American folk music.

We learned that Judge Hand's biographer was Gerald Guenther, a law professor out in California. We wrote to him: Did Salinger ever write any letters to the judge? Yes, he did, came the reply, thirteen of them, according to the Guenther files. To see photocopies of these we would need the permission of the Harvard Law Library and of Judge Hand's literary executor, his son-in-law, a lawyer in New York. We wrote off for these permissions, got them, and within weeks yet another bundle of Salinger's private correspondence was in our hands. And, yes, it covered the years 1955–61. Judge and Mrs. Hand used to spend their summers in Cornish, it appeared, and during the winter months Salinger would keep them informed of local events, the weather, his own writing plans, his marital worries (how long would Claire be able to put up with this isolated way of life?), and even on his latest Oriental thoughts—the judge, remarkably, was also something of an expert on Eastern religions. In one especially (to us) useful letter, Salinger admits he is well aware that his new religious preoccupations might turn out to be harmful to his writing, and that he sometimes wishes he could go back to his old methods. But it seemed to him that there was little he could do about controlling the direction of his work. Again we get this sense of the "work" having a life (a mind, almost) of its own, of the Glass children being like real children—hard to handle sometimes but always to be treated with great care.

The tone of *these* letters was weightily respectful, reverential even.

If Hamish Hamilton was for a time the older brother, Judge Hand was surely the kind of father Salinger might wish to have had. And it is to Judge Hand, in December 1955, that he announces his own transformation into fatherhood. "Raise High the Roof Beam, Carpenters" was published in *The New Yorker* on November 19, 1955, and three weeks later the Salingers received their own "guest in the house." Margaret Ann Salinger was born on December 10.

2

THE CATCHER CULT CATCHES ON was a typical mid-fifties headline. The so-called teenage revolution had begun in 1954, and by 1956 adolescent outsiderism was thoroughly established as a market force: Films like *The Wild One* and *Rebel Without a Cause* scored huge popular successes, and *Rock Around the Clock* was about to do the same. Editorialists spoke darkly of a "youthquake." On university campuses Salinger's five-year-old novel had suddenly become the book all brooding adolescents had to buy, the indispensable manual from which cool styles of disaffection could be borrowed. *The Catcher in the Rye* was middle class and it gave voice to the malaise of the advantaged; it offered a college-boy version of Marlon Brando's leather jacket—a pacific, internalized manner of rebellion, soft of heart but toughly comic. Holden Caulfield began topping "Best Loved" student polls across the country, and J. D. Salinger was elevated to the rank of in-demand celebrity, a spokesman and a guru for the young.

The manner of *The Catcher in the Rye*'s ascent remains mysterious. After its first impact, there had been a lull. In 1951, Salinger himself had been glad to see the end of what he called the book's "season of success." For five years it had presumably made its way by word of mouth: Between 1951 and 1956 only three articles on Salinger (apart from book reviews) are listed in the bibliographies; between 1956 and 1960 no fewer than seventy pieces (on *The Catcher in the Rye* alone) appeared in

American and British magazines.² A feature of the youthquake was, of course, that students could now tell their teachers what to read.

By 1956, then, Salinger had a new version of himself to cope with. He had originally chosen Cornish as a retreat. From now on it would seem to him more like a fortress. By the time he began work on his next long story, he was aware that his status in the public view had changed, that he was now a literary star. And his response was curious. In life, he withdrew into a deeper, more consciously constructed anonymity. In his work, he bustled mischievously to the center of the stage, addressing the audience with the wordy, casual artifice of one who knows that he is loved.

In "Zooey" we are introduced to a refashioned Buddy Glass, transformed now from the rather pale and passive figure who narrates "Raise High the Roof Beam, Carpenters." This new Buddy has two functions. Working in the third person, he narrates and stars in a fresh chapter of the Glass family saga—a continuation of "Franny" in which the distraught heroine, just back from her harrowing weekend with Lane Coutell, is preached to by her brother Zachary, or Zooey. In the first person, Buddy is Salinger's own mouthpiece, whimsically deployed.

In both persons, Buddy is presented as having almost everything in common with his author. Like J. D. Salinger, Buddy is a professional short story writer who has reached a turning point in his career. People are "shaking their heads" over the mystical, religious slant of his new work, but he knows what he is doing—he has been writing since he was fifteen. Like Salinger, he lacks a university degree and lives as remotely as he can; he has no telephone (his mother hates this: "No one has any desire to invade his *privacy*, if that's what he *wants*, but I certainly don't think it's necessary to live like a *hermit*"), and he once wrote a story about the suicide of Seymour Glass. And here the teasing differences begin. Seymour is Buddy's brother, given to him by the brotherless J. D. Salinger. Also, Buddy has a job, the kind of job that Salinger himself would loathe—he teaches Advanced Writing 24-A at an unfashionable college. Indeed, over the years, Buddy has been obliged to move his "literary whore's cubicle" from one campus to another—a cruel punishment indeed for Salinger to heap upon *his* alter ego—rather like me forcing *my* companion to write poetry.

But Salinger needs Buddy to have these links with academia so that he himself can plausibly give further voice to his impassioned views on education, so that—via Buddy—he can say things like "education by any means would smell as sweet, and maybe much sweeter, if it didn't begin with a quest for knowledge at all but with a quest, as Zen would put it, for no knowledge." "Zooey" is a story about education, and it reminds us just how much of Salinger's fiction turns on a teacher-pupil dialogue. Phoebe teaches Holden, Seymour teaches Buddy, and Buddy teaches Seymour's teaching to Franny and Zooey. There are sacred texts and relics: Allie's baseball mitt, Seymour's diary, Buddy's letter to Zooey after Seymour's death. Buddy and Seymour are both teachers. They took charge of Franny and Zooey's education from the start, introducing them to the Upanishads, the Diamond Sutra, and the rudiments of Zen:

... we wanted you both to know who and what Jesus and Gautama and Lao-tse and Shankaracharya and Hui-neng and Sri Ramakrishna, etc., were before you knew too much or anything about Homer or Shakespeare or even Blake or Whitman, let alone George Washington and his cherry tree or the definition of a peninsula or how to parse a sentence.

Now Buddy wonders if this was the right approach. Zooey, it seems, suffers from the same perfection complex that afflicted Seymour. He is an actor by profession, but Buddy fears that he is already "demanding something from the performing arts that just isn't residual there," that he too will end up in the woods: "I know how much you demand from a thing, you little bastard."

In many ways, "Zooey" is an attempt to rewrite Ramakrishna's gospel for the 1950s. That gospel was also framed as a teacher-pupil drama, the chief character being a kind of Seymour Glass, dispensing wisdom to the dazzled young. Salinger, his head spinning with the Eastern verities he has gleaned from five years of (we assume) dedicated study, and now granted a huge audience, evidently feels some sort of masterlike impulse to pronounce. He appoints Buddy as his spokesman and then arranges for Zooey to pretend to be Buddy, on the telephone, so that Franny will listen the more respectfully to what he—Zooey-Buddy—has to say, to what he has to teach. Mrs. Glass believes the similarity between her two sons is uncanny, and she lectures Zooey thus:

You either take to somebody or you don't. If you do, then you do all the talking and nobody can get a word in edgewise. If you *don't* like somebody—which is most of the time—then you just sit around like death *itself* and let the person talk himself into a hole. . . . Neither you nor Buddy know how to talk to people you don't like . . . Don't love, really.[3]

3

"Zooey" was published in *The New Yorker* in May 1957. Salinger and his wife had intended to take a summer trip to Europe when the story was completed, but by June, "Zooey" had already begun to spill over into a new chapter of the Glass romance—a chapter in which the mysterious Seymour would at last step from the shadows. Salinger found it impossible to put this work aside. He had built himself a workplace separate from the main house at Cornish, and he had a routine that he dared not disturb. In his letters to the Hands he repeatedly praises Claire for her tolerance, but even during the long harsh winter of 1957–58 there is no sense that he himself would prefer to take a trip to warmer climes.

In February 1958, Roger Machell was in New York and once again he urged Salinger to join him there for dinner or an evening on the town. Salinger's refusal makes little effort to spare Machell's feelings. But Machell had some time ago decided that Salinger was "perhaps the most brilliant but certainly by far the nuttiest author I've ever known," and he was not offended.[4] Machell knew that, for Salinger, he belonged to a despised species: He was a publisher and Salinger's hatred of publishers had been steadily deepening as his books had become more widely bought and read. As Machell commented: "His real mania is publishers. He realises books must be published but wishes they didn't . . . I would say he has a profound hatred of all publishers."

One story put about by Gavin Douglas has Salinger in town, against his will, to attend a meeting with his publisher and "a representative of the English firm that handled him":

Jerry was in an arrogant, nasty mood. And he told them that he'd meet them at the Stork Club. When they got there, they sat down and started talking and then along came Claire and this friend of hers called Kay, slinking in acting like call girls. Jerry pointed them out to the publishers as examples of "that kind of woman" and asked if they would like a closer look. He asked the girls over to their table and for an hour or two they went on with it, talking tough and casting sly glances at the Englishman. I don't know if Jerry ever told them [the publishers] what was really up.[5]

The contempt implied here seems to have been typical. Salinger believed that publishers enjoyed excessive profits, that they exploited their writers by promotional gimmicks and cheapskate presentation; he distrusted the new paperback revolution, believing it had further lowered standards and had prompted a vulgarizing alliance between publishers and academics.

In a letter to Machell, Salinger mentions he has been sent an English contract for the paperback of his short stories. This letter caused some consternation back at Hamish Hamilton in London. There was indeed a contract to be signed—with Harborough Publishing—for a paperback edition of *For Esmé—with Love and Squalor,* but Salinger ought not to have seen it. And Hamish Hamilton had good reason to be nervous. Harborough was an enterprising outfit that had come up with the then-novel ploy of marketing highbrow novels as if they were cheap trash. The reasoning seems to have been that what really mattered in the bookstores was the artwork; if it took a sleazy blurb and an enticing blonde to shift the masterpiece in question, then so be it. This was not a philosophy that J. D. Salinger could have been expected to warm to. The Harborough imprint was called Ace Books, and the cover of their edition of *For Esmé* was indeed all blonde: a pouting, doe-eyed invitation to misread the "Love and Squalor" of the title—a title Salinger had not wanted in the first place. Just above the girl's head it was announced: EXPLOSIVE AND ABSORBING—A PAINFUL AND PITIABLE GALLERY OF MEN, WOMEN, ADOLESCENTS AND CHILDREN. Hamish Hamilton himself describes what followed as the "unhappiest experience of my career":

Eunice Frost, who more or less ran Penguins, refused the book and it went to another house, which provided it with a jacket of singular vulgarity. Jerry, not unnaturally, was furious and held me personally responsible. Nothing I could say could persuade him that the hardcover publishers had no influence over paperback jackets. I did everything in my power, including offering to go to America, but to no avail. Roger and my wife both wrote to him, with no success (he liked them and hated me). We had an option on his next novel, but Jerry said he would rather not be published in England than by me.[6]

"A tragic falling out between well-meaning people" was Roger Machell's description of the incident.[7]

Henceforth Salinger would insist on supervising the production of all his books, and he had special clauses written into contracts giving him the power to prohibit illustrated covers, biographical blurbs (except those written by himself), and quotations from reviews; his vigilance on these matters would extend even to the remotest foreign publication of his work. After their quarrel came to a head, he never spoke to Hamish Hamilton again.

4

In the spring of 1959, Salinger did in fact make it to New York, although not in order to dine with Roger Machell. His work on the long "Seymour" story had been dogged by minor illnesses during the fall of 1958, and now there was pressure from *The New Yorker* for a firm date on which they could expect to clear almost an entire issue for Salinger's new work, his longest since *The Catcher in the Rye*. In March he even took a hotel room in Atlantic City in an effort to complete a draft. After that, he had a spell in *The New Yorker* office. It was during this time that he met a number of his co-contributors: Mollie Panter-Downes, Kenneth Tynan, Winthrop Sargeant. Mostly, these were corridor encounters, although Sargeant does recall that Salinger would now and then drop in on him to talk Eastern religions.[8]

His New York sojourn, though, lasted only a few days. He caught flu and retreated to Cornish. By May the work was done. He made one more visit to New York to make some final revisions, and "Seymour: An Introduction" appeared in *The New Yorker* on June 6, 1959. The title almost certainly carried an element of mockery: mockery of the general reader to whom it is sardonically addressed, but mockery also of the author's own pretense that what he is about to offer will be cordial and clear. In fact, the story is an introduction to an introduction—further background reading on a man we might never actually *get* introduced to.

Once again Buddy Glass is the narrator, and he does indeed tell us more about his dead brother than we knew before; but the new material is mainly scraps and details—there is no attempt at anything resembling an orthodox characterization. Seymour is, quite simply, an embodiment of excellence, a great poet, a reincarnated seer, and an infallible judge, jury, executioner in matters moral and aesthetic. He committed suicide, as we have heard before, in 1948. Still in mourning, Buddy Glass wants us to worship Seymour as he does, and this is the avowed purpose of his introduction.

"Seymour: An Introduction" is not even mainly about Seymour. The real star of the show is Buddy, and Buddy, we already know, is Salinger's own representative on earth. The rather sketchy portrait we were given in "Zooey" is here substantially fleshed out. Buddy, we learn, once wrote a very successful novel about an adolescent. He also published (and here Salinger's identification with his spokesman is complete) two stories about Seymour: one in 1949, about his suicide; the other, about his wedding, in 1955. Salinger, of course, did likewise. Buddy has become successful, a kind of hero to the young, but he feels victimized by his admirers. He doesn't give interviews to the Sunday newspapers; he ignores all the wild and fallacious rumors he hears about himself—for instance, that he spends half his life in a Zen monastery and the other half in a mental institution. Are these rumors that Salinger has heard about himself? Or is this just his cheeky way of *starting* rumors? Bear in mind here that we have pretty well been *told* to think of Buddy as his author's mouthpiece: The whimsical planting of false rumors seems weirdly inconsistent with Salinger's supposed shrinking from the attentions of biographers and gossips. Or is it just what you'd expect?

Buddy, much of the story is devoted to assuring us, despises the culture that has made him famous. He loathes the current "intellectual aristocracy"; he calls it "a peerage of tin ears." Intellectuals these days are obsessed by psychoanalysis, for which Buddy has no time. He also has no time for biographical symptom seekers and time-serving weekly journalists, and would wish to make it clear to his young campus readers that if literary stardom means keeping company with beats, dharma bums, unskilled guitarists, and Zen faddists, then he for one will readily forgo their adoration.

The story that Buddy is here engaged on—"Seymour"—is in fact designed to disappoint, to thwart all puerile expectations: The author will not "get the hell on with his story" in the way an ordinary, low-grade fiction reader might prefer him to. On the contrary, he will indulge himself with verbose digressions, vast parentheses, and even scholarly footnotes. And his prose, he says, will be as "heart-shaped" and self-serving as it wants to be. Now and again he might break off to throw the reader a small crumb of apology, or he might warn him that a particularly hard-to-read paragraph is imminent. Otherwise, there will be no concessions.

"I've waited a good many years to collect these sentiments and get them off," says Buddy as he weighs into "our busy neo-Freudian Arts and Letters clinics," into the publishers and academics, the mediocre poets, and all those of his so-called fellow artists who collaborate with the corrupt metropolitan literary machine—those who write about one another's work or give "unreluctant" interviews about their "working methods." "Seymour" pretends to be a song of praise, and it is full of arch, self-deprecating charm, but the energy that keeps it going is essentially sour and retaliatory. J. D. Salinger may not give interviews, but here—uninvited—he is bending everybody's ear. Even poor Seymour's merits as a poet in the Oriental style are used chiefly as a means of drubbing the non-Oriental culture he is trapped in.

Seymour's 184 marvelous poems have not been published: Buddy is not able to quote from them without permission from the poet's widow, who is very strict about such things. This seems a rather cumbersome fictional device, but it is more than just a means of avoiding the insuperable problem of how to show a fictional great writer's fictional great works. Such is the purity of Seymour's gift that Buddy would not wish to have it knock around in the literary marketplace as if it were just another contender for the worthless praise of second-rate reviewers. Art of this order needs to be protected:

I feel something close to a conviction that we have had only three or four *very* nearly nonexpendable poets, and I think Seymour will eventually stand with those few. Not overnight, *verständlich. Zut,* what would you? It's my guess, my perhaps flagrantly over-considered guess, that the first few waves of reviewers will obliquely condemn his verses by calling them Interesting or Very Interesting, with a tacit or just plain badly articulated declaration, still more damning, that they are rather small, sub-acoustical things that have failed to arrive on the contemporary Western scene with their own built-in transatlantic podium, complete with lectern, drinking glass, and pitcher of iced sea water. Yet a real artist, I've noticed, will survive anything. (Even praise, I happily suspect.)[9]

It will be remembered that Salinger himself is said to have led a secret life as an unpublished Oriental poet, and that it was during the months leading up to his "breakdown" that he was having his poems rejected by the magazines. Also, his first postbreakdown story was about a poet whose poems were *never* rejected by the magazines.

5

Assisted by the flirtatious half disclosures of "Seymour: An Introduction," the Salinger legend was now gaining ground: He was popularly spoken of as a hermit, a recluse, "the Greta Garbo of American letters," and his young readers were heartened by the spectacle of an author whose life seemed to honor the instructions of his art, a celebrity who had high-mindedly declined to take delivery of low rewards. Salinger, it was claimed, had taught a generation of young thinkers to suspect the grown-up phonies who controlled their lives, and his own conduct was therefore susceptible to special scrutiny. That he should so triumphantly pass all the tests endowed his "message" with a rare sort of authenticity.

If the young had any qualms about their hero, these had to do with his apparent disdain for any sort of involvement in political or social realms. Seymour Glass had had similar qualms about *his* own disaffiliation: He sometimes thought his poems read like the work of an ingrate, someone who had turned his back on the real world he lived in. "He said he ate his food out of our big refrigerators, drove our eight-cylinder American cars, unhesitatingly used our medicines when he was sick, and relied on the U.S. Army to protect his parents and sisters from Hitler's Germany, and that nothing, not one single thing in all his poems, reflected these realities. Something was terribly wrong." Seymour may have expressed worry on this score, but it did nothing to alter what he wrote, and, aside from Seymour's fleeting self-critique, Salinger is usually happy to let his characters transcend the here and now. In his own person, he signed no petitions, and although from time to time in his letters there is some railing against Eisenhower or Nixon, he mostly took pride in being apolitical.

It was therefore something of an event when, in December 1959, he wrote a letter to the *New York Post*. The letter was written in reply to an article that had appeared in the *Post* some months earlier on the subject of the New York penal system. Salinger's particular concern was with the predicament of lifers: In New York State, there was no provision for a lifer to seek parole after having served "20 or even 30 years" in jail. This was surely "justice-without-mercy . . . the bleakest, coldest combination of words in the language." Something ought to be done about it, Salinger declared. "Can it be brought to the attention of the Governor? Can he be approached? Can he be located? Surely it must concern him that the New York State lifer is one of the most crossed-off, man-forsaken men on earth."[10]

The likelihood is that this—Salinger's only known public statement on a public issue—had its origins in conversations he had had with Learned Hand. Or he may have learned about the lifer's plight from a New York police chief friend named John D. Keenan, who had served with him in the CIC. According to one witness, Salinger was for some years in regular correspondence with a long-term prisoner in New York's Sing Sing Prison. Whatever the source or the circumstances, there is surely a poignancy to be discovered in the notion of the man-forsaking begging mercy for the man forsaken, in the image of Salinger in his self-constructed Cornish bunker joining thoughts with the lifelong prisoner in his cell.

Chapter 11

1

After the 1959 appearance in *The New Yorker* of "Seymour: An Introduction" it was widely assumed that Salinger would very soon publish a Glass family novel or collection. It was by now more than six years since *Nine Stories* and almost a decade since *The Catcher in the Rye*. One of the odd aspects of Salinger's burgeoning celebrity was that it had seemed not to need the nourishment of regular book publication. Indeed, the legend was well served by his evident reluctance to rush into hardcovers: The work—or some of it—was almost as hard to get hold of as the man. "Franny," for example, had by 1959 become a famous story, much mused on in the quarterlies, but the text could not be purchased in bookstores, and *The New Yorker* had long ago exhausted its stock of back issues.

Sooner or later, though, there would have to be a Book; an astute publicity man could not have devised a more titillating buildup. It began as early as May 1960, with a long article in *Newsweek* by Mel Elfin. Elfin was the first professional journalist to set about cracking the Salinger mystery: "Although Salinger pursues privacy with the same passion that some men pursue pleasure, his name bobs up oftener in current literary conversations than that of any other American writer—

including Hemingway." Elfin would attempt to break down Salinger's "iron curtain" of secrecy by visiting "Cornish, N.H. (population 1,000) and speaking to those who knew him best." Elfin knew that an interview with Salinger himself would not be countenanced, but in search of "atmosphere" he set off "up the unpaved country road where Salinger's one-story redwood cottage stands on a crest of a thickly wooded hillside overlooking the green mountains of Vermont in the distance. Surrounded by stands of white birch and hemlock, the house is remote enough to discourage all but the most persistent idol-hunters."[1]

So far there had been none more persistent than Mel Elfin. He talked to everyone who would talk to him. He talked to Salinger's mailman, to his local storekeepers, to the town librarian (who kept *The Catcher in the Rye* on his restricted shelf). He made a trip to Dartmouth College, where he discovered that Salinger "frequently uses the facilities of the Baker Memorial Library." He discovered that Salinger was a chain smoker, a registered Republican, and that he and his wife now and then turned up at town meetings. Rebuffed by Judge Learned Hand as he had been rebuffed in New York by Dorothy Olding and by William Shawn, Elfin nevertheless managed to build up a more detailed profile of his subject than had been available before.

His main scoop was to extract confidences from the painter Bertram Yeaton, who had at one time allowed Salinger to make use of his telephone. Yeaton gave Elfin an account of Salinger's work methods, the kind of account Salinger hated to see in regular literary interviews. It was revealed that this famous author rose at 5:00 or 6:00 A.M. and walked "down the hill to his studio, a tiny concrete shelter with a translucent plastic roof." There he would spend fifteen or sixteen hours a day at his typewriter:

Jerry works like a dog. He's a meticulous craftsman who constantly revises, polishes and rewrites. On the wall of the studio, Jerry has a series of cup hooks, to which he clips sheafs of notes. They must deal with various characters and situations, because when an idea occurs to him, he takes down the clip, makes the appropriate notation and places it back on the proper hook. He also has

a ledger in which he has pasted sheets of typewritten manuscript on one page
and on the other he has arrows, memos, and other notes for revisions.

At Dartmouth, Elfin also picked up a few nuggets. A bookshop assistant (who regularly supplied Salinger with detective fiction) said that he
had once, on behalf of a friend, approached Salinger for an informal
interview: "Jerry didn't say anything, he just turned his back and
walked away." And a professor of comparative literature confided that
"many faculty members would like to get to know Salinger, but he
seems to avoid any contact with them."

Elfin's other quotes were not attributed: "friends say," "other friends
recall," and so on were the favored formulations, suggesting that much
of his material had been passed on to him in confidence. The anecdotes
he garnered were on the whole too general or too trivial to provide
much of a *frisson:* "He can talk for hours about things he likes—music,
detective novels, Japanese poetry. In fact, whenever Japan is mentioned, his face seems to light up"; "There was a time when he used
to stand on his head. But that was before he got married." One Elfin
story, though, has passed into legend and will not be easy to dislodge.
"Not long ago, stage director Elia Kazan was supposed to have cor-
nered Salinger and pleaded for permission to stage *The Catcher* on
Broadway. After listening to Kazan's sales talk, Salinger . . . replied: 'I
cannot give my permission. I fear Holden wouldn't like it.' " Of this
Kazan himself recalls: "I asked J. D. Salinger by letter if he'd be interested. He wrote back no, no thanks. That's all there was to it. He gave
no reasons."

Mel Elfin's story appeared in *Newsweek* on May 30, 1961, with two
rather forlorn-looking photographs attached; one was a snap of Salinger's mailbox (S. J. Perelman once said that Salinger "may be a recluse
but I'll bet he gets down to the mailbox just as fast as everybody else")
and the other a long-range portrait of the house as perceived through
a small forest of birch trees. *Newsweek* had hired a local photographer
to get a close-up of Salinger himself, and the story of this botched

assignment was written up a year later when the *New York Post*'s Edward Kosner set out to follow Elfin's lead:

Salinger's definitive statement on the matter [of his privacy] was given to a local photographer hired by *Newsweek* last year to snap his picture for a feature story. Knowing his reputation for avoiding publicity, the photographer decided to park his car on the road near Salinger's house and ambush his man.

But when he saw Salinger strolling along, unaware, with his young daughter, the cameraman's resolve melted. He stepped from his car, introduced himself and explained his mission. "Salinger was very polite," recalls Nelson Bryant, editor of the *Claremont Eagle*. "He thanked the man for his discretion and for not trying to 'sneak' a picture. But he told him: 'My method of work is such that any interruption throws me off. I can't have my picture taken or have an interview until I've completed what I set out to do.' "[2]

Kosner followed Elfin's pioneering *Newsweek* route. He spoke to Dorothy Olding ("This man wants his privacy"), to William Shawn ("Salinger simply does not want to be written about"), and to Judge Learned Hand ("He wants to be alone"), and he made visits both to Cornish and to Dartmouth College. His interviews, though, added little to the Elfin file. Indeed, much of the Kosner story reads like a rehash of the *Newsweek* piece: "His friends in New Hampshire say he can talk for hours about music, detective stories and Japanese poetry"; "Yeaton agrees with the others who've seen Salinger at work that he is a meticulous craftsman who writes each story in drops of his own blood."

Kosner's most endearing witness, though, was a college student who once worked as a night office boy at *The New Yorker*—presumably in 1959. The boy's recollection ran as follows:

He was in New York working on "Seymour." He'd come up to the office at night and there'd be just the two of us in this big, dark building. He was writing seven days a week and it was the hardest work I've ever seen anyone do. But he was never too busy to stop, light a cigarette and have a cup of coffee and talk to me.

He's the kind of guy who, even the first time you talk to him, impresses you that he's really interested in you and what you have to say. He *listens*. I was very mixed up at the time—I had a lot of problems—and he helped me a lot. I'm very grateful to him.[3]

Telephoned twenty years after writing his *New York Post* story, Edward Kosner understandably could not recall the student's name. Nor could he provide the identity of the "friend" who, he'd reported, "was inspired not long ago to suggest that Salinger hold a press conference to 'take some of the heat off.' " Salinger declined, and the friend confessed that he hadn't seen much of him since he broached the idea.

By the time Kosner's piece appeared on April 30, 1961, the "heat" was getting close to boiling point. It had been announced that Salinger's new book would be appearing in the summer. This news, wrote Kosner, had "prompted his paperback publishers to plan a substantial reprint of *The Catcher in the Rye,* even though there are already 1,250,000 copies of it in print." It also prompted the editors of *Time* and *Life* to begin work on a "major investigation." Cover stories were planned to coincide with the inevitable new surge of interest that would accompany the publication of *Franny and Zooey. Time* set a whole team of reporters to dig up everything they could about their subject's past, and *Life* dispatched Ernest Havemann to Cornish to make an all-out bid for Salinger's cooperation.

Havemann set off for Cornish, he recalls, with highish hopes. He admired Salinger's work and felt so sympathetic to his general position that "I was sure that he would see me." He drove up to the house and called hello over the now-famous fence: "It was a tremulous hello, I confess it. I was intimidated by that fence." After a time, the gate opened and Claire Salinger peeped out—"a young woman with blondish hair, barefoot and without make-up . . . holding her startled baby in her arms." Havemann introduced himself, explained his mission, and then stood back as Mrs. Salinger declared, "O Lord, not another one!" She told Havemann that she "has a set piece for visitors who want to meet her husband, the gist of it being absolutely no. There was no point in making her repeat it." Havemann withdrew, mumbling his good-byes to Mrs. S., "who was looking more distressed by the moment, and the gate closed."

Havemann's next move was to track down Shirley Blaney, the girl from Windsor High School who had secured an interview with Salinger in 1953. Shirley was twenty-four and just married, but she was still a keen student of Salinger's "life-style." She advised Havemann to hang around the Windsor town center—sooner or later, Salinger would drive in to do his shopping at the local supermarket. Havemann set up a patient vigil, cruising through Windsor "time and again, morning and afternoon," watching out for the ancient Jeep or the new gray Borgward he had seen parked outside Salinger's house. Neither vehicle appeared. He then learned that on Sundays the Salinger family often took lunch at the Howard Johnson restaurant in White River Junction. Come Sunday, he staked out the joint. Once again, Salinger refused to show. At this, Havemann decided to give up:

> I had better things to do than sweat out a glimpse of a man who did not want to be glimpsed. . . . I started to drive home, through a drizzle that had replaced the morning rain, and on impulse I took a little detour and drove once again up the hillside, and past the mailbox and the impenetrable fence.
>
> The Borgward was in the clearing: the Jeep was gone. Salinger had eluded me. Perhaps everything about him had eluded me. . . . And then I saw him. His Jeep was well past the house, well down the hillside, parked at a reckless angle next to the little snow fence and garden patch. He was inside the Jeep, half hidden by the curtains, wearing a rain jacket, puffing reflectively on a pipe. . . .
>
> I had heard about that snow fence from the neighbors. He had been having trouble with woodchucks in his garden, and he had built the fence to try to discourage them. Woodchucks, however, can burrow; they are no respecters of fences; they can try a man's soul.
>
> I don't know what Salinger was thinking. Perhaps Zen thoughts. But he looked to me at that moment like any other city-bred gardener frustrated by varmints; he looked a little miserable himself, like the Fat Lady, and I only wished that I could have expressed my sympathy.[4]

Ernest Havemann's personalized, varmintlike approach was rather more manageable, from Salinger's point of view, than the kind of onslaught that was being organized in the same month by the editors of *Time*. Salinger had by now grown accustomed to coping with the odd hopeful visitor to Cornish. The *Newsweek* investigation had depressed him, and he had not spoken since to those he had identified as Elfin informants. He had changed supermarkets and stopped buying his detective yarns in Dartmouth. But he could presumably console himself that *Newsweek*'s piece had worn an air of mild defeat.

The *Time* operation was quite different, though. Under the command of Henry Anatole Grunwald (then senior editor of the *Time* book section) the magazine's team of detectives began digging into Salinger's past, locating school friends, army buddies, relatives, and friends. They began by covering the now-familiar Cornish route, and here their chief triumph was to chance upon a pair of neighbors who, when the Salingers were out of town, had actually scaled the six-and-a-half-foot fence to take a look at the inside of his house:

What they saw behind a cluster of birches was a simple, one-story New England house painted barn-red, a modest vegetable garden, and—100 yards and across a stream from his house—a little concrete cell with a skylight. The cell contains a fireplace, a long table with a typewriter, books and a filing cabinet. Here the pale man usually sits, sometimes writing quickly, other times throwing logs onto the fire for hours and making long lists of words until he finds the right one. The writer is Jerome David Salinger, and almost all his fictional characters seem more real, more plausible than he.[5]

Time's chief reporter, Jack Skow, did manage to contrive a face-to-face encounter with "the pale man," but it was brief:

I met him at the steps of the Post Office and asked him if he had a few minutes to talk. He stared at me for a second and ran down the steps and the rest of his way to his Jeep, executed a great U-turn and was out of town. He didn't say a word to me.[6]

With Havemann's experience in mind, Skow made this his first and last attempt to speak with Salinger. He checked out a few more of Salinger's by now quite fluent neighbors, and returned to the New York operations room, where reports were already pouring in from McBurney School, from Valley Forge, from Washington, D.C. (where *Time*'s man had somehow uncovered an outline of Salinger's army record and a list of the men who had served with him). There was an account too of an "interview" with Salinger's sister, Doris, who had been waylaid in Bloomingdale's (she worked there in the Town and Country women's wear department). The reporter's notes in the *Time* archive read as follows:

August 15, 1961. Doris—tall handsome woman in late forties—hair medium brown—well-groomed—she acted put-upon: "I wouldn't do anything in the world my brother didn't approve of. I don't want to be rude, but you put me in a v. difficult position. Why don't you leave us alone. *Hundreds* of people want to write stories about him." . . .[7]

There were other rebuffs of this nature—Peter de Vries told the magazine's reporter, "No, I don't want to hear your questions. If you asked me how to spell his name, I wouldn't feel free to tell you. If there are gaps in your story, they're gaps Salinger *wants* in the story."

Salinger wanted gaps in his story. For the *Time* sleuths this could mean only one thing. Salinger had Something to Hide. To judge from the narrative that can be pieced together from *Time*'s archive (a bulging folder of notes, telexes, memos, and dispatches), it was not long before a distinct line of investigation started to emerge: that the key to Salinger's reclusiveness, or furtiveness, could be fathomed by decoding his two most celebrated stories—"A Perfect Day for Bananafish" and "For Esmé—with Love and Squalor." The stories had two things in common: a hero whose nerves had been badly damaged in the war and a little girl heroine who for a moment seems to offer him salvation. "Bananafish" was thought to be the more significant of the two because it inaugurates Salinger's weird obsession with the family Glass.

"Why did Seymour kill himself?" *Time* wondered. If the story was based on Salinger's own life, then two lines of questioning had to be pursued. First, who and where was Salinger's first wife? Was she the Muriel of "Bananafish" and of "Raise High the Roof Beam, Carpenters"? Second, who and where was Sybil, the little girl Seymour/ Salinger befriends on the beach in Florida? *Time* operatives were dispatched across the land with orders to locate the real-life counterparts of Muriel and Sybil.

In the *Time* archive, there is a telex from the magazine's West Coast correspondent that reads: WE HAVE FOUND A LEAD THAT MAY FINALLY OPEN MR. SALINGER'S CLOSET OF LITTLE GIRLS, and this does rather crisply encapsulate the spirit of the magazine's inquiry. The "lead" in question here (based on a tip-off by Richard Gehman, Salinger's old *Cosmopolitan* adversary) had to do with the identity of "Sybil." It appeared that in 1950 or thereabouts Salinger had proposed marriage to a schoolgirl. The girl's parents had opposed the match, but the friendship had lasted some two years. *Time* tracked down the girl's father, who testified that some ten years earlier (i.e., in 1950 or thereabouts) he and his family had met Salinger at a hotel in Daytona Beach, Florida. "He was an odd fellow. He didn't mingle much with the other guests. He fastened on to my daughter, J—— and spent a lot of time with her. He was—well, is he Jewish? I thought that might explain the way he acted. Oh, I mean I thought he might have a chip on his shoulder. The fact that he didn't mingle much, I mean." As to his daughter: "Maybe she was crazy about him. I just don't know."[8]

This somewhat threadbare confidence produced an eager memo from the *Time* reporter: "This establishes that J (the girl) met JDS in Florida. Check pub. dates of Esmé and Bananafish to determine whether J, at 16 or 17, could have been the wellspring for either of these fictional girls. Secondly we should redouble efforts to find a divorce record in vicinity of Daytona." The theory here seems to have been that J. might have precipitated Salinger's divorce, as Sybil had precipitated the suicide of Seymour Glass.

Disappointment was in store—a check on the publication dates of

Salinger's two stories would shortly reveal that both "fictional girls" predated the J. encounter by some years—but it did not come soon enough to prevent *Time*'s confronting J. herself, now married, and not in the least anxious to be interrogated on the matter of her bygone relationship with Salinger. Reporter Bill Smith filed his account as follows:

J. tried to be aloof. . . . Didn't remember where she had met Salinger or what he was like. Well, did she deny that, as a child, she had known him in Florida? She puffed on her cigarette a moment, as if debating over which plea to enter: "Yes," she said carefully, "I think I do deny it."

Smith commented: "In view of room-mate's testimony in (Art) Seiden-baum's file—which describes the meeting with Salinger as a young girl, the difficulties with her parents over Salinger, the probability that she visited him at least once in Cornish etc—there is only one reasonable conclusion: that she is lying, presumably to protect Salinger."[9] Here again, the dates refused to fit: By the time Salinger moved to Cornish the girl J. (born 1934) was in her eighteenth year. The quest for Sybil was called off.

Not all of *Time*'s researches were as sleazily fanciful as this, but disturbing reports of what the magazine was up to had been leaking back to Salinger in Cornish, and he was taking steps to block any further leads. *Time*, he seems to have known, would shortly encounter its star witness:

We ran him to ground in Venice West—digesting a recently consumed ½ gallon of white wine. Age 30, lank blond hair, mouthful of bad teeth, hypnotically steady blue-green eyes. In the few moments of clarity that hit him as we dragged through three bars and a restaurant he confessed that he was Claire Salinger's brother, Gavin Douglas.[10]

At this first encounter, Douglas was too drunk to make a lot of sense; he kept mumbling about having just received a telegram from the

Salingers saying that his "remittance" from Claire's stepfather had been increased and adding that "he should not tell anyone anything." *Time*'s second interview was more coherent; this time, they had bailed Douglas out of the drunk tank of the local jail, and he evidently thought he should repay them. He didn't feel too bad about talking, he declared, because "after all, Jerry invaded my privacy. People who know I'm related to Jerry are always asking me if I'm Holden Caulfield, or Seymour, or someone. Well, I'm not." Strange logic, but it came as music to the ears of *Time:* Here at last was an insider who actually *wanted* to tell all. Over the next few days Douglas gave *Time* a series of interviews, providing "background" on Salinger's marriage, his life in Cornish, his writing plans. It was Douglas's testimony that provided the basis of the article which eventually appeared as the magazine's cover story on September 15, 1961.

This was the week of publication for Salinger's *Franny and Zooey*, but there was no celebrating in Cornish. The *Time* investigation, we are told, is what Salinger had in mind when he wrote to us of his "unspeakably bitter experience." And it could hardly have come at a worse time: On August 18, Judge Learned Hand had died of heart failure at New York's St. Luke's Hospital. He was eighty-nine: "We who knew him will miss him and so will the millions of Americans to whom his concept of justice was an invisible force for good in their daily lives." So said the mayor of New York on the day Hand died; and as Roger Machell commented to the *Time* reporter he was meeting secretly in London, "Not even J. D. Salinger could resist that fantastic man. Jerry will miss him now he's dead."

Franny and Zooey, to no one's surprise, was an immediate best seller, with some bookstores reporting early-morning lines on publication. On Salinger's instructions, Little, Brown had made strenuous efforts to prevent prepublication sales and special discount offers; it had issued advertisements that simply stated the book's author and title; and it had refused overtures from all book clubs. Even so, within two weeks the book had sold 125,000 copies; it rose swiftly to the head of the Sunday *Times* list and stayed there for six months. As an artifact, it was triumphantly austere: black lettering on white with a green spine, and a typeface borrowed from the first edition of one of Holden Caulfield's best-liked books, Isak Dinesen's *Out of Africa*. On the jacket flap Salinger provided a throwaway self-interview (throwaway in every sense, since the words are not repeated in the body of the actual book):

The author writes: FRANNY came out in *The New Yorker* in 1955, and was swiftly followed, in 1957, by ZOOEY. Both stories are early, critical entries in a narrative series I'm doing about a family of settlers in twentieth-century New York, the Glasses. It is a long-term project, patently an ambitious one, and there is a real-enough danger, I suppose, that sooner or later I'll bog down, perhaps disappear entirely, in my own methods, locutions, and mannerisms. On the whole, though, I'm very hopeful. I love working on these Glass stories, I've been waiting for them most of my life, and I think I have fairly decent, monomaniacal plans to finish them with due care and all-available skill.

A couple of stories in the series besides FRANNY and ZOOEY have already been published in *The New Yorker*, and some new material is scheduled to appear there soon or Soon. I have a great deal of thoroughly unscheduled material on paper, too, but I expect to be fussing with it, to use a popular trade term, for some time to come. ("Polishing" is another dandy word that comes to mind.) I work like greased lightning, myself, but my alter-ego and collaborator, Buddy Glass, is insufferably slow.

It is my rather subversive opinion that a writer's feelings of anonymity-obscurity are the second-most valuable property on loan to him during his working years. My wife has asked me to add, however, in a single explosion of candor, that I live in Westport with my dog.

If *Time*'s editors had been experiencing any qualms about their invasion of Salinger's "anonymity-obscurity," they would have felt a lot better after reading this. What they called the "coy fraudulence" of Salinger's jacket blurb ("I live in Westport with my dog") could surely be interpreted as a teasing kind of challenge, a "Catch me if you can." And was there not a taunt to be detected in his naming of Buddy Glass as his "collaborator"? *Time* thundered in reply that "the dark facts are that he has not lived in Westport or had a dog for years."

Even here, though, there was scope for doubt. When Ernest Have-mann's piece appeared in *Life* some weeks later, it was illustrated with a few born-of-desperation photographs, the best Havemann could mus-ter: the Salinger mailbox, the Salinger driveway with two cars; a college yearbook picture of Claire Douglas. Across half a page there was spread a portrait that *Life* evidently thought of as a scoop: Most of this por-trait—about four fifths—was solid fence; at the bottom of the fence, through the perhaps six-inch gap that separated fence from ground, the reader was instructed to detect "the *family dog* taking an unSalingerlike peek at passers-by." "Peek" seems about as accurate as "passers-by." The dog, a sort of wolfhound, is crouched in what can (or should) only be described as the pounce and destroy position.

Nineteen Sixty-one had been a harrowing year for Salinger, but he could take some satisfaction from the way it ended: with America's two wealthiest and most resourceful newsmagazines unable to agree on the matter of whether or not he owned a dog.

2
─

A harrowing year, this year of ordeal by journalism. Harrowing for Salinger and harrowing to write about for us. There was a certain hypocrisy, we knew, in our snooty attitude to news gatherers like Elfin, Havemann, Seidenbaum, and Skow. We weren't like them, because we didn't do what they did. We weren't like them because we had our precious ground rules, our taboos, and because our background and our ultimate intent were literary critical, not journalistic. We didn't speak about closetsful of little girls, nor attempt crude life-art linkups of the "search for Sibyl" type. Even my companion shrank from being brack-eted with *Time* and *Newsweek* and, you might have noticed, has made little or no effort to roughen the easy superiority of tone that comes naturally to me when I write about the methods of magazines like these.

But why don't we confess that in more than a few areas of our "research," we have had our dirty work done for us by these unfastidious professional "reporters"? The *Time* cover story has for more than a quarter of a century been a major source for all students of Salinger: There is no neat dividing line to be drawn here between the news desk and the college library. Indeed, it could be said that Henry Grunwald was making just this point when he edited, in 1962, a book called *Salinger: A Critical and Personal Portrait.* [11] In this he prints a selection of academic and highbrow literary essays (some taken from journals such as the *Western Humanities Review* and *American Speech*) alongside an expanded version of his own *Time* magazine investigation.

When we visited Grunwald in 1983 in the mogul splendor of his thirty-fourth-floor office in New York, he was by then known to the world as the mighty editor-in-chief of the entire Time-Life magazine empire. But he was better known to us as the editor of *Salinger: A Portrait.* It was an odd meeting, and perhaps specially so for him. He stared at the cover of his own book (which we had brought along) for what must have been a full two minutes, as if he were trying to remember what this old enthusiasm of his had been all about. The book was now twenty years old and was, he told us, his only hardcover publication. He then buzzed for a secretary and issued orders for us to be admitted to the *Time* archive, a rare privilege indeed for an outsider—or so the secretary pointed out to us as she reluctantly released the no-longer-confidential files. My companion fell on these with some avidity, and has had few scruples about transmuting their contents into "pure" research. As he has explained to me, it was our mission to imagine what this *Time* onslaught of 1961 must have been like for Salinger. And "harrowing," it seems, was the word we finally decided on (although "unspeakably bitter" were two other dandy words that came to mind). And there was worse to come, although the next attack was from a regiment in which we like to think we're more at home.

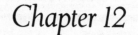

Chapter 12

1

J D. Salinger was now a popular success, but it was more than eight years since he had had to face any sort of public interrogation by the arbiters of highbrow literary taste. Students adored him, the lower reaches of academia had built a thriving industry around the two books he had published, and the book columnists were all too happy to collaborate in the perpetuation of his "legend." But there was a higher, harsher court, and Salinger was soon in its eyes to be found guilty of contempt. In "Seymour: An Introduction," he had given *his* disdainful view of the current intellectual aristocracy, calling it a "peerage of tin ears." With the publication of *Franny and Zooey* in book form, that aristocracy now had the opportunity to make reply.

In 1959, Norman Mailer had provided a foretaste of what lay in store. He described Salinger as "everyone's favorite" and went on to demur:

I seem to be alone in finding him no more than the greatest mind ever to stay in prep school . . . of course this opinion may come from nothing more graceful than envy. Salinger has had the wisdom to choose subjects which are comfortable, and I most certainly have not; but since the world is now in a state of acute discomfort, I do not know that his wisdom is honorable.[1]

In the same year, George Steiner took a similar line: He denounced the "Salinger industry" as largely of Salinger's own making:

The young like to read about the young. Salinger writes *briefly*. . . . He demands of his readers nothing in the way of literacy or political interest. . . . Salinger flatters the very ignorance and moral shallowness of his young readers. He suggests to them that formal ignorance, political apathy and a vague tristesse are positive virtues. This is where his cunning and somewhat shoddy use of Zen comes in. Zen is in fashion. People who lack even the rudiments of knowledge needed to read Dante, or the nerve required by Schopenhauer, snatch up the latest paperback on Zen.[2]

In both Mailer's and Steiner's pronouncements a distaste for Salinger's audience shades all too readily into a distaste for Salinger himself. Commercial success was suspect, but how much more darkly suspect when the readership was underage? Salinger, it was implied, had cold-bloodedly set out to manipulate the shallow susceptibilities of his youthful audience, had exploited their known fads and tastes, encouraged their apathies, endorsed their disaffection, and so on. And, presumably, he had done all this in order to be rich and famous, to be loved.

This proved to be a common theme as the reviews of *Franny and Zooey* began to trickle in. In the week of publication the two most significant notices came from John Updike in the *New York Times* and from Alfred Kazin in the *Atlantic Monthly*. Both these reviewers gave the impression of *wanting* to be generous, and Updike, particularly, made it clear that he was writing more in sorrow than in anger.

As Hemingway sought the words for things in motion, Salinger seeks the words for things transmuted into human subjectivity. His fiction, its rather grim bravado, its humor, its morbidity, its wry but persistent hopefulness, matches the shape and tint of present American life.

But even he could not suppress his misgivings on the matter of Salinger's Glass family:

Seymour defines sentimentality as giving "to a thing more tenderness than God gives to it." This seems to me the nub of the trouble. Salinger loves the Glasses more than God loves them. He loves them too exclusively. Their invention has become a hermitage for him. He loves them to the detriment of artistic moderation.[3]

And this seems just and decent—proof that it was possible to talk about Salinger's shortcomings without reference to his popular success. But Updike was alone—at any rate among the heavyweight literary critics who (it must have seemed to Salinger) were lining up to give their views. Alfred Kazin's piece, although level and humane in its approach, could not shake off an obsession with the "audience"—"that enormous public of sophisticated people which radiates from *The New Yorker* to every English department in the land." Kazin conceded Salinger's considerable gifts, but accused him of an excessive "cuteness," a "self-conscious charm and prankishness," and of encouraging a cozy, self-regarding pose of alienation in his bored and affluent young readers:

Salinger's vast public, I am convinced, is based not merely on the vast number of young people who recognize their emotional problems in his fiction and their frustrated rebellions in the sophisticated language he manipulates so skillfully. It is based even more on the vast numbers who have been released by our society to think of themselves as endlessly sensitive, spiritually alone, gifted, and whose suffering lies in the narrowing of their consciousness to themselves, in the withdrawal of their curiosity from a society which they think they understand all too well, in the drying up of their hope, their trust and their wonder in the great world itself.[4]

This is what Salinger—and Holden Caulfield—would think of as podium sonority, but it carried no ill will. There is a residual fondness for the early work, and a readiness to accept that Salinger might not be totally to blame for his success. Not so with the strictures of Joan Didion. In the *National Review*, Didion denounced *Franny and Zooey* as "finally spurious":

However brilliantly rendered (and it is), however hauntingly right in the rhythm of its dialogue (and it is), *Franny and Zooey* is finally spurious, and what makes it spurious is Salinger's tendency to flatter the essential triviality within each of his readers, his predilection for giving instructions for living. What gives the book its extremely potent appeal is precisely that it is self-help copy: it emerges finally as *Positive Thinking* for the upper middle classes, as *Double Your Energy and Think Without Fatigue* for Sarah Lawrence girls.[5]

And Leslie Fiedler in *Partisan Review* agreed, throwing in a few well-turned extras of his own:

Salinger of course speaks for the cleanest, politest, best-dressed, best-fed and best-read among the disaffected (and who is not disaffected?) young: not junkies and faggots, not even upper-Bohemians, his protagonists travel a road bounded on one end by school and on the other by home. They have families and teachers rather than lovers or friends, and their crises are likely to be defined in terms of whether or not to go back for the second semester to Vassar or Princeton, to Dana Hall or St. Marks. Their *angst* is improbably cued by such questions as: "Does my date for the Harvard weekend *really* understand what poetry is?" or "Is it possible that my English instructor hates literature after all?"[6]

Most vitriolic of all, though—and reportedly the review that Salinger himself was most angered by—came from Mary McCarthy. It appeared first in the London *Observer* in a full-page spread to coincide with the British publication (by Heinemann) of *Franny and Zooey,* and then reprinted in *Harper's* under the heading "J. D. Salinger's Closed Circuit—A suggestion that the literary hero of the younger set—the Great Phoney-slayer—may, just possibly, be a bit of a phoney himself":

And who are these wonder kids but Salinger himself, splitting and multiplying like the original amoeba . . . to be confronted with the seven faces of Salinger, all wise and lovable and simple, is to gaze into a terrifying narcissus pool. Salinger's world contains nothing but Salinger. . . .

Why did Seymour Glass kill himself? asks McCarthy. After all, is he not the presiding genius of all this "self-loving barbershop harmony"?; he is always so "happy," so worshipful of his wife's "simplicity, her terrible honesty"; he takes pleasure in the performance of his own astounding gifts. How *could* he commit suicide? Was it because all along "he had been lying, his author had been lying, and it was all terrible, and he was a fake?"[7]

"Fake," "spurious," "narcissistic," "cute"—the hurtful adjectives were piling up, and it was not to be expected that they would be disowned when Salinger, in 1963, followed *Franny and Zooey* with his two other long Glass stories, "Raise High the Roof Beam, Carpenters" and "Seymour: An Introduction," brought together in a single volume. The response to *Franny and Zooey* might not have been so snappishly vindictive if the reviewers had not already, in 1959, felt the lash of Seymour's scorn in *The New Yorker*. Now that he too was issued in book form, the Salinger verdict could be consolidated, set in marble, made to last. Almost unanimously it was agreed that "Raise High the Roof Beam" represented Salinger's farewell to the real world and that he was now set on a path "so infernally clever, so precious and inwrought that it gives you the sense of being toyed with."

The *Seymour* book (if we may call it that) carried a message from the author. When writing this message, Salinger would have been digesting the reviews of *Franny and Zooey*, or failing to digest them. He dedicates this new book to the very audience his assailants had so busily maligned; to an audience, that is to say, untainted by any kind of literary professionalism:

If there is an amateur reader still left in the world—or anybody who just reads and runs—I ask him or her, with untellable affection and gratitude, to split the dedication of this book four ways with my wife and children.

(Salinger's son, Matthew, had been born in 1960.) Once again, there is some throwaway self-revelation on the dust jacket. Salinger had published these two Glass stories in a single volume because, he says, he wanted them

to avoid unduly or undesirably close contact with new material in the series. There is only my word for it, granted, but I have several new Glass stories coming along—waxing, dilating—each in its own way, but I suspect the less said about them, in mixed company, the better.

Oddly, the joys and satisfactions of working on the Glass family peculiarly increase and deepen for me with the years. I can't say why, though. Not, at least, outside the casino proper of my fiction.

There is a touching defiance in all this, and we should keep in mind that this jacket blurb will turn out to be Salinger's last direct address to his readership. Two years earlier, he had spoken of the risk of getting bogged down, of maybe disappearing entirely "in my own methods, locutions, and mannerisms." He knew now that in the literary world's judgment he had failed to skirt or overcome these hazards and that in any case his "locutions and mannerisms" had been largely treated with derision. He also knew that his precious Glass family was widely viewed as a blind alley from which he ought to extricate himself but fast. And yet here he was, impenitent to the extent of promising "several new Glass stories," of vowing—in effect—to burrow deeper and deeper into a fictional world which, whatever anybody else might think, was for him a world of "joys and satisfactions."

2

Salinger appeared in print for the last time in *The New Yorker* of June 19, 1965, with a long story called "Hapworth 16, 1924." The story is in letter form: the seven-year-old Seymour Glass writing home from summer camp. More than twenty years earlier Holden Caulfield had written a letter datelined CAMP GOODCREST FOR SLOBS and reported to his family: "This place stinks. I never saw so many rats." Seymour's view of Hapworth Camp is less forthright than Holden's, and his manner less endearing:

The majority of young campers here, you will be glad to know, could not possibly be nicer or more heart-rending from day to day, particularly when they are not thriving with suspicious bliss in cliques that insure popularity and dubious prestige.

Seymour's forty-year-old letter has been only lately chanced upon by Buddy Glass, who "for a good many years of my life—very possibly all forty-six" has felt himself "installed, elaborately wired, and, occasionally plugged in, for the purposes of shedding some light on the short, reticulated life and times of my late, eldest brother, Seymour Glass, who died, committed suicide, opted to discontinue living, back in 1948, when he was thirty-one." Buddy intends here to type up an exact copy of Seymour's letter, "word for word, comma for comma. Beginning here: May 28, 1965."

And so he does—all twenty thousand words of it. It is addressed to Seymour's parents, Les and Bessie, and to Boo Boo, Walter, and Waker. Buddy himself—"that magnificent, elusive, comical lad (aged five)"—is with Seymour at the summer camp. Seymour, needless to say, is revealed as a child of staggering precocity and self-assurance. He has lately been studying a book on sentence formation, and his letter, he warns, will be a kind of exercise in fine writing. He asks his parents to watch out for "any slang or merely sloppy errors in fundamental construction, grammar, punctuation or excellent taste."

"Hapworth" adds up to a weird, exasperating tour de force. Much of its charm—if it is meant to have charm—should derive from Seymour's literary trapeze act: the seven-year-old boy masquerading as an all-knowing man of letters. Pretentious fluency repeatedly (and—is it hoped?—endearingly) stumbles into tautology, misplaced epithets, and comic faults of tone. Seymour has key words that he has just learned and cannot help repeating—"charming," "touching," "magnificent," "heart-rending," "humorous"—and which therefore keep on forming not quite appropriate attachments. "This is often a stimulating and touching place"; "past a certain touching point . . ."; "Here and elsewhere on this touching planet . . ."; "He is excellent, touching, intelligent company."

Now and then Seymour falters into slang: "You would make me a lot happier, quite frankly spoken, if you didn't press that kind of painful and erroneous crap on me over the phone again," but he mostly aims for altitude. His apostrophes have a jarring first-night ring to them: "Jesus, you are a talented, quite magnificent couple," "O God, the human body is so touching!" and there are other actorlike formulations that Seymour, actor's son and expert tap dancer, seems unable to avoid: "It quite takes my personal breath away"; "I regret with my entire body to say . . ." Are we meant to chuckle indulgently at these displays of summer camp? It is impossible to say.

"Hapworth 16, 1924" provides some new Seymour revelations, but not as many as we have the right to expect in a first-person document of such forbidding length. We learn, for example, that Seymour is ugly or thinks he is: "a foul nose and a chin as weak as water"; that he possesses psychic powers—he can stop himself feeling pain, and he can look into the future; that this is his third appearance on earth and that he will be quitting in his thirties; that women excite him and that he is troubled, he thinks, by "unlimited sensuality"—Mrs. Happy, the pregnant wife of the camp counselor, has "unwittingly aroused" him. He reports, "Considering my absurd age, the situation has its humorous side, but merely in simple retrospect, I regret to say."

This situation with Mrs. Happy does indeed have its humorous side, and there is a brief, hopeful moment when it seems as if Salinger will take advantage of it. But no, there are more solemn matters to attend to, such as Seymour's reading list. This takes up several pages of the story and it is the familiar Salinger curriculum: Vivekananda, Tolstoy, Flaubert, Blake, Jane Austen, etc. And there are asides to be worked in about the corrupt practices of certain academics.

"O my God! I am relishing this leisurely communication," Seymour

more than once exclaims, and leisurely it is. In the manner of "Seymour: An Introduction," there is much wandering off into lengthy
digression and parenthesis, and the letter form of the story means that
this time there is no requirement to offer apologies to the short-tem-
pered reader. In "Hapworth" the reader is blithely disregarded: "Take
it or leave it" is Salinger's unmistakable retort to any grumbles from
the nonamateurs among his audience and he seems fairly certain (indeed *makes* certain) that most of them will leave it. The boy Seymour
really is writing to his family. The Glass family has, in this last story,
become both Salinger's subject and his readership, his creatures and his
companions. His life is finally made one with art.

In a prophetic moment, Seymour looks forward to the present day—
that is to say, May 28, 1965—and gives us what he calls a "stunning
glimpse" of Buddy Glass, gray-haired, smoking a cigarette, looking
thoughtful and exhausted. Buddy Glass, we know, is J. D. Salinger,
himself now aged forty-six. "You would think," Seymour says, "this
particular glimpse would pierce the casual witness's heart to the quick,
disabling him utterly." But it shouldn't, because Buddy-Salinger is
exactly where he wants to be: in a room with a skylight, surrounded
by books, pencils, writing paper, and typewriter:

It is all his youthful dreams realized to the full! . . . Oh my God! He will be
overjoyed when he sees that room, mark my words! It is one of the most
smiling, comforting, glimpses of my entire life, and quite possibly with the least
strings attached. I would far from object if that were possibly the last glimpse
of my life.[8]

And for us, this *was*—we thought—our own "last glimpse" of Salinger, the writer and the man. We had tracked him to the disappearing
point, it seemed: in life, in art, in life as art. His "writing life," so far
as we had any authorization to speak of it in public, was complete: J.
D. Salinger, 1919–65. We would add an appendix or an epilogue to bring
the bare facts up to date, but we would do this in a neutral, so-we-
understand narrator's voice, and leave it there.

Before signing off, I looked back to my original synopsis for the book. It spoke seductively of the adventures my invented biographer figure was in line for, and it ended, I noticed, with the hope that Salinger (whom I'd portrayed in my outline as somewhat more playful in his reclusiveness than we knew him now to be) would, under pressure from our mischievous "research," be lured into the open. To round the book off, there might even be some sort of amusing confrontation, a final scene in which *he* would try to outsmart *us*. Some hope.

Chapter 13

1

S ince 1965, Salinger has been silent. In 1970 he repaid (with interest) a $75,000 advance he had accepted from Little, Brown after the publication of *Franny and Zooey*, and since then he has privately made it clear that he will countenance no further publication of his work. He has continued writing. I am assured by one who knows (but prefers not to be named) that he has at least two full-length manuscripts locked in his safe.

He still lives in Cornish, although he was divorced from Claire in 1967. There have been occasional sightings of him in the press: making a speech at a retirement dinner in New York for his ex-army colleague John Keenan, escorting a TV actress to an opening, attending the first night of a Broadway play in which his son, Matthew, had a leading role.

There have been Salinger spoofs: In 1977, *Esquire* published a story called "For Rupert—with No Promises" and there were rumors that Salinger had written it (the piece was actually composed by the magazine's fiction editor, Gordon Lish), and in 1982 a full-page advertisement in the *New York Times* carried a cute message from one Buddy Glass—a plug for a forthcoming book called *Benedictus*—and lawyers wrote to the paper denying any Salinger connection. Also in 1982 a

young journalist tried to sell a fake Salinger interview to *People* magazine. Salinger sued him for "impersonation": The case was settled out
of court. And in this same year W. P. Kinsella published a novel,
Shoeless Joe, in which a character called "J. D. Salinger" is kidnaped and
taken to a baseball game by the book's fixated hero; in the course of the
narrative, "Salinger" speaks freely of his life and work.

Over the years there have been several "scoop" articles on The
Recluse—in *Newsweek*, *People*, and even in the *Paris Review*. They have
each followed the same formula: a note left for Salinger at his local post
office; a brief encounter which, with luck, elicits about five sentences
of copy; and a sneak photograph of Salinger striding off toward his
Jeep. None of these stories has added anything substantial to the record,
but each has helped to serve the myth.

2

This, then, was where, chronologically, my book came to an end, my
J. D. Salinger: A Writing Life—a book somewhat different from the one
you're reading now. The manuscript of that earlier book was delivered
to Random House in July 1985. After a couple of weeks, news came that
it had been accepted for publication. A further sum of money was
released, and I was advised that the Random House lawyers would need
to "clear" my text before it could be sent to press.

A few more weeks later, a legal questionnaire arrived: a routine set
of queries to do with possible libels. Was Captain Horace Aitken alive
or dead? If dead, no problem. If alive, might it be possible to change
his name? I was also asked about the book's several quotations from
Salinger's letters. I had quoted from these fairly extensively, anxious as
I was to communicate my subject's tone. The lawyers wanted to know
how much I'd quoted, what proportion of the whole? I did a count and,
where I could, I worked out what percentage of each letter had been
used. Sometimes I could not do this because I did not have the original,
or a copy of it, but it was usually possible, from memory, to make a

decent guess. In the end it was assumed, I think, that "fair use" would apply to unpublished as well as published writings. The book was passed for press.

In the fullness of time, proofs arrived, then page proofs, and, in the spring of 1986, bound galleys. Publication was scheduled for the autumn, and it was proposed that the bound sheets, marked ". . . please do not quote for publication, . . ." should be sent out to possible reviewers. A proof of the jacket was prepared and a photograph was taken of me up against a wall. And the same kind of thing was happening in England. The lawyers for Heinemann in London had checked out the manuscript and passed it for publication—or at any rate they had not raised any strenuous objections. One formed the impression that they would quite like to see what happened in the States before taking the plunge themselves. Even so, the book was set in type, a jacket was designed, and, after a bit, an English set of bound galleys was in modest circulation. *The Observer* had bought British serial rights and discussions were begun about which extracts, if any, they might use.

So far, so good. I can't say that I was actually looking forward to publication of the book. It was not, in those days, really the book I had wanted it to be. It was too nervous and respectful, and in many ways disabled by my anxiety to assure Salinger that I was not a rogue. But it was workmanlike, it had far more facts about the man than you could find anywhere else, it had (thanks to the letters) something of his tone of voice, his presence. And in its literary-critical aspects, it did, I thought, have some useful things to say about the relationship between the author's life and work. It was *all right*. All the same, I could predict that if it was to be pushed as a biography, there might be some disappointed buyers. Hence my subtitle: "A Writing Life." Whatever its merits, the book had by no means solved the mystery of Salinger. It had rendered, with supporting evidence, a semispeculative portrait: In order to get much out of that portrait you would need to have read, or be prepared to read, Salinger's collected (and uncollected) works with some attention. The original concept, of a quest-type literary adventure yarn, had in the end been lost, it seemed to me. The biographer, far from being a character in his own tale, had become in this version routinely anonymous, an offstage murmurer, a critic.

But still, if the hype could be contained, and if no misleading or inflated claims were made, the book might well enjoy a quiet, if not thoroughly reclusive, life in campus bookstores. To people who asked me about it at this stage, I'd tend to say, "It isn't much. Don't get the idea that it's a *biography*, because it isn't. But it's not too bad." The one or two prepublication notices I saw during the early summer of 1986 (in *Kirkus* and *Publishers Weekly*, for example) suggested that this, or something rather like this, would be how most critics would eventually react. Well, so what? At least Salinger couldn't complain that he had been reglamorized. Indeed, I think I still believed that he might rather like my book. He more than anyone would know what I'd left out. He would know which leads I'd elected not to chase after. He would understand the book's essential sympathies and warm to them.

On May 25, 1986, a letter arrived at the offices of Random House from the Manhattan law firm Kay Collyer and Boose. The same letter, give or take a few formalities, was also delivered to my home in London and to the offices of Heinemann and *The Observer*. It stated that J. D. Salinger had read bound galleys of my "biography," that he was displeased by my use of his unpublished letters, and that unless these quotations were removed forthwith, he would take all necessary legal steps to have the book enjoined.

At first I was not too worried. It was a disappointment that Salinger didn't like what I had done, but then I had no doubt been a trifle foolish to imagine that he would. As to the legal angle: Well, we were presumably standing on safe ground. After all, had not the Random House lawyers declared my quotations to be fair use? It had never really occurred to me to wonder if they might be wrong. I telephoned them from London, expecting to be reassured that Salinger's mouthpiece was merely trying it on and that he didn't stand a chance. Thus calmed, I could go back to wondering what Salinger had thought of those rather extensive sections of the book that *didn't* use his letters. I now knew for certain that he'd *seen* the book. It was an eerie thought, but also a relief. Surely, apart from this letters business, he must be relieved also . . .

The voice at the other end of the line, although controlled and cordial, somehow lacked the airy depth that I'd expected. I wouldn't say it sounded anxious; at the same time, though, it wasn't picking up on my offhand opening remarks. There was a chance, it seemed to be saying, that we might have a problem. Yes, it was quite true that they, the lawyers, had judged my quotations to fall within the limits of fair use. In the light of Salinger's intervention, however, it might be politic to examine the fair use definition just a bit more closely. Also, it might turn out to be a matter for concern that the word counts I had done were not precisely accurate. I had often failed to include in my counts odd words and phrases from Salinger's letters that I had deployed as links *between* actual quotations. By the end of this exchange, I had begun to sense a slight frosting of the atmosphere. Trouble was perhaps at hand, and someone would have to take the blame. I already knew enough about organization men to suspect that the someone would be me.

Soon after, I was summoned urgently to New York—so urgently that my arrival coincided with the beginning of a public holiday. When I eventually made contact with my summoners, it was put to me that I should reduce the amount of direct quotation in the book so as to make it more acceptable to the other side. I spent a week hacking and juggling so that no more than ten words remained from any single letter. The excised quotations I rewrote as reported speech, taking care not to use Salinger's own expression. Some of this labor seemed to me ludicrous, but after a bit I began to take a certain abstract pride in making my reports fit, exactly, the space taken by the original Salinger quotation. Even so, it was unpleasant work and I disliked having to throw out most of Salinger's best lines. In almost every instance, I was deadening his language; I was making him seem duller than he was. Whose interests did this serve? Salinger's earliest letters are all style, all show. There was never a great deal of factual content. The "fact" I wanted to communicate was that he wrote letters in the way he did. But—in law—is that a fact? Certainly, in my version, the original's distinctive sparkle couldn't be preserved. Something like it was really not like it at all.

This was not, by now, the sort of grumble to be raised at Random House. For a start, there was no one I could raise it with. The editorial department had fallen silent, and the law department had a job to do. No wonder Max Perkins is remembered as a saint. In the offices of American publishers these days an author can measure his current rating, and perhaps his future prospects, as soon as he steps out of the elevator and presents himself at the front desk. If your stock is high, you will immediately be recognized, your name will have been remembered. More likely than not, you will be kept waiting no more than a few minutes before you are ushered into the almost-genial presence of your Editor. As you move through the corridors, between the desks, you will perhaps be greeted with a wave, a nod, an upbeat "Hi, there" from the Team, of which you might now feel yourself to be an honored, if honorary, member. I have had one or two such golden moments and I treasure them. If things are going less then well, however, if, alack, there is any sort of Problem with your Project, then you will soon enough be made to know it. The receptionist will have forgotten who you are, and will ask you to spell your name a couple of times before she eventually phones it through. The Team will be polite enough, but strained. Your Editor will be, shall we say, preoccupied. You will be given the feeling that you (just like your manuscript) have suddenly become provisional, sub judice.

I exaggerate, of course. In a truly harsh world my publisher could, I am aware, have easily backed off: It could have withdrawn the book, apologized to Mr. Salinger, and sent me off to be remaindered, pulped. The news from Britain indicated that the intrepid *Observer* had already canceled its serialization plans and was demanding reimbursement of all moneys paid. I could hardly expect Random House to thank me for having raised some interesting points of law, for sharpening up its thinking on the matter of fair use. Random House was, after all, prepared to back me in the courts. And was not my invisible editor's assistant, the splendid Sarah Timberman, working all hours to help me save what could be saved of my imperiled text? And would I actually recognize the receptionist if I was to bump into him/her in the lobby? Was I becoming like Salinger—phobic about publishers? Certainly I was getting more than a bit touchy on all fronts. After all, look what had come to pass. J. D. Salinger, my admired quarry, had finally been forced to speak, and his first words had been: "It's you I hate. You are a snooper and a thief."

And it was no good looking to my old companion-biographer for reassurance or consolation. He regarded Salinger's letters as a coup, and was in no mood to equivocate. His job was done. After all, he would have said if he'd been asked, here is a public figure who takes pleasure in withholding even the most elementary facts about himself, however timidly he is approached. And here are these libraries that are, in the end, no more than giant, well-heeled information stores. What we couldn't get out of Salinger, we had got from them. And the fair use angle made it good and legal.

He would also have been confident that Salinger would not press his lawsuit. Sooner or later, if Salinger did persevere, he would be obliged to make a personal appearance—in either a courtroom or in the offices of the Random House attorneys. He would be required, at the very least, to give a deposition. That is to say, an interview. And as we knew all too well, this man didn't give interviews. Relax.

3

By September, the rewriting had been done. There were now only about two hundred of Salinger's words left in the manuscript. The revised text was set in type and a second set of galleys was produced. A copy of the new book was dispatched to Salinger's lawyers on September 18. The confident prediction was that they would appreciate our efforts and allow the project to go forward without further challenge.

This confidence seemed to be well founded. Although we might have begun to have our fleeting doubts, there surely was in U.S. law a concept of fair use. Indeed, as I now learned, the rule is codified as follows:

In determining whether the use made of a work in any particular case is a fair use the factors to be considered shall include:

1. The purpose and character of the use, including whether such use is of a commercial nature or is for nonprofit educational purposes;
2. the nature of the copyrighted work;
3. the amount and substantiality of the portion used in relation to the copyrighted work as a whole; and
4. the effect of the use upon the potential market for or value of the copyrighted work.

On 1 we would plead that *J. D. Salinger: A Writing Life* was a sober, responsible work of scholarship, that even though we could not (or could we?) describe its purpose as "nonprofit," we could certainly claim it to be educational. On 3 we would simply say that from more than thirty thousand words we had quoted a mere two hundred. And on 4 we would contend that Salinger would never put these letters up for sale, nor publish them himself. In other words, there was no "potential market . . . value."

It was with 2 that we envisaged the chief difficulty. After all, these letters were unpublished. Nearly all of the available precedents were concerned with material that had already been in print. Random House was heartened, though, by its memory of a 1966 ruling in which it had been able to repel efforts by the Hemingway estate to squash an unauthorized biography. The issue there had turned on some hitherto unpublished correspondence. And it was also deemed helpful that Salinger was a notorious recluse. Random House had done battle in the past with Howard Hughes, and in that case it had been pleaded that "Hughes has almost an obsession as to his privacy and his right thereto. However, when one enters the public arena to the extent he has, the right of privacy must be tempered by a countervailing privilege that the public have some information concerning important public figures." "Unpublished," in Salinger's case, almost certainly meant "never to be published."

And it was in this respect that the Salinger case (as it was now beginning to be called) differed most strikingly from the case that his lawyers were citing as "their" precedent: the case of Harper & Row versus *The Nation* magazine. In this dispute, the text in question was some three hundred words from an autobiography by Gerald Ford. Harper & Row was the publisher and it had sold serial rights of the book to *Time*. Before *Time* was ready to publish its extracts, *The Nation* jumped in with a substantial quotation from Ford's most (perhaps only) newsworthy chapter, the one in which he reveals his feelings about the pardoning of Nixon. *Time* canceled its serialization contract and Harper & Row sued *The Nation*, eventually securing a Supreme Court judgment in its favor. On the face of it, this judgment had scant bearing on the detail of our problem: It was a dispute about commerce, about the right to sell. Salinger was defending his right not to sell.

Even so, his lawyers evidently felt that by this ruling the balance of judicial sympathy had been tilted against any fair use line of defense (the line taken by *The Nation*). A week after receiving the new galleys, the "September galleys" as they were henceforth called, Salinger filed suit, asserting that my book still drastically infringed his copyright and that he would be "irreparably harmed" if publication and distribution were allowed to proceed. On October 3, 1986, a New York district court granted Salinger a temporary restraining order. This meant simply that the book had to be delayed so that both sides could have a chance to marshal their arguments.

As part of this marshaling, I was required to swear an affidavit. In this, I described my finding of the Salinger letters and my reasons for wanting to include material from them in my book. I also had to describe the damage that would befall me if my book was to be banned: damage not just to the pocket but also to the reputation. And I also had to make it clear that I had gone to some lengths to placate Salinger and to avoid any copyright infringement. I claimed, for instance, that I had "made every effort to avoid quoting the expressive heart of any letter. . . . What I attempted to do . . . was to give a true account of events without impinging on Mr. Salinger's word-choice and expressive devices." This was the first time I had heard, let alone used, the phrase "expressive heart." So it wasn't just a matter of not stealing Salinger's exact words: Each of his letters was, it seemed, a living thing and had a heart that also could be stolen.

In New York, Salinger was required to formalize his accusations. In his affidavit he described himself as an "author of some renown" who had "elected, for personal reasons, to leave the public spotlight entirely." He had shunned all publicity for twenty years and was now a private citizen. On reading my book, he had been "utterly dismayed" to find that a large part of it—"the core"—was, as he put it, *in my own words.* (The underlining here was one of the very few flickers of authentic Salingerese to appear in his testimony.) He recognized that in the September galleys some changes had indeed been made, but these were merely "cosmetic." For all my "inartful" fiddling with word order and vocabulary, I was still effectively a thief. I had used his literary property to "flesh out an otherwise lifeless and uninteresting biography." Although it was true that he had no thoughts of ever publishing these letters, he nonetheless claimed that they were worth a lot of money, and he didn't see why someone else—someone like me—should pick up any part of it. His "past literary successes," "particularly in context with [his] twenty years of public inaccessibility, or 'silence' " rendered his letters "most uncommonly valuable literary property."

All in all, the document made for a depressing read. Salinger, obliged to give an account of himself at last, speaks in a voice that is not even remotely like his own. He would never, in real life, I could have sworn, describe himself as an author of renown, or boast—as he did here—of the "bestsellerdom" his books had "most fortunately" managed to achieve. Now and again a word like "inartful" or "cosmetic" did seem as if it might have fallen from his lips, but otherwise, this—his first autobiographical statement for two decades—was written in what one might call "litilingo," the language of the courts. The whole thing, I was pretty sure, had been drafted by Kay Collyer and Boose. And when these worthies did try to pep things up, the effect almost always was to demean their client even further—as when they had him say that if my book was to reach the stores, the injury to Salinger would be "grave and wholly irreparable" because "the proverbial cat will be let out of the bag."

The cat? The bag? Could Salinger really have said this, or something like it? Or was this but another irony in this case of many ironies: J. D. Salinger, protecting his own words but forced to do so in the words of others? If over the past twenty or so years this man of mystery had ever made gratified reference to the money value of his "silence" and "inaccessibility," a large lump of his mystique would have evaporated. In law, however, nobody's language is encouraged to demonstrate "expressive heart," not even when matters of "expressive heart" are claimed to be the stuff of the dispute. Salinger can hardly be blamed for the prose style of his affidavit (not by me, anyway, whose own effort was no masterpiece) but all the same there was a sadness and absurdity in the spectacle of two authors speaking to each other in this strenuously mediocre way.

The case, I soon heard, would come up sometime in December. In the meantime, there would need to be further low-grade dialogue between the principals: between Salinger and his loathed "biographer," myself. Each of us was required to give a deposition; in other words, to be interrogated by lawyers from the other side. This was the moment that we, the defendants, had been waiting for and thought would never happen, the moment when poor Salinger would at last be forced to leave his Cornish lair. His affidavit might easily have been prepared by mail or on the telephone; his deposition, though, would have to be in person. He would have to submit to an interview, face to face, with lawyers representing *me*. For myself, I was convinced he wouldn't do it. But he did.

Salinger came to New York on October 10, 1986, and was inter-

viewed by Robert Callagy of the law firm Satterlee and Stephens
(representing Random House and me). Callagy, who has confessed to
feeling mildly awed by the prospect of conducting the first-ever extended "Salinger interview," described his sixty-eight-year-old victim
as "remarkably well preserved, though somewhat deaf. . . . He is gray-
ing, with stark features. He is well dressed and appears quite athletic.
He comes across more as a businessman than an author. He sort of
objected to the fact that he had to be questioned at all." Salinger was
polite and accommodating, but somewhat aristocratic in his manner,
not to say disdainful.

Throughout the actual questioning, Salinger was well protected by
his attorney, Marcia Paul. Whenever he showed signs of perhaps wishing to expand one of his answers, Ms. Paul would enter an objection
or instruct him to say nothing. Again, the notion of Salinger's having
to be instructed *not* to speak was somewhat piquant. It is clear from the
transcripts of his deposition that the "witness" was not as extensively
familiar with the detail of my text as I, the not-so-proud author, might
have wished. He had read, or skimmed, each version once and then
simply given his attorneys the green light to sue. Asked to point to
specific passages in which my paraphrases ran too close to the originals,
he was unable to make more than the most cursory response. It was the
whole thing he objected to.

Salinger's humor, though, could not have been improved by Robert
Callagy's unmerciful attachment to correct procedure. Each letter had
to be shown to Salinger so that he could acknowledge his authorship,
and with each one he was asked to identify its "expressive heart" and
to say how much of this he thought I had stolen. What was the "main
purpose" of each letter? Which was its "most important" section? Since
there are nearly one hundred letters in the overall collection, this chapter of the deposition took up several hours, with Salinger every so often
wondering if there was not some swifter method of proceeding, since
in each case his answer was going to be the same: He didn't know or
could not remember. Surely the letters simply said what they said?

In his letter to me three years earlier, Salinger had asked me not to "break into the privacy . . . of a person not reasonably suspected of criminal activity." I was reminded of this plea more than once during my reading of the transcripts of his deposition:

Q. Mr. Salinger, when was the last time you wrote any work of fiction for publication?

A. I'm not sure exactly.

Q. At any time during the past 20 years, have you written a work of fiction for publication?

A. That has been published, you mean?

Q. That has been published.

A. No . . .

Q. At any time during the past 20 years, have you written any fiction which has not been published?

A. Yes.

Q. Could you describe for me what works of fiction you have written which have not been published?

A. It would be very difficult to do . . .

Q. Have you written any full-length works of fiction during the past 20 years which have not been published?

A. Could you frame that a different way? What do you mean by a full-length work? You mean ready for publication?

Q. As opposed to a short story or a fictional piece or a magazine submission.

A. It's very difficult to answer. I don't write that way. I just start writing fiction and see what happens to it.

Q. Maybe an easier way to approach this is, would you tell me what your literary efforts have been in the field of fiction within the last 20 years?

A. Could I tell you or would I tell you? . . . Just a work of fiction. That's all. That's the only description I can really give it. . . . It's almost impossible to define. I work with characters, and as they develop, I just go on from there.

Happily, this present-tense line of questioning was not pursued; most of Callagy's questions centered on the Salinger who *had* written works of fiction for publication—the Salinger who had authored the disputed letters. Time and again, Salinger referred to the author of these letters in the third person. When pressed, he would speak of this other J. D. Salinger as "gauche," "callow" or "effusive." Fifty years on, how could he at sixty-eight be expected to know what had gone on in the mind, in the expressive heart, of this "exuberant" young man, this former self? "It's very difficult," he pleaded. "I wish . . . you could read letters you wrote 46 years ago. It is very painful reading." When asked how often the young man wrote to his friends, Salinger replied: "Apart from too often? I don't know."

And a similar kind of reply was made by Dorothy Olding, when she came to give her deposition. Asked if Salinger had known about the "secret" meeting she had had with me (which, when I gave *my* deposition, I understood she had confessed to) she said no. Asked why she had met me, she said that she had wanted to warn me off, to dissuade me from proceeding with the book. A little later on, Callagy asked her again why she had met me, and this time she simply said: "I wish I knew." Her attorney reminded her that she had already given a perfectly good answer to this question.

4

Salinger's application for a preliminary injunction went to court on November 5, 1986. On that day, Judge Pierre N. Leval delivered a thirty-page judgment in favor of permitting publication of my Septemberized "biography." The key paragraph of his judgment read as follows:

Upon full consideration of the factors that bear on the question of fair use, it is my view that the defendants have made a sufficiently powerful showing to overcome plaintiff's claims for an injunction. The reasons that support this finding are: Hamilton's use of Salinger's copyrighted material is minimal and insubstantial; it does not exploit or appropriate the literary value of Salinger's letters; it does not diminish the commercial value of Salinger's letters for future publication; it does not impair Salinger's control over first publication of his copyrighted letters or interfere with his exercise of control over his artistic reputation. The biographical purpose of Hamilton's book and of the adopted passages are quite distinct from the interests protected by Salinger's copyright. Finally, although both Random House and Hamilton no doubt hope to realize profit from the sales of the book, it is a serious, carefully researched biography of an important literary figure (of whom little is known); its publication is of social and educational value.

The judge noted that the fair use doctrine has to consider "whether such use is of a commercial nature or is for nonprofit educational purposes," and commented that "in so saying, the statute somewhat unrealistically paints the world into two corners—the venal commercial and the altruistic instructive." But surely, he went on, "a serious scholar should not be despised and denied the law's protection because he hopes to earn a living through his scholarship. The protection of the statute should not turn on sackcloth and missionary zeal":

As an extraordinarily talented and fascinating author, Salinger is a figure of great public interest. His novels are among the most widely admired and sold of the last quarter century. Because of his firmly maintained wish for privacy, little is known of him. Although his desire for privacy is surely entitled to respect, as a legal matter it does not override a lawful undertaking to write about him using legally available resources.

Hamilton's book cannot be dismissed as an act of commercial voyeurism or snooping into a private being's private life for commercial gain. It is a serious, well-researched history of a man who through his own literary accomplishments has become a figure of enormous public interest. This favors a finding of fair use.

From "our" point of view (my own and that of Random House), the judgment could hardly have been more complete, more firmly spoken.

We had won. Letters and telegrams of congratulation began to arrive, newspapers telephoned to ask about my feelings at this hour of triumph, a new publication date was set. *J. D. Salinger: A Writing Life* was now scheduled for spring 1987. And I was not, according to the law, a snooper and a thief. Thus vindicated, how could I ever have had doubts?

There was, however, one minor blemish in Judge Leval's masterly handling of the case. He had granted the opposition time in which to organize an "expedited appeal" against his judgment. At the time this seemed but a kindly sop to Salinger, whom Leval obviously admired. What would be the point of appealing against a judgment so comprehensive and wholehearted, a judgment which had declared that "Salinger has demonstrated no likelihood of success." It would be costly; it would be fruitless. Swollen by victory, I felt almost protective toward my adversary: O stubborn one, will nobody in his lawyer entourage protect him from this folly?

Nobody did. On December 3, Salinger lodged his appeal to the United States Court of Appeals for the Second Circuit. On January 29, 1987, Judges Jon O. Newman and Roger Miner reversed the Leval judgment and granted the appellant a preliminary injunction. SALINGER BIOGRAPHY IS BLOCKED announced a front-page headline in the *New York Times*. " 'We're delighted,' said R. Andrew Boose, the attorney for Mr. Salinger. 'We've told him of the decision, and he is also delighted.' . . . A Random House spokesman said after the appeals court ruling yesterday, 'We are not going to be able to comment until we've had a chance to study the opinion.' " I heard of the decision myself in a five-line paragraph in the one English newspaper that reported it. No telegrams from New York. Indeed, no word at all from Random House. No doubt the front desk was already reunremembering my name.

Eventually, I did manage to get my hands on a copy of the Newman-Miner judgment—twenty-four pages of it. The text lacked Leval's elegant stylistic flourishes and was, I thought, a good deal more philistine in its approach. Undeniably, however, there was a certain bull-

headed impressiveness about it. Where Leval had worked from a reluctance to inhibit what he saw as literary scholarship, these two older men
worked from a deep faith in private ownership. They were prepared
to admit that my book was pure in motive, that it was indeed "educational," as required by Clause 1 of the fair use definition. But they did
not see that this worthiness of purpose entitled me to "any special
consideration." It struck me that there might be a tiny wrinkle in the
logic here, but never mind.

On each of the other three fair use clauses, they disagreed with Judge
Leval. On 2—"the nature of the copyrighted work"—they felt that in
this instance the work's unpublishedness granted it much greater protection than Leval had seemed prepared to offer. Indeed, Leval had not
seemed to care much that the letters were unpublished. Newman and
Miner came close to saying that with unpublished material *there can be
no fair use.*

On 4—the "market value" of the letters—they were similarly fierce.
Salinger's agent had claimed that a collection of his correspondence
would be worth about half a million dollars. Even though Salinger has
said that he will never publish the letters, the appeals court afforded him
"the right to change his mind," and disagreed with Leval's view that
the "marketability of the letters will be totally unimpaired" by my
paraphrasings.

This view, in fact, derived quite fluently from Newman and Miner's
most important disagreement with Leval. This was on the matter of
clause 3—"the amount and substantiality of the portion used in relation
to the copyrighted work as a whole." In Leval's judgment, it was found
that the portion used was "minimal" and to support this finding the
judge had produced a meticulous, color-coded analysis of my treatment
of the letters: "all direct quotations in red, all impermissibly close
paraphrase in yellow, all non-copyrightable material in orange, and all
reports of facts and ideas that did not include expression in green and
blue." The appeals court was unimpressed by this, arguing in reply that
Leval had been far too lenient with his yellow markings, in too many
instances seeming to accept that mere changes of vocabulary and word

order were sufficient to deprive Salinger of copyright protection. For example, Salinger might have said of X: "He's the kind of guy who sends his wife down to the bookstore to check out his sales," and I might have rendered this as "He's the sort of fellow who would ask his wife to monitor how many of his books had been shifted by the corner store." Leval would have found this acceptable. Newman and Miner would have considered it too close to direct quotation; and worse, even, than verbatim theft, because it gives or might give, the impression that Salinger actually uses words like "monitor" and "fellow." Thus, I had appropriated Salinger's "expressive device"—the wife/booksales flight of fancy—and I had also misrepresented the skill with which the device had been employed. For Newman and Miner, an acceptable treatment would have read: "Salinger believed X was vain," or "Salinger believed X was too interested in how his books were selling," or "Salinger believed X was wont to send his wife on errands that might boost his self-esteem."

Newman and Miner also believed that Leval had been overready to contend that certain words and phrases in Salinger's letters were too "ordinary" to warrant copyright protection: They were clichés or common turns of speech, Leval had argued, and could not therefore be thought of as the property of any single author. According to Newman and Miner, though, "in almost all of those instances where the quoted or paraphrased passages from Salinger's letters contain an 'ordinary' phrase, the passage as a whole displays a sufficient degree of creativity as to sequence of thoughts, choice of words, emphasis and arrangement to satisfy the minimum threshold of required creativity. And in all of the instances where that minimum threshold is met, the Hamilton paraphrasing tracks the original so closely as to constitute infringement." In other words (and how differently *that* phrase now falls upon the ear), I had been wasting my time changing "movie" to "motion picture," "rat" to "rodent," "applauding madly" to "clapping her hands in appreciation," and so on. That elusive, yet-to-be-defined "expressive heart" was indeed a suffusing sort of essence, untransplantable.

The appeals court judges summarized as follows:

On balance, the claim of fair use as to Salinger's unpublished letters fails. The second and third factors weight heavily in Salinger's favor, and the fourth factor slightly so. Only the first factor favors Hamilton. . . .

To deny a biographer like Hamilton the opportunity to copy the expressive content of unpublished letters is not, as appellees contend, to interfere in any significant way with the process of enhancing public knowledge of history or contemporary events. The facts may be reported. Salinger's letters contain a number of facts that students of his life and writings will no doubt find of interest, and Hamilton is entirely free to fashion a biography that reports these facts. But Salinger has a right to protect the expressive content of his unpublished writings for the term of his copyright, and that right prevails over a claim of fair use. . . . Public awareness of the expressive content of the letters will have to await either Salinger's decision to publish or the expiration of his copyright. . . .

In fact, public awareness of the "expressive content" of Salinger's unpublished letters was instantly extended the day after this judgment was released. The *New York Times* felt itself free to quote substantially not from my paraphrases but from the Salinger originals that I had so painstakingly, and—it now seemed—needlessly attempted not to steal. And the same thing has happened since in several other newspapers and magazines. Simply leafing through the ones I happen to have on my desk this morning, I have counted no fewer than five hundred copyrighted words from Salinger's unpublished writings, in papers ranging from *The Times Literary Supplement* to *New York* magazine. Injunctions, of course, can work only if you know in advance that there is a plan to publish. I don't expect that Salinger will sue these journals retrospectively. If he doesn't, can we assume that these five hundred words have been released into the public domain, that they are no longer "unpublished"? Would Newman and Miner now let me *put them back* into my book?

For Random House, the next step was to ask for a rehearing of the appeal, this time *en banc*—that is to say (I think), they wanted it to be heard by the Second Circuit's full lineup of sixteen appeals court judges. This application, however, had to go up before the very two judges whose opinion it set out to challenge: Not surprisingly, Judges Newman and Miner decreed that there was no need for such a challenge.

By this stage of the case, the world at large had had a chance to consider the appeals court verdict. In the legal community, there was a flurry of excitement. This new ruling had raised all sorts of juicy possibilities. Fair use had taken a bad knock. So too had paraphrase. Copyright law might never be the same again. Although none of the outside legal opinions canvassed by the press came down at all firmly on one side or the other, the general feeling seemed to be that here was an important, if not crucial, clash between the right to privacy and the right to know. The Newman-Miner verdict had brought the Copyright Act into direct collision with the First Amendment.

Meanwhile, Salinger was getting more feature-length attention in the press than would surely have resulted from the unimpeded publication of my "writing life." After all, was there not a rich new fund of Salinger information to be tapped? For a start, there was my book, which by now the whole of New York seemed to have a copy of, in photostat. Also, for a fee of ten dollars, anyone could drop in to the copyright office in Washington and consult the full collection of "unpublished letters"—chronologically arranged and neatly packaged. In order to bring his legal action, Salinger had had to copyright each letter individually, thus making them accessible at a price well below what Random House would have been asking for my book. Armed with all this handily placed data, *New York* magazine ran a seven-page story called "The Salinger File," and *Newsday* published a pull-out supplement. As *New York* opined: "In the course of this well-documented lawsuit, the public is learning more about Salinger than it has at any time during the last 34 years. And if the precedent-setting case is finally decided in favor of Salinger, the elusive author's influence on future biography, journalism and nonfiction could prove as indelible as his mark on modern fiction." The same story (which also described the lawsuit as "the ultimate literary joke") quoted generously from Salin-

ger's deposition and reproduced in facsimile the letter he had written
to me back in 1984: the one in which he spoke of not being able to bear
any further loss of privacy. To date, more than one hundred newspaper
and magazine articles on Salinger have appeared since he filed suit.

In one of these, Robert Callagy is quoted as saying: "If you take this
opinion [the appeals court judgment] to an extreme, what it says is that
you can't quote anything that has not been published before, and if you
attempt to paraphrase you are at serious peril. Copyright law was
created to protect an author in a property right, not to obliterate the
past." Random House, it transpired, had decided to go to the Supreme
Court, and its petition had support from two important-sounding bod-
ies—the Association of American Publishers and the Organization of
American Historians—as well as several distinguished historians, biographers, and journalists. Earlier, we had enjoyed support from two
newspaper chains. None of them had any particular interest in J. D.
Salinger, nor in the fortunes of my book: They had been made uneasy
by a judgment that seemed likely to make their jobs more difficult. As
one publisher speculated: What if "a news reporter discovers Oliver
North's private diary, but can neither quote nor paraphrase from it
because it is unpublished?"

In September 1987, Random House applied to the Supreme Court for
a writ of certiorari, asking for three questions to be pondered. There
was no guarantee that the court would agree to ponder them, since out
of more than four thousand cases offered to them each year, the nine
justices accept only about two hundred. These questions, though, were
made to sound most weighty:

1. Is the decision of the Court of Appeals for the Second Circuit that the
   Copyright Act bars virtually any quotation at all from or any fair use of
   technically unpublished letters of the prominent subject of a biography,
   even when those letters have previously been publicly disseminated, consistent with this Court's ruling in *Harper and Row, Publishers, Inc.* v *Nation
   Enterprises.* 471 U.S. 539 (1985), the Copyright Act and the First Amendment to the United States Constitution?

2. Did the Court of Appeals correctly resolve the question left open by this Court in *Harper and Row* as to what constitutes the taking of "expression" as opposed to use of ideas and facts under the Copyright Act?

3. Is it consistent with the Copyright Clause of and the First Amendment to the United States Constitution for a prior restraint to be entered against publication of a scholarly biography because it contains brief quotations and paraphrases from technically unpublished but publicly disseminated letters?

The petition described in detail the background to the case, and it mounted a spirited attack on the appeals court verdict, claiming that it imperiled the writing of all biography, but most particularly the writing of literary biography. By their nature, literary biographies "are histories of the thoughts and ideas of writers, works on the process of imagination of writers. Such works would often be nearly pointless, not to say superficial, if biographers were not permitted to make some fair, if modest, reference to the full range of published and unpublished writings that illuminated the creative process." Biographers, it went on to say, were now placed in a "double bind": Their job required them to hunt down "primary sources," "to gather information from sources as yet untouched." But what was the point of such diligence if "they are not at liberty to quote or convey any of the richness of those materials without facing the risk—perhaps the likelihood—of an injunction?" The court of appeals "had little or no sympathy for the biographer faced with this dilemma."

On the other fair use clauses, the petition argued that the appeals court had taken an "overly restrictive" attitude to my paraphrasings and was thus "protecting ideas, not expression, under the guise of copyright," and that the "market value" element was insignificant. Not even the appeals court had judged money to be central to this case: "Nevertheless, in order to prevent only a slight or non-existent injury to the marketability of technically unpublished letters, the Court of Appeals restrained the biography of an important public figure."

"Prior restraint" means "ban." It can also mean "censor." American courts don't like to think that they do either of these things. The Random House petition pointed out that "in every previous instance in which a plaintiff has attempted to invoke the copyright laws to prevent the appearance of unauthorized biography or history," the courts had ultimately sided with the sued and that now, "for what may well be the first time in the history of American scholarship, an appellate court has countenanced the effort of a public figure to veto publication of a book of which he disapproves."

So, history was on our side: legal history, that is to say. The application's rhetoric was plangent and persuasive, and was even buttressed with a tag from Thomas Jefferson about letters being the diary of a man's soul. Waiting for the outcome, some two years after having handed the book in to Random House, I asked myself from time to time: Why don't I feel more victimized, why do I tend to shift my gaze, as Holden Caulfield did, when people yell at me "Good luck!"? Maybe it's because, when I really ask myself how this whole thing began, I have to confess that there was more to it than mere literary whimsy. There was more to it than mere scholarship. Although it will seem ludicrous, perhaps, to hear me say so now, I think the sharpest spur was an infatuation, an infatuation that bowled me over at the age of seventeen and which it seems I never properly outgrew. Well, I've outgrown it now. The book I fell for has at last broken free of its magician author. But even so I can't rejoice that, whatever happens, my name and J. D. Salinger's will be linked in perpetuity as those of litigants or foes, in the law school textbooks, on the shelves of the Supreme Court, and in the minds of everyone who reads this, the "legal" version of my book.

On October 5, 1987, the Supreme Court denied our petition for certiorari.

NOTES

Chapter 1

1. Warren T. French, *J. D. Salinger* (Indianapolis: Bobbs-Merrill, 1963; revised 1976).
2. Ibid., p. 21.
3. Ernest Havemann, "The Search for the Mysterious J. D. Salinger: The Recluse in the Rye," *Life*, November 3, 1961.
4. *New York Times*, June 2 and 7, 1941.
5. Rian James, *All About New York* (New York: John Day, 1931), p. 245.
6. William Maxwell, "J. D. Salinger," *Book-of-the-Month Club News*, July 1951, pp. 5–6.

Chapter 2

1. Warren T. French, *J. D. Salinger* (Indianapolis: Bobbs-Merrill, 1963), p. 22.
2. Handbook from the Valley Forge Military Academy, Wayne, Pennsylvania.
3. This is one of several replies received in response to my form letter of December 1984. Certain of Salinger's co-students have asked not to be identified. My thanks, however, to Richard P. Gonder, Franklin H. Hill, Paul E. Sheldon, Harry R. Smith, and Harry R. Taylor.
4. *Time* magazine archive, 1961.
5. Ibid.
6. Milton Baker to JDS, March 11, 1963.
7. *Crossed Sabres*, 1936, p. 27.
8. Ibid., p. 28.
9. Ibid., p. 138.
10. Ibid., p. 131.

Chapter 3

1. *New York Times,* June 2 and 7, 1941.
2. E. J. O'Brien, ed., *The Best Short Stories, 1934* (London: Jonathan Cape, 1934), p. 11.
3. Arnold Gingrich, ed., *The Esquire Treasury* (London: Heinemann, 1954), p. xv.
4. "Talk of the Town," *The New Yorker,* May 25, 1935, p. 12.
5. JDS, "A Girl I Knew," *Good Housekeeping,* 126 (February 1948), pp. 37, 191–96.
6. Ibid., p. 37.
7. JDS, "Autobiographical Note," *Story.* In *Esquire,* September 1941, p. 24, the story goes as follows: "He visited pre-Anschluss Vienna when he was eighteen, winning high honors in beer hoisting. In Poland, he worked in a ham factory and slaughterhouse . . ."
8. William Maxwell, "J. D. Salinger," *Book-of-the-Month Club News,* July 1951, pp. 5–6.
9. Handbook, Ursinus College, 1985.
10. All quotations from Salinger's co-students at Ursinus are from letters written to IH, 1984–85. Grateful acknowledgment to Helene E. Berger, Roberta Byron Bodley, J. D. Davis, Frances T. Glassmoyer, Annabel G. Heyen, John F. Rauhauser, Geraldine Y. Voss, and Paul L. Wise.
11. Frances T. Glassmoyer to IH, February 12, 1985.
12. JDS, "The Skipped Diploma," *Ursinus Weekly,* October 10, 1938, p. 2.
13. Ibid., December 12, 1938, p. 2.
14. Ibid., November 7, 1938, p. 2.
15. JDS, "Strong Cast Scores in Priestley's Somber Post-War Drama," *Ursinus Weekly,* December 12, 1938.
16. JDS, "Seniors Present Comedy, Ball as Final Social Contributions," *Ursinus Weekly,* December 12, 1938.
17. Roberta Byron Bodley to IH, February 7, 1985.

Chapter 4

1. JDS, *The Catcher in the Rye* (New York: Bantam, 1977), p. 173.
2. Hallie and Whit Burnett, *Fiction Writer's Handbook* (New York: Harper & Row, 1975), preface by Norman Mailer.
3. William Maxwell, "J. D. Salinger," *Book-of-the-Month Club News,* July 1951, pp. 5–6.
4. Burnett, *op. cit.,* "A Salute to Whit Burnett" by JDS, pp. 187–88.
5. Whit Burnett, interview with *Time* magazine, 1961, (*Time* archive).
6. Burnett, *op. cit.,* p. 105.
7. JDS, "The Young Folks," *Story,* March–April, 1940.
8. Ibid.
9. JDS, "The Hang of It," *Collier's,* July 12, 1941, p. 22.
10. JDS, "The Heart of a Broken Story," *Esquire,* 16 (September 1941), pp. 32, 131–32.
11. Jack Woodford, *Trial and Error: A Key to the Secret of Writing and Selling* (New York: Garden House, 1940).
12. George Jean Nathan, *The World in Falseface* (New York: Alfred A. Knopf, 1923).

Chapter 5

1. JDS to Elizabeth Murray, November 2, 1942 (Harry Ransom HRC).
2. JDS to Milton G. Baker, December 12, 1941.
3. Milton G. Baker, "To Whom It May Concern," July 1942.
4. Whit Burnett, "To Whom It May Concern," July 1942 (Firestone Library).
5. Army booklet on OCS applications (Governor's Island, 1943).
6. JDS, "The Long Debut of Lois Taggett," *Story*, September-October 1942, p. 30.
7. Arthur and Barbara Gelb, *O'Neill* (New York: Harper & Row, 1962), p. 850.
8. JDS, "Once a Week Won't Kill You," *Story*, November-December, 1944, pp. 23–27.
9. *History and Mission of Counter Intelligence Corps in World War II* (CIC School, Counter Intelligence Corps Center, Fort Holabird, Maryland, 1945).
10. JDS, "Last Day of the Last Furlough," *Saturday Evening Post*, July 15, 1944, pp. 26–27, 61–64.
11. Ibid., p. 62.
12. Ibid., pp. 61–62.
13. Ibid., p. 64.
14. Robert Lowell, interview in *Paris Review*, 25, Winter-Spring, 1961, pp. 56–95; the poet under discussion was W. D. Snodgrass.

Chapter 6

1. JDS, "Soft-Boiled Sergeant" (originally "Death of a Dogface"), *Saturday Evening Post*, April 13, 1944, pp. 18, 82, 84–85.
2. Whit Burnett to JDS, April 14, 1944 (Firestone Library).
3. JDS to Whit Burnett, May 2, 1944 (Firestone Library).
4. Official histories: 12th Infantry Regiment and 4th Infantry Division, U.S. Army (probably 1946).
5. Official history, 12th Infantry Regiment, U.S. Army (probably 1946).
6. *Time* archive.
7. Warren T. French, *J. D. Salinger* (Indianapolis: Bobbs-Merrill, 1963), p. 25.
8. Jack Altaras and Joseph Kadellac, interviews with *Time* reporters, 1961 (*Time* archive).
9. Official history, 12th Infantry Regiment.
10. Mack Morriss, "With the Fourth Infantry Division in Huertgen Forest," *Yank* magazine, January 5, 1945; reprinted in *Combat*, edited by Don Congdon (New York: Dell, 1958).
11. JDS, "The Stranger," *Collier's*, December 1, 1945, p. 18.
12. Ibid., p. 77.
13. "Contributors," *Story*, 25, November-December, 1944.
14. "Backstage with *Esquire*," *Esquire*, October 24, 1945, p. 34.
15. JDS, "For Esmé—with Love and Squalor," *Nine Stories* (New York: Bantam, 1971), p. 114.
16. Don Congdon, interview with IH, September 1985.
17. Whit Burnett to Dorothy Olding, December 5, 1963 (Firestone Library).
18. "Backstage with *Esquire*," *loc. cit.*

Chapter 7

1. Army records in *Time* archive.
2. *Time* archive.
3. JDS to Elizabeth Murray, July 13, 1944 (Harry Ransom HRC).
4. Elizabeth Frank, *Louise Bogan: A Portrait* (New York: Alfred A. Knopf, 1985), p. 338. *New Yorker* poetry editor Louise Bogan wrote to William Maxwell in November 1944 that a young man, J. D. Salinger, "has been bombarding me with poems for a week or so."
5. "Mlle. Passports," *Mademoiselle*, 25 (May 1947), p. 34.
6. A. E. Hotchner, *Choice People* (New York: Morrow, 1984), pp. 65–66.
7. Ibid., p. 66.
8. Ibid.
9. JDS, "The Inverted Forest," *Cosmopolitan*, 123 (December 1947), pp. 73–109. "The Inverted Forest" could easily have turned out to be Salinger's first novel. On August 14, 1947, he wrote to Elizabeth Murray that Harcourt Brace might publish it in book form after its appearance in *Cosmopolitan*.
10. Hotchner, *op. cit.*, pp. 100–101.
11. Herbert Mayes, *The Magazine Maze* (New York: Doubleday, 1980), pp. 46–47.
12. William Maxwell, "J. D. Salinger," *Book-of-the-Month Club News*, July 1951, pp. 5–6.
13. Robert Giroux, letter to IH, May 2, 1984.

Chapter 8

1. Gavin Douglas, interview with *Time* reporters, 1961 (*Time* archive).
2. JDS quoted in *Saturday Review*, July 14, 1951, pp. 12–13.
3. Douglas, *loc. cit.*
4. Robert Giroux, letter to IH, May 2, 1984.
5. Don Congdon, interview with IH, September 1983.
6. *New York Herald Tribune Book Review*, August 19, 1951, p. 2.
7. Angus Cameron, telephone interview with IH, June 1986.
8. William Maxwell, "J. D. Salinger," *Book-of-the-Month Club News*, July 1951, pp. 5–6.
9. Eloise Perry Hazard, "Eight Fiction Finds," *Saturday Review*, 35 (February 16, 1952), p. 16. The other "finds" include James Jones, William Styron, and Hortense Calisher.
10. E. B. White, quoted in *E. B. White, A Biography* by Scott Elledge (New York: W. W. Norton, 1984), p. 317.
11. E. B. White to JDS, December 17, 1951. *Letters of E. B. White,* collected and edited by Dorothy Lobrano Guth (New York: Harper & Row, 1976), p. 347.
12. Brendan Gill, *Here at the New Yorker* (London: Michael Joseph, 1975), p. 151.
13. Ibid.
14. Leila Hadley, interview with IH, November 1983.
15. Ibid.
16. *The Gospel of Sri Ramakrishna,* translated by Swami Nikhilananda (New York: Rama-krishna-Vivekananda Center, 1973), introductory matter.
17. Ibid., p. 341.
18. Swami Vivekananda, *Raja Yoga* (Mayavati Almora, UP: Advalta Ashrama, 1928), p. 75.

19. JDS, "Teddy," *Nine Stories* (New York: Bantam, 1971), p. 183.
20. *The Gospel of Sri Ramakrishna*, p. 81.
21. Mr. and Mrs. John Dodge (former owners of the Cornish property), interview with *Time* reporters, 1961 (*Time* archive).

Chapter 9

1. Hamish Hamilton to JDS, November 25, 1952.
2. Ibid.
3. JDS, *The Catcher in the Rye* (New York: Bantam, 1977) p. 173.
4. Interviews with *Time* reporters, 1961 (*Time* archive).
5. Ernest Havemann, "The Search for the Mysterious J. D. Salinger: The Recluse in the Rye," *Life*, November 3, 1961.
6. Shirley Blaney, "Twin State Telescope," *Claremont* (N.H.) *Daily Eagle*, November 13, 1953.
7. Gavin Douglas, interview with *Time* reporters, 1961 (*Time* archive).
8. Roger Machell, interview with *Time* reporters, 1961 (*Time* archive).
9. JDS, *Franny and Zooey* (New York: Bantam, 1969), pp. 29–30.
10. Ibid., p. 37.
11. *The New Partisan Reader*, edited by William Phillips and Philip Rahv (New York: Harcourt Brace, 1953), p. vi.
12. Douglas, *loc. cit.*
13. JDS, "An Ocean Full of Bowling Balls," unpublished ms. (Firestone Library).

Chapter 10

1. *The Spirit of Liberty: Papers and Addresses of Learned Hand*, edited by Irving Dillard (New York: Alfred A. Knopf, 1952).
2. Jack R. Sublette, *J. D. Salinger: An Annotated Bibliography, 1938–61* (New York and London: Garland Publishing, Inc., 1984).
3. JDS, *Franny and Zooey* (New York: Bantam, 1969), pp. 98–99.
4. Roger Machell to IH, June 26, 1984.
5. Gavin Douglas, interview with *Time* reporters, 1961 (*Time* archive).
6. Hamish Hamilton to IH, June 26, 1984.
7. Machell, *op. cit.*
8. Winthrop Sargeant, telephone interviews with IH, November 1983.
9. JDS, "Seymour: An Introduction," *Raise High the Roof Beam, Carpenters and Seymour: An Introduction* (New York: Bantam, 1971), p. 135.
10. JDS, "Man-Forsaken Men," *New York Post Magazine*, December 9, 1959, p. 48.

Chapter 11

1. Mel Elfin, "The Mysterious J. D. Salinger . . . His Woodsy, Secluded Life," *Newsweek*, May 30, 1960, pp. 92–94.
2. Edward Kosner, "The Private World of J. D. Salinger," *New York Post Magazine*, April 30, 1961, p. 5.

3. Ibid.
4. Ernest Havemann, "The Search for the Mysterious J. D. Salinger: The Recluse in the Rye," *Life*, November 3, 1961.
5. "Sonny: An Introduction," *Time*, September 15, 1961, pp. 84–90.
6. Jack Skow, letter to IH, December 1983.
7. *Time* archive.
8. Ibid.
9. Ibid.
10. Ibid.
11. Henry Anatole Grunwald, ed., *Salinger: A Critical and Personal Portrait* (London: Peter Owen, 1964).

Chapter 12

1. Norman Mailer, "Evaluation: Quick and Expensive Comments on the Talent in the Room," *Advertisements for Myself* (New York: Putnam, 1959), pp. 467–68.
2. George Steiner, "The Salinger Industry," *Nation*, November 14, 1959, pp. 360–63.
3. John Updike, "Anxious Days for the Glass Family," *New York Times*, September 17, 1961, Section 7, pp. 1, 52.
4. Alfred Kazin, "J. D. Salinger: Everybody's Favorite," *Atlantic Monthly*, 208 (August 1961), pp. 27–31.
5. Joan Didion, "Finally (Fashionably) Spurious," *National Review*, November 18, 1961, pp. 341–42.
6. Leslie Fiedler, "Up from Adolescence," *Partisan Review*, 29, Winter 1962, pp. 127–31.
7. Mary McCarthy, "Franny and Zooey," (London) *Observer*, June 3, 1962; reprinted as "J. D. Salinger's Closed Circuit," *Harper's*, 225 (October 1962), pp. 46–48.
8. JDS, "Hapworth 16, 1924," *The New Yorker*, June 19, 1965, p. 43

INDEX